Advance Praise

Girmitiyas and the Global Indian Diaspora takes the reader from India to Natal, Fiji, Trinidad and Surinam. Using new source material such as folklore in the vernacular languages and photographs, the 10 chapters offer bold and fresh perspectives on the transformative experience of Indians who migrated overseas to work on colonial plantations. The focus is on being and the never completed process of becoming. Particularly insightful are the chapters dealing with the recruitment of indentured women, ageing on plantations and migration as resistance to caste oppression. This is an excellent addition to the literature on indenture and migration.

Nira Wickramasinghe, Leiden University

Bringing together leading and emerging voices in the history of indenture today and from across the globe, this crucial volume takes the field towards new concerns around memory, diaspora and identity. At a time when the legacies and after-effects of coerced labour are at the forefront of public and institutional discussions, this is a valuable intervention which foregrounds South Asian labourers and subaltern peoples. It also admirably and innovatively stretches the chronology of the story through decolonisation and to the present, working with the premise that this history continues to live on, needing interrogation and urgent and wide consideration by all of us.

Sujit Sivasundaram, University of Cambridge

This collection of essays provides new and interesting perspectives on the study of indenture in the colonial and post-colonial eras. Untapped archival sources reveal the changing identities of the South Asian labour diaspora globally. The volume details the various difficulties encountered by indentured labourers, including growing older in a foreign society, losing their Indian identity, trying to maintain a sense of belonging in the post-colonial host nations, and adjusting to the new political and social realities and challenges they had encountered as minorities in those nations.

Brij Maharaj, University of KwaZulu-Natal

This refreshingly readable collection of essays offers new insights into the study of indenture and its afterlives, exploring the furthest reaches of the archive and the museum for underutilized sources and excavating evolving identities in the global South Asia labour diaspora.

Marina Carter, author of *Servant, Sirdars and Settlers: Indians in Mauritius, 1834–1874*

Girmitiyas and the Global Indian Diaspora combines in-depth analysis of the history of indentured migrations from India and the many impacts to societies such as Fiji, South Africa, Surinam and Trinidad. Moving beyond mere quantitative studies of numbers and dusty colonial reports, the assembled essays tackle issues of recruitment, gender, ageing, citizenship, folklore, biography and anti-caste activism in *girmitiya* spaces across the globe. In doing so, this collection offers numerous insights into one of the most important facets of South Asian contributions to the making of the modern world.

Neilesh Bose, University of Victoria

GIRMITIYAS AND THE GLOBAL INDIAN DIASPORA

Many Indians journeyed out of India to supplant the loss of slave labour in the former European plantation colonies of Mauritius, South Africa, Fiji and the Caribbean from the early nineteenth century onwards. This book aims to highlight the careers of these migrants who served as vital agents in building the global society of the twenty-first century. It explores the transformative experiences of those who migrated, and the memories of those who did not return after expiration of their contracts but chose instead to stay in their respective host countries. It describes the many challenges they faced – ageing in a society far from home, the loss of their formal Indian identity after Indian independence, their efforts to preserve a sense of community in the post-independence societies of South Africa and the Caribbean, and their adaptation to the new political and social realities they faced as minorities in the countries in which their ancestors had adventurously determined to settle and live.

Ashutosh Kumar is Associate Professor of history at Banaras Hindu University, Varanasi, India. He was a fellow at the University of Leeds, United Kingdom, the Centre for the Study of Developing Societies (CSDS), New Delhi, at the Centre for the Study of Slavery, Resistance and Abolition at Yale University, Indian Institute of Advanced Studies, Shimla, and at Nehru Memorial Museum and Library, New Delhi. His publications include *Coolies of the Empire: Indentured Indians in the Sugar Colonies, 1830–1920* (Cambridge University Press, 2017); *The Indian Labour Diaspora*, authored with Professor Crispin Bates (2017); *Re-visiting the First World War: Indian Soldiers in the Global Conflict*, edited with Professor Claude Markovits (2021); and *Warfare Society in British India, 1757– 1947*, edited with Kaushik Roy (2022).

Crispin Bates is Professor of modern and contemporary South Asian history at the University of Edinburgh and holds an Honorary Visiting Professorship in the Graduate School of African and Asian Studies, Kyoto University. He completed his PhD at Cambridge University, where he was also a junior research fellow at Churchill College. He has held visiting professorships in Paris, Kolkata, Beijing, Kyoto, Tokyo and the National Museum of Ethnology in Japan. He has authored, co-authored and edited a total of 15 books including a history of South Asia from 1600 to the present entitled *Subalterns and Raj* (2010), and a series of seven volumes concerning the history of the Indian Uprising of 1857, entitled *Mutiny at the Margins* (2013–17).

GLOBAL SOUTH ASIANS

Throughout the modern era, South Asia and South Asians have been entangled with global flows of goods, people and ideas. In the context of these globalised conditions, migrants from the subcontinent of India created some of the world's most extensive and influential transnational networks. While operating within the constraints of imperial systems, they nevertheless made distinctive and important contributions to international trade, global cultures and transnational circuits of knowledge. This series seeks to explore these phenomena, placing labourers, traders, thinkers and activists at the centre of the analysis. Beginning with volumes that seek to radically reappraise indenture, the series will continue with books on the mobility of elite actors, including intellectuals, and their contributions to the global circulation of ideas and the evolution of political practice. It will highlight the creativity and agency of diasporic South Asians and illuminate the crucial role they played in the making of global histories. As such it sets out to challenge popular misconceptions and established scholarly narratives that too often cast South Asians as passive observers.

Books in the series

GIRMITIYAS AND THE GLOBAL INDIAN DIASPORA

Origins, Memories, and Identity

Edited by

ASHUTOSH KUMAR
CRISPIN BATES

Shaftesbury Road, Cambridge CB2 8EA, United Kingdom

One Liberty Plaza, 20th Floor, New York, NY 10006, USA

477 Williamstown Road, Port Melbourne, VIC 3207, Australia

314–321, 3rd Floor, Plot No. 3, Splendor Forum, Jasola District Centre, New Delhi – 110025, India

103 Penang Road, #05–06/07, Visioncrest Commercial, Singapore 238467

Cambridge University Press is part of Cambridge University Press & Assessment, a department of the University of Cambridge.

We share the University's mission to contribute to society through the pursuit of education, learning and research at the highest international levels of excellence.

www.cambridge.org
Information on this title: www.cambridge.org/9781009342612

First published 2024

Printed in India by Avantika Printers Pvt. Ltd.

A catalogue record for this publication is available from the British Library

ISBN 978-1-009-34261-2 Hardback

CONTENTS

FIGURES AND TABLES

FIGURES

TABLES

ABBREVIATIONS

ABH   Aryan Benevolent Home

ASM   Adiwasi Samta Manch

AYS   Arya Yuvak Sabha

BEE   Black Economic Empowerment

BJP   Bharatiya Janata Party

CAALAS   Centre for Asian, African and Latin American Studies

CASSS   Centre for Alternative Studies in Social Sciences

CBD   Central Business District

DUT   Durban University of Technology

GHDS   Guyana Hindu Dharmic Sabha

IIP   Indian Immigration Papers

ISS   Institute of Social Sciences

IT   information technology

IUAES   International Union for Anthropological and Ethnographic Sciences

MP   member of parliament

NGO   non-governmental organization

NGR   Natal Government Railways

NIC   Natal Indian Congress

NIO   Natal Indian Organisation

NP	National Party
NRI	non-resident Indian
OCI	overseas citizens of India
PIO	person of Indian origin
SAI	state-aided Indian (school)
SAIC	South African Indian Council
SAIO	South African Indian Organisation
SDMS	Sanatan Dharma Maha Sabha
SRC	Sugar Refining Company
STI	sexually transmitted infection
UP	Uttar Pradesh

INTRODUCTION

Crispin Bates and Ashutosh Kumar

This book concerns what has been called the 'first wave' of Indians who travelled overseas to work on colonial plantations in the nineteenth and early twentieth centuries.[1] It was a migration facilitated and supervised by the British colonial government of India under what became the indentured labour scheme. Under this scheme, workers would sign a contract, popularly known as a *girmit*, or agreement, which bound them to work for a single employer at a fixed wage for a fixed period of three–five years.[2] Indentured migrants identified themselves with specific terms such as *angaze* in Mauritius, *kontraki* in Suriname and *girmitiya* in Fiji. However, the British commonly called them 'coolies' – a term already familiar to them from its usage in South India and China.

The indenture system was introduced to overcome the crisis that emerged from the banning of slavery in the British Empire by the British Parliament in 1833. The system attracted huge criticism and opposition from the very beginning; however, it continued until 1917 when it was finally abolished, under pressure from Indian nationalists and the greater importance of moving troops and supplies during the global conflict of World War I. Another reason was the crisis in the sugar industry as the production of sugar beet undermined the demand for plantation sugar cane in global markets.

This volume explores the transformative experiences of those who migrated, and the memories of those who did not return after expiration of their contract, but chose to stay in their respective host countries. These communities of South Asians abroad struggled to adapt to their new situations, standardizing the languages spoken and preserving some cultural and folk traditions, whilst discarding others (notably many of the distinctions of caste) – in short, forging for themselves entirely new identities as 'diasporic Indians'.

Many books and essays concerning the history of Indian indentured migration in the colonial period begin with numbers. They attempt, with overused tropes, to generalize in a few lines the experience of labour migration across multiple destinations throughout the globe and a period of more than a century. However, the numbers themselves are uncertain. Many more millions of South Asians migrated without contracts of indenture as 'free migrants', otherwise known as 'passenger Indians'. And many re-indentured, or re-migrated from colony to colony, without ever returning home (what Reshaad Durgahee has termed 'subaltern careering') – thus evading enumeration in official statistics.[3] We know most about the lives of workers who were indentured in the Indian subcontinent to work overseas, since their migration was required by law to be carefully documented by the various colonial governments involved. It is these migrants and their descendants who are the subject of this volume.

Too often the study of South Asian overseas labour migrants has concentrated on the most difficult experiences of pioneers in the early years between the 1830s and the 1860s. Rarely do they go beyond, into the era of steam travel, when conditions were vastly different.[4] Many accounts also tend to generalize based upon statistics and discussions of colonial policy, which predominate in colonial archives. Rarely do they allow much agency for the migrants themselves. In more recent research – especially that coming out of the diaspora itself – this has begun to change.[5] While the grand paradigm of victimhood was challenged by historians in the 1980s,[6] other recent writings on labour migration in the nineteenth century have contextualized and apparently diminished the importance of indentured Indians.[7] Historians have also highlighted the uniqueness of the indenture system among systems of labour employment, both in in terms of workers' rights and welfare, and the legal framework that provided a new language of freedom and contract.[8] Other publications have emerged offering a more global and longer-term perspective on the experience of South Asian migration. The 'Tinkerian' paradigm, as it has been called, of perpetual victimhood has been set aside. There is more emphasis instead on indentured migration as part of a global system of labour power, which industrially transformed the Global South.[9]

In this volume, our focus is not on the economic aspects of migration, but on issues of memory and identity and the ways in which South Asians migrated and adapted to their overseas destinations. Diasporic communities are constantly adapting and positioning themselves in relation to the new societies in which they live. In describing his own experience of migration, Stuart Hall observed that

> identity is not a set of fixed attributes, the unchanging essence of the inner self, but a constantly shifting process of positioning. We tend to think of identity as taking us back to our roots, the part of us which remains essentially the same across time. In fact, identity is always a never-completed process of becoming – a process of shifting identifications, rather than a singular, complete, finished state of being.[10]

Thus, the experiences which migrants choose to remember about their past play a large part in determining their social and political experiences in the present day. They can be memories of rupture and loss and a sense of liminality or in-betweenness. They can be memories of solidarity, assertion and resistance. They can be memories of nostalgia or memories of integration and achievement. What is remembered and how it is represented in the stories we tell ourselves (as argued by Hayden White) play a large part in the construction of identities in the present. They also help to delineate the 'third space' described by Homi Bhabha in which alternative possible futures are imagined, including the possibilities for hybridity in which 'we may elude the politics of polarity and emerge as the others of our selves'.[11]

ORIGINS

This volume is presented in two halves: 'origins', narrating the experiences and memories of the very first South Asians who migrated as indentured workers, and 'afterlives', describing the memories, transformative adaptation and quest for identity among those migrants overseas following the end of indentured migration, the collapse of European global empires and the establishment of sovereign independent nations in their wake.

The motives of those South Asians who migrated overseas were diverse and played a significant part in determining whether they stayed or eventually returned home. These could include the desire of the landless to acquire land or to escape religious, caste or gender discrimination. Otherwise, many were motivated by the quest for economic security, to acquire the means to marry or to escape the immiseration of widowhood. The largest number of migrants came from the fertile, but agriculturally unstable riverain districts prone to flooding in Bengal, Bihar, eastern Uttar Pradesh (UP), Tamil Nadu and Andhra Pradesh. But poverty and famine in colonial India could strike anyone at any time, and research has shown that migrants came from all sections of society.[12] The most famous critics of indenture, who wrote of their experiences in Fiji in the late nineteenth and early twentieth centuries were Baba Ram Chandra and Totaram Sanadhya: both high-caste Hindus, who migrated as indentured workers, loathed the experience and returned home to north India at the earliest opportunity. The only other surviving memoir of indenture (a far more positive account) was written by Munshi Rahman Khan, who enlisted to work as a labourer in Suriname in 1898 – a role which he soon escaped by buying land, becoming a farmer, marrying and raising a family.[13]

The very earliest labour migrants, recruited to work on sugar plantations in Reunion, Mauritius and Martinique, were predominantly male. However, most colonies were not content to recruit only able-bodied men on a short-term basis, but were keen to establish self-sustaining communities to feed the demand for labour. Thus, Mauritius, the largest destination for indentured migrants, offered free passage to women and children from the 1840s.[14] A similar policy was pursued in South Africa until the beginning of the twentieth century, when the post-Boer War economy fell into recession, and the South Asian community had become so numerous (and successful) that the official attitude towards migration reversed and increasingly became hostile.

In the first decades of indentured migration in the nineteenth century, barely one in five migrants was female, a clearly unsustainable proportion for orthodox community life to be established, so a target of around 30 per cent (or 100 men and 40 women) was set by most colonies.[15] This target was difficult to achieve, not least of all as it was hampered by a profound prejudice in the originating districts against the migration of females who were neither attached to a father nor a husband. In the first chapter in this volume, Kalpana Hiralal examines these and other issues arising in the recruitment of women immigrants under indenture. Attempts to overcome the disparity between the sexes created many problems for recruiting agents, colonial officials and employers. Socio-economic conditions, the difficulty in gaining consent to the legally required medical examinations, and the patriarchal and misogynistic attitudes of colonial officials stood in the way of recruiting female workers. Through an examination of these aspects of indenture, Hiralal provides rich insights into recruitment practices and procedures concerning women workers and the factors that shaped their decision to emigrate.

In the second chapter, Archana Kumari scrutinizes life for labourers under the indenture system on the sugar plantations of South Africa and Fiji, examining their everyday experiences, ritual observances and social interactions. The chapter uses memoirs and contemporary sources to enrich our understanding of the changes wrought by migration upon those who entered into contracts of indenture. The social background of migrants in their home country is also briefly analysed in order to form a basis for this evaluation. The testimonies used reveal the discriminating mentality of the Indian Brahminic system, but crucially they also expose how the disruption of this institution in the colonies gave birth to a new society and a community which was forced to be less partisan. This was not necessarily borne out of an anti-caste consciousness, but rather the circumstances in which people found themselves. In further examining the impact of indentured migration on life, marriage and relationships, the celebration of religious and cultural festivals and the working conditions of migrants are discussed. The prevalence of malpractices and the challenges faced by women in their working lives are included in the complex picture that emerges. The core contention of this chapter is that migration fundamentally altered the sociocultural lives of migrants. However, this does not mean that indentured Indians did not retain many important religio-cultural practices of their homeland, including festivals such as Holi, Diwali, Muharram and Muruga. These religious practices were a syncretic composite of previous Indian beliefs and practices, which came in the colonies to elide what were in India profound differences. In this way, Indian indentured migrants formed a distinctive culture in relation to other ethnic groups in the colonies. Plantation life was filled with hardship, struggle and injustice, but it simultaneously provided a unique environment that unavoidably impacted the economic, social and cultural dynamics of migrant society.

During the period from 1834 to 1916, Indians were enlisted as indentured labourers in countries as far-flung as Mauritius, British Guyana, Trinidad, Natal, Suriname and Fiji. Native societies were greatly changed by the influx of Indians, and the lives of these indentured migrants in their 'receiving countries' are well documented. However, lives were changed at their point of origin in the Indian subcontinent as well. In the third chapter, Ashutosh Kumar explores the folklore of *girmitiya*s, which has been passed down through oral culture, and endeavours to identify the continuities and changes within it. The songs of Bhojpuri migrants stemmed from north Indian songs that lamented the separation which accompanies the joy of marriage for women, as well the sadness attendant to the world of migratory work. While discussing the content and context of folk songs in Bhojpuri–Hindi collected in Fiji and Suriname, Kumar argues that their new home compelled Bhojpuri migrants to modify their folklore as they came into contact with new languages, cultures and societies. For indentured Indians, folk songs especially were a form of expression through which *girmitiya*s expressed their pain and sorrow and memories of the experiences of their ancestors. Hence, Kumar argues that the content and context of folk songs became an important means for plantation workers to express their humanity. They can also be seen as a form of resistance, not only on the colonial sugar plantations of the past, but against discrimination experienced in the present day as well. Folk songs are thus an important resource for historians. They are cathartic and poetic forms of expression and should not be received naively as immediate reflections of reality. Nonetheless, they allow us an insight into a creative aspect of the culture of migrant workers and their descendants as they struggled to establish new lives for themselves overseas, an aspect which is otherwise obscured in political discourse and the dry statistics and policy documents of the colonial archive.

When the ships carrying the first indentured migrants from north India docked in Suriname in 1873, they encountered a society in which only a small proportion of the inhabitants was Dutch. The majority of the population were of African, Chinese or Portuguese descent or were indigenous Indians. The dominance of Creole and European culture in Suriname meant that Indian indentured labourers had to reconstruct their identity upon arrival, amending their social habits and adapting to their new environment. The fourth chapter, by Sarojini Lewis, uses archival Surinamese photographs, particularly those that feature Bhojpuri women, to interrogate the ways in which Surinamese society influenced the sitters' identity formation. These photographs can be mined not just for their historical value as documents but also for what they aesthetically communicate through their staging. The ethnicities present in Suriname were divided under the colonial system through ethnographic photographic projects, their allocated daily labour and physical living arrangements. However, the photographs featured in this chapter point towards mixed ethnicities and identities, and sometimes even reflect the potential agency of the Bhojpuri-speaking women who arrived on those boats. By exploring these images and their social context, and by comparing them to colonial photographic studies made elsewhere in the Indian diaspora, Lewis argues it is possible to access aspects of the realities of cultural diversity in Suriname in the colonial era.

In the fifth chapter, Bobby Luthra Sinha examines how the first generation of indentured Indians came to terms with an ageing body, in an environment designed primarily to be a place of work rather than a home. Pointing to the gap on this issue in academic and non-fictional studies, Sinha argues how ageing in the context of indentured Indians cannot be seen only as a simple biological process of moving towards the 'end of life'. Their bodies became a site of contestation between those aspiring to control Indian labour and the aspirations of the labourers themselves, who might not wish or even be able to return to families in India to live out the final years of their lives – as colonial officials and planters might prefer. Elderly *girmitiya*s who survived their 'cooliehood' had to be content with scarce social planning and limited familial resources for managing the fragilities of old age. An example is taken from Natal in South Africa, where in the early 1900s the first generation of indentured Indians found avenues to manage their old age, despite the absence of extended families to whom they might turn for support. The chapter points to the need to look at the ageing body of indentured labourers from a contextual view of ageing on sugar plantations, where even 35-year-olds could be considered too old and unfit for work in the field. This was a new situation, in which men were forced to share an experience more common to women in India, of ageing and dying alone, without the benefit of offspring to support them. The chapter points to the need for a grounded, ethnographic understanding of ageing, and the various private and state-led humanitarian recourses and initiatives that were taken as newly formed migrant societies began to assume responsibility for their citizens at each and every stage of life.

AFTERLIVES

Subsequent to the winding down of indentured labour migration during and after World War I, substantial communities of Indians – Hindus and Muslims, Tamil, Telugu and Bhojpuri speakers, and many others – were left scattered across the globe in former plantation colonies. In some countries, such as Malaysia, they remained a valued and welcome addition to the sparse local labour force. However, in other destinations, they were victimized by racist, local nationalist movements, which demanded that employment opportunities be reserved for locals alone. The first such movement arose in Canada and the United States from the 1870s, then South Africa in the aftermath of the Boer War and finally in Burma (Myanmar) during the years of the Great Depression, as recounted by Adam McKeown (2008). These measures were resisted both in London and New Delhi. However, eventually, in 1943, the Government of India felt obliged to respond by introducing the Indian Reciprocity Act, which legislated sanctions against colonies, countries and their citizens in India that mirrored the legislative restrictions placed on Indians in those areas. The sixth chapter, by Heena Mistry, contextualizes the Indian Reciprocity Act of 1943 within the politics of the Indian diaspora between the two world wars. Following the abolition of indenture, so-called Indian moderates who sat at imperial decision-making tables appealed to the idea of imperial reciprocity to guarantee the extension of white settler rights to British Indian subjects settled overseas – an idea which met with support in some circles, but also encountered powerful local resistance. Mistry argues that debates surrounding the Indian Reciprocity Act indicate the dialogue between imperial reformism and anticolonial nationalism in the Raj's final years, especially when thinking about the future of the relationship between Indians overseas and those in India.

As the independent nations of India and Pakistan were finally born in 1947, whatever ties remained between the two new nations and Indian-born subjects overseas were abruptly ruptured. The aftermath of Partition was awful enough, without India or Pakistan having to cope with a tide of returnees from around the globe. The then Indian prime minister, Jawaharlal Nehru, therefore strongly encouraged Indians overseas to remain where they were and to become loyal citizens of the countries in which they found themselves. Not everyone did so, and several mass migrations ensued, but those who chose to remain were faced with the need to rethink their identities once again. In the Caribbean islands furthest away from the Indian subcontinent, whence the possibilities of return were always more remote, this process had already been ongoing for some time. In the seventh chapter, Satnarine Balkaransingh uses the occasion of the 2017 centennial anniversary of the end of indenture held in Trinidad to reflect on the changes South Asians had brought to the Caribbean and the changes the Caribbean had wrought upon them.

When indentured Indians disembarked in Trinidad, they carried their entire worldly possessions tied up in bundles on their heads or their shoulders. This was their *jahaji bandal* – a reference to this baggage coming off the ship, or *jahaj*. The bundle was, however, not only physical. Inside their heads and their hearts were, figuratively speaking, bundles containing their spiritual, philosophical, religious, intellectual, linguistic, artistic and other cultural characteristics, their norms of behaviour, attitudes, values, traditions, heritage and rituals, and feasts and festivals. Prior to their arrival, Trinidad already hosted a mosaic of races and cultures (its twin-island, Tobago, has always been less economically industrious and therefore more homogeneous). This diversity was the result of its separate and distinct historical antecedents and heritages and remains reflected in today's population statistics. Balkaransingh argues that this diversity is also manifested in the performative traditions of Trinidad: its fasts, feasts, rituals and festivals. Within these, the Indo-Trinidadian contribution is significant. Following the recent centennial anniversary of the end of the Indian indenture system, he asks: what does Trinidad and Tobago have to show, artistically, for the presence of successive generations of Indians in the country? In this regard, he identifies eight diverse events or traditions that take place in both India and Trinidad and seeks to compare and contrast them, endeavouring to trace common influences and the impact of cultural adaptation. The festivals examined include Ramlila, Diwali, Christmas, Maha Shivaratri, Carnival, Phagwa and Hosay. The argument that follows reveals significant continuities and changes in them in terms of form, format, festivities and gender relations that contribute to the unique phenomenon that is Indo-Trinidadian culture.

Aside from ethnicity and culture, caste remains a much diminished but still important issue within the Indian diaspora. In the eighth chapter, Gajendran Ayyathurai argues that caste-based exclusion, historically associated with the invention and oppression of self-privileging-caste groups in India, is also to be found within the Indian diaspora, and that the diaspora is often described in terms of a falsely homogenous Hindu and Brahmanical identity. However, Ayyathurai contends that this is not the only discernible narrative; many Indians emigrated against caste or casteism and found religio-cultural self-emancipation overseas, collectively transforming their social life in faraway lands, such as the Caribbean. Following the introduction of indentured labour, the virulence of colonialism and casteism may have continued to 'disembed' marginalized Indians from their local life-worlds, but contracts of indentured migration allowed them to 're-embed' themselves in a casteless time and space overseas. Ayyathurai explores how migration enabled migrants to forge new identities. This process allowed those Indo-Caribbeans who believed in privileged castes to claim Brahmin and Kshatriya ancestry, but more compellingly, allowed others to reject the labels of caste altogether. A detailed comparison between the brahmanical and non-brahmanical Kali or Amman temples and religious practices of the Indo-Guyanese today highlights the continued existence and inclusive character of the 'caste-free' Indian diaspora. The active connection between the modern diaspora and its formative years in the nineteenth century is thereby revealed.

Whilst the transition to freedom in Mauritius, Trinidad and Guyana was comparatively smooth, by Indian standards, in South Africa, a whites-only political organization, the National Party, seized power in 1948 and began enforcing policies of rigorous racial segregation. What became known as the apartheid regime confined Indians and Africans to the status of second-class citizens and lasted, despite sanctions and international condemnation, for the next 46 years. The largest Indian community was that in Durban in the Natal province, which soon found itself ghettoized within discrete areas of the city. One of these was the Grey Street Complex, a long-established hub of Indian and, more broadly, South Asian enterprise. In a study based upon historical records as well as oral evidence, the ninth chapter, by Tashmica Sharma, explores nostalgia, memory and the reality of culture and education in the Grey Street Complex in downtown Durban. The aim of this chapter is to assess the rise of cultural hubs in the Grey Street Complex during the apartheid era, presenting a historical background to the area and analysing the role of culture, memory and nostalgia in influencing the historical connection of former and current residents. The precinct (presently renamed after Yusuf Dadoo, an anti-apartheid activist) formed the node where many former indentured and passenger Indians in Natal established cultural bodies and educational institutions from the late-nineteenth century onwards. Often called 'home away from home' for former Grey Street residents, this complex encapsulated a rich and rare cultural ambience (religious, educational and recreational). Even though apartheid ended in 1993, and to some extent the Indian community has since become more dispersed, it is evident that the community of the precinct still share a strong spatial connection with the Grey Street Complex. This they recall in their memory of common events, similar experiences at particular locations in the precinct and a shared yearning and nostalgic sentiment based on their mnemonic attachments.

Following the collapse of apartheid in South Africa, Indians in Durban acquired a new-found confidence; there was a renewal of ties between India and South Africa and a heightened interest in the descendants of indentured migrants seeking to trace their roots to the 'motherland'. The final chapter in this volume, by Goolam Vahed and Ashwin Desai, follows the remarkable life of M. L. Sultan, an indentured labourer who left a lasting legacy in South Africa, bequeathing a considerable sum of money to education. This survives into the present day, in the form of the M. L. Sultan Charitable and Educational Trust, and its creation, the Durban University of Technology (DUT). The power of this chapter derives in many senses from the afterlife of Sultan, whose family sought to trace his roots back to India. Through an amazing set of lucky breaks, they chanced upon a man who unfolded letters, newspaper clippings and photographs that he had lovingly kept, hoping one day to show it to the family long lost in Africa. It is a remarkable story of an indentured labourer who built a fortune and left a legacy, and the tenacity of his family in finding their roots back in South India. The family is scattered across the world, but in the end, it came down to one small village and one man in his eighties with a bundle of memorabilia to bring them together, as recounted in this chapter.

History writing is often about archives, commissions of inquiry and court cases, but just as frequently it is about the human quest to make the journey back in time, to make connections, to do basic detective work. It can end in disappointment, or, as in the case of the Sultan family, it can strike a rich vein of bloodlines to rescue what was on the edge of erasure. Vahed and Desai vividly illustrate what can be achieved, if the effort is made by historians to take oral history and material culture seriously. It is an important project that remains to be embarked upon in all of the countries of the South Asian diaspora, before it is too late. It is only by such endeavours that we may begin to know the true diversity and scale of South Asia's social, economic and cultural contribution to the development of the Global South during the past two centuries. Through such methods we can learn to appreciate the extraordinary cultural achievements of diasporic South Asians, their hard work and inventiveness, their syncretic innovations and the amazing hybrid cultures that they have created in locations throughout the First World and across the Global South.

NOTES

1. Bates (2017).
2. The word *girmit* (from 'agreement') was initially used by those Indian indentured workers who went to Fiji. This term is now used by the

descendants of many indentured in receiving countries to denote the indenture system under which their grandparents worked as labourers. See Kumar (2017). In some places, such as Natal, the contract was at first made for three years. However, it was soon formalized for five years. See Bhana (1991).

3. Hurgobin and Basu (2015); Bates and Carter (2021); Durgahee (2021, ch. 4).

4. See Kumar (2017, ch. 4).

5. See, for instance, the many published volumes on indentured Indians originating from the conferences 'Legacy of Slavery and Indentured Labour: Past, Present and Future', held in 2013, and 'Legacy of Slavery and Indentured Labour', held in 2018, both at Anton de Kom University of Suriname. These volumes are edited by Maurits S. Hassankhan and published by Manohar Publishers, New Delhi, and Routledge, London.

6. For early attempts to contradict the 'Tinkerian paradigm', see Lal (1983); Emmer (1986); Carter (1995). More recently, Kumar (2017) has produced further evidence challenging established stereotypes in the history of Indian overseas migration.

7. See McKeown (2004).

8. See Kumar (2021); Sturman (2014).

9. Bose (2021); Beckert and Sachsenmeier (2018); Mongia (2018).

10. Hall (2017, 16).

11. Bhabha (2004, 56).

12. Lal (1983); Bates (2017, 14–15).

13. Baba Ram Chandra (previously known as Shridhar Balwant Jodhpurkar) was a Maharashtrian Brahmin from Gwalior state who migrated to Fiji in 1905. In August 1913, he published a letter entitled 'The Wails of a Woman', attributed to an Indian migrant woman named 'Kunti' in the Calcutta newspaper *Bharat Mitra*. It became a *cause célèbre* in the Indian nationalist campaign against overseas labour migration. Baba Ram Chandra went on to become an intrepid campaigner for peasants' rights in Bihar and eastern UP (whence many of the migrants originated). See Kumar (2017, ch. 6). Totaram Sanadhya, a Brahmin by caste, was born in Firozabad, UP. He migrated to Fiji as an indentured labourer in 1893, but soon educated himself and became a priest. When he returned to India in 1914, he published his immensely popular and controversial memoir – *Fiji Dveep Mein Mere Ikkis Varsh* (My twenty-one years in Fiji) – with the help of Banarasi Chaturvedi, a Hindi journalist, which added further to

the anti-indenture campaign. Munshi Rahman Khan shipped to Suriname via Calcutta in 1898. A locally well-known poet and authority on both Hinduism and Islam, his autobiography was completed in manuscript form in 1943 but was not translated and published in English until 2005.

14. Carter (1994, 29, 32).

15. Northrup (1995, 74–78).

BIBLIOGRAPHY

Bates, Crispin. 2017. 'Some Thoughts on the Representation and Misrepresentation of the Colonial South Asian Labour Diaspora'. *South Asian Studies* 33 (1): 7–22.

Bates, Crispin, and Marina Carter. 2021. 'Remigration of Indian Subalterns in the Colonial Indian Ocean'. *Journal of Colonialism and Colonial History* 22 (1): 1–30.

Beckert, Sven, and Dominic Sachsenmeier (eds.). 2018. *Global History Globally: Research and Practice around the World*. London: Bloomsbury.

Bhabha, Homi. 2004. *The Location of Culture*. 2nd ed. London: Routledge.

Bhana, Surendra. 1991. *Indentured Indian Emigrants to Natal, 1860–1902: A Study Based on Ships' Lists*. New Delhi: Promilla and Co.

Bose, Neilesh (ed.). 2021. *South Asian Migrations in Global History: Labour, Law, and Wayward Lives*. London: Bloomsbury.

Carter, Marina. 1994. *Lakshmi's Legacy: The Testimonies of Indian Women in 19th Century Mauritius*. Stanley, Rose-Hill, Mauritius: Éditions de l'Océan Indien.

———. 1995. *Servants, Sirdars and Settlers: Indians in Mauritius, 1834–1874*. New Delhi: Oxford University Press.

Durgahee, Reshaad. 2021. *The Indentured Archipelago: Experiences of Indian Labour in Mauritius and Fiji, 1871–1916*. Cambridge: Cambridge University Press.

Emmer, P. C. 1986. 'The Great Escape: The Migration of Female Indentured Servants from British India to Surinam, 1873–1916'. In *Abolition and Its Aftermath: The Historical Context 1790–1916*, edited by D. Richardson, 245–266. London: Routledge.

Hall, Stuart. 2017. *Familiar Stranger: A Life between Two Islands*. Durham, NC: Duke University Press.

Hurgobin, Yoshina, and Subho Basu. 2015. '"Oceans without Borders": Dialectics of Transcolonial Labor Migration from the Indian Ocean World to the Atlantic Ocean World'. *International Labor and Working-Class History* (87): 7–26.

Khan, Munshi Rahman. 2005. *Autobiography of an Indian Indentured Labourer: Jeevan Prakash*. New Delhi: Shipra.

Kumar, Ashutosh. 2017. *Coolies of the Empire: Indentured Indians in the Sugar Colonies, 1830–1920*. Cambridge: Cambridge University Press.

———. 2021. 'Subaltern Mobility and Labor Contract: Indian Indenture in New World History'. *Journal of World History* 32 (1): 19–28.

Lal, Brij V. 1983. *Girmitiya: The Origin of the Fiji Indians*. Canberra: Journal of Pacific History.

McKeown, Adam. 2004. 'Global Migration 1846–1940'. *Journal of World History* 15 (2): 155–189.

———. 2008. *Melancholy Order: Asian Migration and the Globalization of Borders*. New York: Columbia University Press.

Mongia, Radhika. 2018. *Indian Migration and Empire: A Colonial Genealogy of Modern State*. Durham, NC: Duke University Press.

Northrup, David. 1995. *Indentured Labor in the Age of Imperialism, 1834–1922*. Cambridge: Cambridge University Press.

Sanadhya, Totaram. 1914. *Fiji Dveep Mein Mere Ikkis Varsh*. Firozabad: Bharti Bhawan Press.

Sturman, Rachel. 2014. 'Indian Indentured Labor and the History of International Rights Regimes'. *American Historical Review* 119 (5): 1439–1465.

White, Hayden. 1987. *The Content of the Form: Narrative Discourse and Historical Representation*. Baltimore, MD: Johns Hopkins University Press.

PART I

ORIGINS

1

'COOLIE CATCHING'

THE RECRUITMENT OF INDENTURED WOMEN TO COLONIAL NATAL

Kalpana Hiralal

In the nineteenth and early twentieth centuries, labour migration led to the settlement of Indians throughout the British Empire. Fiji, Mauritius, British Guyana and South Africa became key labour procuring colonies. Thousands of men, women and children crossed the oceans to work on plantations and estates under contracts of indenture. Studies on indentured migration are well documented. Its gendered aspects have been the subject of research examining issues such as mobility, agency, resistance and citizenship. In most instances, the gendered experiences of indenture are discussed in the place of destination – that is, life on the plantations and estates.[1] However, the narratives around recruitment practices concerning women immigrants have primarily been an untapped area of analysis.

Carter, Lal, Hoefte and Reddock have alluded to some aspects in their studies of women indentured immigrants to Mauritius, Fiji and the Caribbean, examining colonial attitudes towards women as well as the role of women recruiters in labour mobilization to the colonies.[2] In South African historiography, while several publications have explored varied aspects of female experiences in the migration process, no extensive study has been done on the recruitment practices surrounding women's migration to Natal.[3] This gap is explored in this chapter. The unequal ratio between men and women labourers migrating to Natal created many problems for recruiting agents, colonial officials and employers. Securing the 40 per cent set quota for women immigrants was at times hampered by socio-economic conditions in India, depot medical examinations and colonial attitudes towards female labour.[4] An analysis of these aspects of indenture will provide rich insights into recruitment practices and procedures concerning women immigrants to Natal and the factors that shaped their decision to migrate.

HISTORICAL BACKGROUND

Indentured immigration to Natal began in 1860 at the request of sugar planters. In 1874, the Natal government agreed to indenture labourers from the southern and northern areas of India. They entered a contractual agreement for five years. Those who re-indentured were entitled to claim a return passage to India or a small piece of land for settlement after 10 years. Many immigrants took advantage of this concession, and by 1891 it is estimated that there were approximately 30,000 Free Indians in Natal. However, they, together with 'passenger'[5] Indians, began to compete with the colonialists in trade and agriculture and soon generated widespread protests in the colony. Between 1891 and 1895, discussions were held between the governments of Natal and India regarding the conditions of service of indentured labourers as well as their return to India on completion of their contract. It became clear that the Natal government was not keen on the settlement of Free Indians in the colony.[6] After much negotiation, both governments sanctioned Act 17 of 1895 which led to the imposition of an annual licence payment of 3 pounds if a labourer refused to return to India. This was the first significant effort to prevent further settlement of Indians in Natal, and the tax weighed heavily on ex-indentured Indians. Moreover, grievances against employers continued, and after several real attempts to adjust differences, the Government of India responded to the pressure of public opinion in India and prohibited the emigration of Indian labourers to Natal in 1911.[7]

INDENTURED WOMEN IN NATAL

Between 1860 and 1911, 152,184 indentured Indian immigrants were shipped to Natal.[8] Indentured women who arrived in Natal were heterogeneous in terms of place of origin, age, language, caste and religion. The main areas of embarkation were Madras and Calcutta. Several villages and towns in Madras (in the south) and Calcutta (in the northwest) became prime areas of recruitment. The majority of women came from the south, via the Madras Presidency from villages and towns such as Chittoor, Gudiyatam, Poloor and

Vellore. Immigrants from Calcutta originated primarily from the United Provinces of Agra and Oudh, particularly from areas such as Allahabad, Bustee and Gonda, as well as Patna in the Bengal Presidency.[9] The vernacular languages of the immigrants were predominantly Tamil, Telugu and Hindi. Caste backgrounds varied among immigrants, many being from 'middling to low caste composition'.[10] Among the Madras passengers, the commonly cited caste groups were those with an agricultural background such as Cavarai, Padiachy, Palla and Odda. The vast majority were Hindus, followed by Muslims and Christians.[11] The age of women upon arrival varied. A perusal of the shipping list of indentured women who arrived indicates that women's ages often ranged between 18 and 50. Infants, toddlers and children accompanied their indentured parents. For example, in 1899 the total number of immigrants who arrived at the port of Natal was 1,300 of whom 868 were adult males, 327 adult women, 55 boys, 27 girls and 23 infants (13 boys and 10 girls).[12]

COLONIAL ATTITUDES TOWARDS WOMEN

Indentured migration to the British colonies in the nineteenth century was characterized by a huge gender disparity in terms of quotas. Initially, the proportion of women to men was set at 35 per cent, but this changed to 40 per cent in 1858.[13] Indentured migration to Natal began only in 1860, and the quota for women was set, initially, following in the wake of other colonies, at 33 per cent. This was mainly because colonial officials, capitalists and planters were targeting the male labourer, who was the primary workforce. They were seeking cheap, reliable and sustainable labour that would be economically viable for the colonists. Beall argues that in the early years of indentured labour migration to Natal, the female was regarded as 'dead stock'.[14] Planters were far more interested in recruiting 'well built', 'strong' men who would 'render good service'.[15] The protector often reported favourably when this requirement was met. Reporting on new male immigrants in 1900, he stated, the 'men introduced from Madras during the year were a well-built and muscular body of people and compare very favourably indeed with any introduced during the previous years'.[16] Beall adds that these gendered attitudes towards women resulted 'in the haggling by planters over the "price" to be paid for each labourer'.[17] Initially, the planters were to pay two-thirds of the immigrants' travel expenses, and the difference was covered by the Natal government. However, by the end of the nineteenth century, after ongoing complaints from many employers, the latter were no longer required to sustain the costs of women assigned to them.[18]

Women were seen as adjunct migrants during indentureship. There was not much interest, initially, in recruiting women because they were considered a financial risk due to childbearing and child-rearing.[19] Moreover, women usually did not fit the category of possessing a 'muscular body' and hence were likely to be less diligent as agricultural labourers. They were perceived as 'delicate' and 'should prove useful labourers on the tea estates, especially, where they are principally employed in gathering the leaf which is, of course, very easy and light work'.[20]

These gendered attitudes towards women and labour were one of the reasons why family migration was discouraged. G. P. Staunton, surgeon superintendent, the depot medical doctor in Madras, expressed his annoyance at 'dependants'. He examined six dependants on board the SS Congella before its departure from Madras to Natal in 1891: 'With regards to dependents, either male or female, I must say that after considerable experience with such people as these, I would much rather they were not shipped. They are under no contract and give an immense amount of trouble'.[21] Similarly, the protector of emigrants at Calcutta noted that 'the object of encouraging female emigration is the promotion of colonisation; for this purpose, the exportation of any but virtuous women is essentially a mistake'.[22]

However, attitudes towards female migration gradually changed in the colonies. In Mauritius, by the mid-nineteenth century, it became evident that 'increased female migration was vital in social and moral terms'.[23] Subsequently, in Mauritius, the ratios of women to men were changed from 35 per cent in 1857 to 40 per cent in 1858 and 50 per cent in 1859.[24] Similar attitudes also prevailed in Natal with regard to increasing the quotas for women. Both the governments of India and Natal in the 1870s raised grave concerns about the 'evils arising from a paucity of women …'.[25] Rangasammy, an Indian hotel keeper in Verulam, a town north of Durban, giving evidence to the 'Coolie Commission' in 1872 noted that the 'paucity' of women fractured familial relations on the plantations. 'As to marriages, among Coolies we first imported, too many males were single, and the scarcity of females caused many debauches, and in many cases they committed suicide …'.[26] Also, planters 'discovered that the vulnerability of women could be used to the planters' advantage'.[27] Settled family life would create a stable labouring population that would undoubtedly be beneficial to the employers. Subsequently, the female quotas were increased from 33 to 40 per cent.[28]

However, the new quotas for women became increasingly difficult for recruiters to fulfil. Recruiting strong men was a challenge, but it was even more difficult recruiting women, which constituted the 'greatest problem of all'.[29] Recruiting agents in Madras and Calcutta in the 1880s and 1890s 'searched every nook and corner to obtain labour' and were at pains to highlight this fact.[30] The protector of immigrants in 1880 noted, 'The Calcutta Agent reports that great difficulty in obtaining Emigrants has been experienced in consequence of the stringent regulations concerning the percentage of women which must accompany them'.[31]

Subsequently, emigration agents representing the Natal government in Madras requested a reduction in female quotas, from 40 to 30 per cent.[32] Both the governments of India and Natal agreed to consider the request but took no firm decision on the matter. A decade later, in 1894, the protector of immigrants for Natal noted:

> We have no formal reply to our request, but we gathered that although the Government of India might give permission to the Protector of Emigrants to allow a ship to leave with a smaller number in an exceptional case, the general rule could not be departed from. The reason we asked for an alteration of the regulation was that often Coolies are delayed for considerable periods in Depot at both Ports on account of the requisite proportion of women not having been obtained.[33]

The severe challenges in recruiting women became a constant topic of discussion between the protector of immigrants and recruiting agents in India. On 23 November 1895, the Madras agents for Natal, Messrs Parry & Co., lamented, 'The scarcity of women has been a continual anxiety and were it not for this scarcity, we could have shipped many more Coolies.'[34] In many instances, port authorities at Calcutta and Madras did not allow ships to depart if female quotas were not met. Ships often waited for days, and the recruiters 'in despair then scanned the city and picked up whatever they could'.[35] Yet there is sufficient evidence to reveal that some ships were allowed to leave the ports, despite not fulfilling the quotas. For example, the *Pongola* which departed from Madras in August 1898 with a total of 375 passengers; of these, 216 were adult men (57 per cent) and 85 adult women (22 per cent).[36] The overall average of immigrants from Calcutta and Madras between 1860 and 1902 was 63 per cent male to 27 per cent female.[37] These figures reveal that not only did emigration agents in India have 'great difficulty' in procuring women but also Natal experienced a shortage of women throughout indenture.[38] These conditions inevitably gave rise to fraudulent recruiting practices.

RECRUITING UNDER 'FALSE PRETENCES'

C. F. Andrews, a Christian missionary and social reformer, described the system of indenture as 'inherently evil', and noted that the recruitment process was fraught with 'fraud' and 'deception'.[39] Andrews together with W. W. Pearson headed an independent enquiry on the conditions of indentured labour in Fiji. During their investigations into the plight of Fiji immigrants in 1916, they concluded that 'it is probably not an exaggeration to state that, in the case of 80 per cent of those who were indentured in India, some deceit was practised by the recruiting agent'.[40]

The whole recruitment process was controlled and regimented through a bureaucratic structure of European emigration agents, protectors of emigrants, sub-agents, doctors, interpreters and other personnel in the depots.[41] The Natal government appointed emigration agents at Calcutta and Madras, two key recruiting ports.[42] These agents depended on the protector of emigrants who had jurisdiction at each port and 'specially licensed' recruiters to recruit men and women.[43] Recruiters consisted mainly of Muslim and Hindu men.[44] In the district of Benares between 1882 and 1892, the Muslim recruiters were mostly Pathans, Sheikhs, Saiyids, Moghuls and Hajams, whilst Hindus were Banias, Kayasths, Brahmins, Thakurs and Chhatris.[45] However, it was not the 'specially licensed' recruiters who were the cogs in the recruiting system. Instead, it was the 'arkatis' or 'arkatias', who formed the 'backbone of the recruitment system'; they were 'illegal operators' not recognized by law and 'kept a sharp lookout for people who were in financial distress or in other ways down on their luck'.[46] Many of them often misrepresented themselves as 'subordinate Government officials' to hasten the recruiting process. Added to this were corrupt villagers and police officials who colluded with recruiting agents for bribes.[47] Collectively they preyed on the indigent villager who left his home in search of employment. Andrews and Pearson allude to the 'power' and influence these 'arkatis' exercised in the local villages:

> He [the recruiting agent] becomes not seldom a blackmailer whom the villagers actually bribe in order to live in peace. A typical case of this came under our own observation. A villager, named Fakhira, had his

wife and daughter decoyed from him by a recruiting agent, who offered to return them to him on the payment of a sum of money. Fakhira had not the sum ready to hand and could not borrow it. The wife and daughter were missing. He never saw them again.[48]

However, village communities were not entirely powerless. In the United Provinces, they 'banded together'; unscrupulous villagers and recruiters were followed, hounded and assaulted. Songs were sung from village to village, warning people against these unscrupulous men.[49] This mode of collective resistance forced recruiters to look elsewhere for prospective women immigrants: local markets, *caravanserais*, railway stations, fairs, bazaars and main roads. In many instances, women were away from home when a recruiter approached them. For example, pilgrim centres became key recruiting sites.[50] Often women had lost their way or relations in crowded railway stations whilst they moved from village to village, when the recruiting agent came along and 'tempted them with his story'.[51] Andrews and Pearson allude to this:

> A respectable woman who told us that she had been on a pilgrimage to Benares and had become confused in the strange crowd and separated from her relations. A man had seen her crying and had promised to bring her to her own people. He had taken her instead to the Depot. When she had found out her true plight, she had been too frightened to resist. Asked why she had answered the Magistrate's questions, she said that she was too frightened to do anything else. Asked whether she was told that she was to go on board ship and settle across the sea, she said 'No'.[52]

In Natal, too, there were similar cases of coercion and deception. Abbobaker Amod, a well-known trader in Durban in the 1880s, testified to this before the Indian Immigrants Commission of 1885–1887:

> The coolies are recruited under false pretences in very many instances, for example, I know an Indian woman, a Brahmin, who belonged to Lucknow; through a quarrel with her mother she made a pilgrimage to Allahabad; when there, she met a man who told her that, if she would work, she would be able to get twenty-five rupees a month in a European family, by taking care of the baby of a lady who lived about

six hours sea journey from Calcutta; she went on board and, instead of taking her to the place proposed, she was brought to Natal. I know of many similar cases.[53]

In many cases, family members knew 'nothing about his recruitment'.[54] Prospective immigrants were not told about their real destination until they found themselves 'tossing and sea-sick in the Bay of Bengal'.[55] They were misled with tales of wealth and prosperity. Employment opportunities were described as 'very light' work.[56] Those who wanted out after realizing the real intentions were threatened by recruiters who demanded payments for expenses incurred.[57] For many, once they were lured to the depots, there was no turning back. They were scared, ashamed and felt socially ostracized. For example, a Hindu woman of the Bania caste was lured to the depot. Her 'bitter' and angry husband did not attempt to get her back because once 'she had been inside the depot she was stained'.[58] Andrews and Pearson describe the vulnerability and anxieties of women in the depot:

> [O]nce they had crossed the threshold of the Depot their terror became too great to allow them to turn back. The recruiting agent seemed able to stupefy them with fear. He was then able to coach them in the questions which they had to answer and they very rarely refused to reply according to his directions when the time came.[59]

Thus, recruiting practices were tainted with fraud and deception, and several colonial officials were mindful of this. They were 'suspicious of some secret fraudulent dealing' which they found difficult to detect and regarded as 'dirty work'.[60]

Recruiters were paid per head. In the west of the United Provinces, the price paid for every male was approximately 45 rupees; a higher commission was paid for women, 55 rupees per head. In the east of the United Provinces and Madras, the fee was lower. These modes of recruitment with price per head were associated, according to Andrews and Pearson, with the 'worst features of the old slave system, and are quite indefensible. They offer a premium to a very low class of agents to engage in acts of cunning and fraud'.[61]

The process of signing the indenture contracts was equally deceptive. The emigration agent supplied 'licensed' recruiters with a written or printed statement, signed by the agent and countersigned by the protector of emigrants, of the terms of agreement which the recruiter was authorized to offer, on behalf of the agents, to prospective immigrants. These statements were in English and translated into the vernacular languages of the local area within which the recruiter was licensed to recruit. Once signed, the prospective immigrant was given a copy of the statement.[62] It was thereafter examined by the protector of emigrants or the registering officer. Once approved, the prospective immigrant was registered.[63] However, the statement did not spell out in detail their daily work patterns, hours of work, destination or the penal laws that were to regulate their everyday lives. The length of the contract, five years, also made women susceptible to abuse and exploitation. Andrews and Pearson describe the indenture contract as a 'misleading document'.[64] They add:

> These women are simple, ignorant Indian villagers who have been used to fieldwork. They are told in the agreement that they will have agricultural work to do in Fiji at the minimum wage of nine annas per day for a completed task. They naturally picture to themselves a state of labour in the field, such as they have been used to in India. But when they get to their work in Fiji they find that all is changed. Those who have seen the Indian woman working in the fields in India with her little family playing near her will realise the change when she is told to leave her family behind in the coolie 'lines'. The provision of regulation 'fly proof nurseries' is no compensation to her for the loss of the privilege of looking after her own children and living her own natural life in her own natural way. She is not told, also in the agreement that she will be compelled, under the penal clauses to work incessantly, day in, day out, with no time to cook her own husband's meals or look after her own children. She is never told anything also of the condition of the coolie 'lines' in which she will be compelled to live, without any privacy or even decency for five years, with no possibility of change.[65]

These recruiting strategies were described by some critics as 'very little better than slavery'.[66] The Asiatic Enquiry Commission, convened in 1921 to enquire into Indian grievances in South Africa, noted, 'It should be emphasised that there has been very little spontaneous emigration of the labouring classes from India to South Africa. They were recruited with difficulty and not infrequently by methods which were commonly known in India as "Coolie Catching".[67]

Scholars like Carter, Lal, Hoefte and Reddock have alluded to similar practices in Mauritius, Fiji and the Caribbean.[68] However, others like Tinker have argued otherwise: 'In most cases the recruiter finds the coolie absolutely on the brink of starvation and he takes him in and explains to him the terms of service ... under such conditions, our terms of service are absolute wealth'.[69]

Recruiting under 'false pretences' had profound implications for employers and immigrants. The former often discovered that his recruit lacked experience as a labourer. The protector of immigrants in Natal in 1909 alluded to this:

> [M]uch of the trouble that arises on the estates, through men being introduced unused and unfitted for agriculture. Indeed, far too many of this class have been introduced lately from Madras. When an Indian persistently refuses to work, a single question, 'what work did you do in India?' generally reveals the cause. So much depends on the native recruiter who often schools the intending emigrant as to the answer he shall in a certain eventuality give, and naturally no one is in a position to gainsay the replies.[70]

Women immigrants in Natal did not hesitate to challenge their employers against a system that procured their services under 'false pretences'. They were defiant and laid claims to their labour rights, so much so that employers repeatedly complained of their 'insolence' and frequent desertions. For example, a woman named Rajmanti declined fieldwork because of her caste affiliation: 'I cannot do fieldwork. I am a Brahmin and have never worked with a hoe in India.'[71] A woman named Sonarie on Deepdale Farm in Impendhle raised 'objections' to her work as a domestic servant: 'I was indentured in India to work as a general labourer, not as a domestic servant. I have objections to work in my employer's house. He cannot compel me to do domestic work against my will.'[72]

TREATMENT OF WOMEN AT IMMIGRATION DEPOTS IN INDIA AND NATAL

Once recruited, women were taken to the depots, which 'left much to be desired'.[73] The emigration agent, together with his staff, some of whom lived

at the depot, was tasked with the well-being of the emigrants. At the depots
in Madras and Calcutta, weak, emaciated men and women were fattened to
ensure they passed the medical examinations. Women were inspected by a
nurse or depot surgeon at the port of embarkation. Successful immigrants
were vaccinated and issued with a woman's emigration pass, which stipulated
that the prospective immigrant was free of 'all bodily and mental disease'.
This pass included personal details of the immigrant: name, father's name,
age, caste, height, name of next-of-kin, marital status, district, *taluq*, village
and bodily marks. Thereafter, the woman appeared before the emigration
agent to ensure that she was 'willing to proceed to that country [Natal] to
work for hire and that we have explained to her all matters concerning her
engagement and duties'.[74] Only after the emigration agent was satisfied was
the pass certified.

According to Carter, there were concerns as to how women were treated at
the emigration depots: 'Medical examination of female recruits by European
doctors and other emigration officials was vociferously objected to by their
partners and resisted by themselves'.[75] Similar concerns were voiced in Natal.
Giving evidence at the Wragg Commission, G. Lindsay Bonnar stated:

> Women were examined for venereal disease in India before leaving,
> by nurses and on arrival here all females are examined by a nurse, who
> reserves cases of disease for my inspection. There is no objection to the
> examination of the women by the nurse, but sometimes a little natural
> shyness is manifested to my inspection. I never meet with a decided
> refusal; their husbands sometimes complain.[76]

However, it would appear that, as a general rule, women immigrants were
to be examined only by female nurses. When these rules were transgressed,
medical practitioners came under strong criticism. W. P. Johnstone, surgeon
superintendent of the *Congella* that left Madras for Natal in July 1889, recalls
his experience:

> One female I examined or got permission to examine, as I heard from
> the nurse that she was in a bad way. I treated her, but she did not do
> so well and had slight symptoms remaining. Mr Mitchell told me that
> I had no right whatever to examine females unless I got their special
> permission to do so. Mr Mitchell, of course, is the Agent for Emigration
> at Calcutta.[77]

These medical examinations caused much anxiety amongst recruiters and agents and further added to the burdens of meeting the female quota of immigrants. In November 1895, Messrs Parry & Co., the Madras agents for Natal, remarked, 'During the current year the difficulties of recruiting have not been lessened. The Medical Examination continues to be most severe so much so that many of our recruiters have deserted us and prefer to accept a much lower commission and work for the Straits'.[78]

However, the issuing of the woman's pass was no guarantee that medical examinations were thorough or that the women were in good health. Beall argues that many of these medical examinations were 'superficial ... and virtually all were let through, even when infected with cholera, typhoid, dysentery or venereal disease'.[79] Medical doctors discovered that women were often not physically fit to undertake work immediately upon their arrival. Apart from some women suffering from venereal diseases, other medical conditions included heart ailments, 'chancre' and bronchitis.[80] A perusal of the Indian Immigration Trust Board's medical reports reveals that in some instances, examinations conducted at emigration depots were superficial and at times even waived to meet the quotas for women. Reporting on the new women recruits on board the *Umvoti* that left Madras in December 1888 and arrived in Natal in January 1889, doctors Greene and Moor noted:

> The ages of two Indians are evidently understated. They appear to be eight or ten years older than the ages given.... There are three cases of gleet and gonorrhoea amongst the men, and one of hard chancre amongst the women. The nurse has been remiss in her duties in not reporting the latter to the Surgeon Superintendent.[81]

The protector of immigrants at Pietermaritzburg during the Wragg Commission reiterated this concern: 'I do not believe that there is a personal examination of women before embarkation at Calcutta and Madras and I am sure that the examination is not satisfactory'.[82]

Medical officers and recruiting agents were often requested to be more vigilant in the selection of women immigrants shipped to Natal. However, recruiters ignored these calls; women continued to be despatched despite their unfitness for agricultural work. Doctor Seaton, reporting on the immigrants on board the *SS Umtata* that left Madras for Natal in June 1891, raised concerns regarding some of the passengers' fitness for labour:

Chinnamah, female 30, No. 168. This woman had not been two days on board before it transpired that she was suffering from 'burning feet'. Upon enquiry, I find, she had been under treatment for two months for the disease, and the fact of her suffering from disease was well known.... There being no outward and visible signs of this disease, it is quite impossible for the examining Surgeon Superintendent to detect it. Is it not the duty of the Depot Surgeon and Emigration Agent to withdraw such candidates?[83]

'CLASS' AMONG WOMEN IMMIGRANTS

The urgency to fulfil female quotas and the high number of women detected with venereal disease raised concerns about the 'class' of women immigrants. It became evident to colonial officials and recruiting agents that the 'better class' of women were unlikely to migrate. A despatch from India to the secretary of state for the colony in May 1872 noted, 'The statutory provision of women is hardly ever made up without a large population of prostitutes'.[84] The recruiting agents for Natal in Madras, Messrs Parry & Co., alluded to this fact in 1895: '... the supply of labour from the Madras Presidency has for some months fallen considerably short of the indents sent to the Madras Agents [this was not so in Calcutta], owing to the great difficulty that exists in recruiting the class of people required ...'[85]

A perusal of archival documents, reports of the protector of immigrants and depot medical practitioners reveals that the 'class' of women that landed in Natal was not favourably received. Their dissatisfaction can be discerned from the following phrases used to describe the women:

'The women appear to be of the labouring class and better than the ordinary stamp.'[86]

'The women are of fair average stamp, but are much freer from venereal disease than usual.'[87]

'The women are generally of the usual stamp. We detected venereal disease in one form or other in fifteen of them.'[88]

'The women were in a very dirty condition. They are of about the usual stamp. Six have venereal disease in one form or another.'[89]

'The women from Madras were also of the usual stamp and physique.'[90]

'There is nothing special to remark about the women.'[91]

'The women were rather a better stamp than usual.'[92]

'We have nothing special to note of the women. They were of the ordinary stamp.'[93]

'The women were of the usual stamp and appeared to be a fairly healthy lot.'

'The women were of ordinary physique.'

'The women were not up to the average in development and appearance.'[94]

'The women were landed in a cleanly condition and were of the usual stamp.'

'The women were in rather a dirty condition.'[95]

'There was nothing special to note about the women.'[96]

However, when a 'better' batch of women immigrants did arrive in Natal, the descriptions were not necessarily favourable. Medical reports submitted by depot doctors at Durban after examining new immigrants on board the ships between 1891–1895 noted, 'The women were of more delicate configuration than usual';[97] '[t]he women appear to be of the labouring class, and better than the ordinary stamp';[98] '[t]he women were of slightly better stamp than former shipments'; '[t]he women were a rather better lot than usual and clean'.[99]

The aforementioned descriptions reveal that the most common phrase used by colonial officials was that the 'women were of the usual stamp', which meant that these women were physically weak, diseased and were not a good lot of women. These phrases were disparaging and further exacerbated the stereotype of indentured women immigrants being of low caste, 'immoral' and 'prostitutes'. Colonial officials did not favourably receive the 'class' of women who arrived in Natal. These stereotypes were not only confined to Natal but other British labour-procuring colonies such as Trinidad and Fiji. According to Lal, the Trinidad emigration agent shared similar views:

Of single women, those only will be found to emigrate who have lost their caste, by which all ties of relationships and home are severed, and, having neither religion nor education to restrain them, have fallen into the depths of degradation and vice.[100]

Evidence given at the Wragg Commission linked the high number of cases of venereal disease found amongst women to the 'class' of women who migrated. 'As to the women, some were prostitutes, by profession, before embarkation: as may be expected, they continue their evil practices in Natal not only on the estates to which they are allotted but on all the neighboring estates.'[101] The commission illustrated these concerns by alluding to the emigration certificate of a 20-year-old indentured woman, Thoy no. 33228. She arrived from Madras on board the *Dunphaile Castle* at the end of 1884. Her 'caste' was reflected as 'prostitute', and attached to the certificate was a 'special nurse's certificate' dated 30 October 1894, signed by a 'diplomaed nurse and midwife of Madras' to the effect that she was free from venereal diseases.[102] This is further indicative, as alluded to before, that medical examinations of women were far from stringent. The medical officers and 'the special nurses' tasked with medical examinations were often described as 'insufficient' and 'unreliable'.[103] Statistics further attest to this fact. Between 1874 and the beginning of 1885, 96 women were found on examination after disembarkation at Durban to be affected with venereal diseases; 10 affected were married women.[104]

European employers and colonial administrators believed that the 'class' of women who were most likely to migrate were iniquitous women. The British emigration agent aptly stated:

> In considering this matter, it must be borne in mind that genuine field labourers such as the planters require can be obtained only from among the lowest castes, i.e. from among the non-moral population. A more moral type is found higher in the social scale, but such women would be useless in the fields.[105]

Thus, the argument was that 'respectable' women were unlikely to migrate, as they conformed to traditional Indian gender norms of chastity, seclusion and obedience. Women who did not stay at home and took to wage labour were frowned upon, socially ostracized and labelled 'indecent' and 'immoral'. Colonial officials and agents were seeking to recruit women immigrants who would be of benefit to European employers and capitalists. However, it became evident to colonial officials and recruiting agents throughout indenture that the 'better class' of women were unlikely to migrate.

To attract a 'certain class of women', both in the interests of colonial officials and employers, medical and registering officers at times used their discretion determining who was permitted to migrate. Control was exercised by assessing women's status and class. For example, the *SS Pongola* left Calcutta in March 1891 and arrived in Natal on 20 April 1891. The surgeon superintendent on board, J. von Mengershausen, refused to allow single women with children to migrate much to the frustration of the recruiting agent, who wrote to the protector in 1891:

> On the second day of examination of Emigrants, the ship's Surgeon … declined to pass single women with children. I asked him whether he had any instructions from the authorities in Natal to that effect. He said 'No'. He objected to passing single women with children, because, if they declined to work … they would not be compelled by the Magistrates to do so, and the employer would suffer. I pointed out that it was with great difficulty that women, in the proportion of even forty to one hundred men, could be induced to emigrate, and a number of these were necessarily persons who had lost their husbands or been deserted by them….[106]

Clearly, von Mengershausen was targeting a particular type of woman to migrate, one that was economically productive and would not be a financial burden to both the colony and the employer, yet he had no authority from the protector or any colonial officials to 'reject these people'.[107]

It would be wrong to assume that indentured women immigrants who migrated to Natal and elsewhere in the colonies were of 'immoral' character. Carter argues that they formed a 'decreasing proportion of the female migrant population as legislation forced them out of the towns, and as greater numbers of families began to migrate overseas'.[108] Similar sentiments were expressed by the deputy protector of immigrants, C. Manning, at the Wragg Commission:

> I think that it is a wise provision of the Indian Government that there should be 40 per cent of females, but unfortunately, in practice, there is one evil result – there are not 40 per cent of respectable females who come with their husbands or families, and the proportion has to be made up by touting the cities just before the ship leaves India.[109]

The class of women most likely to immigrate were discussed in a report by James McNeill of the Indian Civil Service and Chimman Lal who were deputed by the Indian government to enquire into the conditions of Indian indentured labour in Trinidad, British Guyana, Suriname, Jamaica and Fiji:

> The women who come out consist as to one-third of married women who accompany their husbands, the remainder being mostly widows and women who have run away from their husbands, or been put away by them. A small percentage are ordinary prostitutes. Of the women who emigrate otherwise than with their husbands and parents the great majority are not, as they are frequently represented to be, shamelessly immoral. They are women who have got into trouble and apparently emigrate to escape from the life of promiscuous prostitution which seems to be the alternative to emigration.... What appears to be true as regards a substantial number is that they ran away from home alone or accompanied by someone by whom they were abandoned, that they drifted into one of the large recruiting centres, and, after a time, were picked up by the recruiter.[110]

McNeill and Lal also alluded to the reasons for women's migration, 'to escape from the life of promiscuous prostitution which seems to be the alternative to emigration'.[111] In Natal, a perusal of the passenger lists between 1860 and 1911, as well as oral biographies, reveal that women who migrated came from diverse social statuses and class backgrounds. Family migration was common. For example, Sugdee migrated as an indentured labourer with her husband around 1888. On completion of her indenture, she remained in the colony for 10 years and returned to India with the free passage, staying there for 18 months. In 1904 she became a return migrant to Natal on board the *Congella* with her daughter Patea (who was in Natal some 12 years ago) and was indentured on the railways and later worked as a domestic for a family in Pietermaritzburg.[112] Sugdee's example illustrates women's agency, both in terms of her independent decision to migrate and her desire to travel alone without a male.

Other women who migrated were prostitutes, women abandoned by their husbands and others escaping family quarrels and the law. Some were just 'simple village people involved in no such trouble'.[113] Widows too migrated, as their 'lives had become almost unbearable after the decease of their husbands'.[114]

Marriage was a universal custom in India, with many young girls having their marriages arranged whilst still in infancy. Indian custom, particularly amongst the Hindus, prevented widows from remarriage, thus forcing women into a life of perpetual widowhood, desolation and poverty. Thus, migration became an 'escape hatch for women who became widows at a young age, who had a low social status, or who were abandoned by their relatives'.[115]

In the late nineteenth century, widows formed a large part of the population. The *Imperial Gazetteer of India* of 1909 noted:

> There is a great category of the widowed, which embraces one-eighteenth of the male and one-sixth of the female population. The number of widowed males under forty years of age was 'insignificant', but among females aged 20–30 no less than one-eleventh are already widowed, and more than one-fifth of those aged 30–40. At 40–60 one half are widowed, and at 60 and over more than four-fifths.[116]

High mortality rates during famines and epidemics further exacerbated widowhood. The higher mortality of males than females and its impact on women can be discerned from the *Report on the Famine in the Madras Presidency during 1896 and 1897*:

> During the 1877 famine, the late Surgeon-General Cornish, then Sanitary Commissioner, found that deaths among men were far more numerous than amongst women. This he ascribed to the exhaustion following the aimless wandering of the men in search of employment that formed a special feature during the famine of that time. With, however, labour provided for the population, as in the present instance, the women have suffered disproportionately owing, it may be presumed, to the special tax upon their vitality in connection with their functions as mothers, and the extra strain involved in fulfilling domestic duties, in addition to the day's work, of a nature most were not accustomed to. The fact that the wife, according to Hindu etiquette, eats what the husband deigns to leave her also cannot be ignored.[117]

Given the attitudes towards widows and the poor socio-economic conditions in India during this period, it is not surprising that unscrupulous recruiters preyed on their vulnerability.

CONCLUSION

In conclusion, the recruitment practices surrounding indentured Indian women reveal the following key issues. First, there is a need to rethink recruitment practices and policies in the context of gendered experiences of fraud and deceit. Throughout indenture in Natal, there was a perennial shortage of women. The difficulty in fulfilling quotas and procuring the 'right' class of women, inevitably, to some extent, led to the recruitment of women under 'false pretences'. The indenture system was not necessarily voluntary, and conspiracy, deception and fraud were an integral part of the recruitment process. It was facilitated by villagers, 'arkatis' and policemen, who collectively acted corruptly.[118] This 'Coolie Catching' was rife and not only provides comprehensive insights into how men and women were recruited but also reveals that the indenture system was fraught with systemic corruption. Second, the recruitment process highlights both the vulnerability and agency of indentured women. Some were lured by false promises, whilst others were kidnapped, exposing these women especially to sexual and physical exploitation. For some women, with the fear of being an outcast and pariah in Indian society, migration became an inescapable fate. Others rebelled as labourers in their new destination and found ways to exercise their newfound freedom.[119] Finally, this chapter shifts the narrative to the place of embarkation rather than the destination. Whilst the latter has become the subject of numerous studies, the former is still wanting in terms of gendered experiences and voices. There is a crucial need to further explore the untold narratives concerning gender within indenture and many of these can be found by continuing to focus on the site of embarkation rather than the destination.

NOTES

1. See Carter (1994); Lal (1985); Reddock (1985); Bahadur (2014); Misir (2018); Pande (2018).
2. Carter (1994, 26–42); Lal (1985, 2012); Hoefte (1987); Reddock (1985).
3. Badassy (2005); Beall (1990); Hiralal (2014).
4. The report of the Coolie Commission, established in 1872 to investigate grievances of indentured labour in Natal, noted that the proportion of 33

per cent was insufficient, and the 'evils arising from a paucity of women are ... serious' (Meer 1980, 129).

5. Indian immigrants who followed in the wake of indentured Indians. They came under normal immigration laws, unencumbered by contractual obligations and originated mainly from western India.

6. British Library, London, Emigration, South Africa, Segregation of Indians, Public and Judicial Department Records, Asian and African Collections, IORL/PJ/8/293, 7–8.

7. British Library, London, Emigration, South Africa, Segregation of Indians, Public and Judicial Department Records, Asian and African Collections, IORL/PJ/8/293.

8. Beall (1990, 147).

9. Bhana (1987, 59–61).

10. Bhana (1987, 78).

11. Bhana (1987, 78).

12. Report of the Protector of Immigrants (1899, A2).

13. Carter (1994, 23).

14. Beall (1990, 151).

15. Report of the Protector of Immigrants (1891–1892, 12–13).

16. Report of the Protector of Immigrants (1900, 4).

17. Beall (1990, 151).

18. Beall (1990, 151).

19. Carter (1994, 11–23).

20. Report of the Protector of Immigrants (1899, 4).

21. Report of the Protector of Immigrants (1891–1892, 5).

22. Cited in Carter (1994, 19).

23. Carter (1994, 21).

24. Carter (1994, 23).

25. Meer (1980, 129).

26. Meer (1980). The Coolie Commission was established in 1872 to look into the grievances of indentured Indians.

27. Bhana (1987, 12).

28. Meer (1980, 129).

29. Meer (1980, 4, 129).

30. Report of the Protector of Immigrants (1904, 13).

31. Report of the Protector of Immigrants (1880, JJ27).

32. Report of the Protector of Immigrants (1885, 10–11).

33. Report of the Protector of Immigrants (1894, 27).

34. Report of Protector of Immigrants (1895, A61).
35. Meer (1980, 4).
36. Report of the Protector of Immigrants, 31 December (1898, 2). Of the 375 passengers, 216 were men, 85 women, 26 boys, 26 girls, 7 infant boys and 15 infant girls.
37. Bhana (1987, 23).
38. Bhana (1987, 23).
39. C. F. Andrews and W. W. Pearson in 1916 investigated the conditions of indentured Indians in Fiji. They noted that the narratives of Fiji indentured Indians tallied with the stories they heard from villagers in the Indian recruiting districts. 'We listened as it were, to the same story from both ends – from the fellow villagers and relations of the recruited coolies in India and from the recruited coolies themselves in Fiji' (Andrews and Pearson 1916).
40. Andrews and Pearson (1916).
41. Hoefte (1987, 56).
42. Meer (1980, 320).
43. Meer (1980, 320).
44. Bhana (1987, 13).
45. Bhana (1987, 13).
46. Bhana (1987, 14).
47. Andrews and Pearson (1916).
48. Andrews and Pearson (1916).
49. Andrews and Pearson (1916).
50. Andrews and Pearson (1916).
51. Andrews and Pearson (1916).
52. Andrews and Pearson (1916). They observed, 'It was noticeable to us how very large proportion of the women whom we questioned were recruited at the pilgrim centres'.
53. Meer (1980, 390). The Indian Immigrants Commission, chaired by Justice Wragg (hence known as the Wragg Commission), was appointed to investigate the grievances of indentured Indians in Natal.
54. Andrews and Pearson (1916).
55. Andrews and Pearson (1916).
56. Andrews and Pearson (1916).
57. Bhana (1987, 14).
58. Andrews and Pearson (1916).
59. Andrews and Pearson (1916).
60. Andrews and Pearson (1916).

61. Andrews and Pearson (1916).

62 Meer (1980, 320).

63. Meer (1980, 320).

64. Andrews and Pearson (1916).

65. Andrews and Pearson (1916).

66. *Indian Opinion*, 25 December 1925.

67. *Indian Opinion*, 25 December 1925.

68. Carter (1994); Lal (1985, 2012); Hoefte (1987); Reddock (1985).

69. Tinker (1974, 54).

70. Report of the Protector of Immigrants for the year ending 31 December 1909, BC 1107/448, 7.

71. Cited in Hiralal (2014, 249).

72. Cited in Hiralal (2014, 252–253).

73. 'Indians Overseas: A Guide to Source Materials in the India Office Records for the Study of Indian Emigration 1830–1950', https://nla.gov.au/nla.obj-506079796/view?partId=nla.obj-506082770#page/n18/mode/1up (accessed 5 September 2019).

74. Indian Immigration Papers (IIP), NCP, 8/ 1/9/1/1, Wharfmaster's Report for the year 1892, 45–46.

75. Carter (1994, 33).

76. Meer (1980, 343).

77. Report of Protector of Immigrants (1888, 50).

78. Report of the Protector of Immigrants (1895, A61).

79. Beall (1990, 150).

80. Report of the Protector of Immigrants (1891–1892, A3).

81. Report of the Protector of Immigrants (1888, 40–41).

82. Meer (1980, 339).

83. Report of the Protector of Immigrants (1891, 87).

84. Cited in Meer (1980, 18).

85. Report of the Protector of Immigrants (1895, A61).

86. Report of the Protector of Immigrants for the year ending 1894, BC 1107/502, A5.

87. Report of the Protector of Immigrants for the year ending 1895, 19.

88. Report of the Protector of Immigrants for the year ending 1895, 19.

88. Report of the Protector of Immigrants for the year ending 1895, 20.

90. Report of the Protector of Immigrants for the year ending 1900, 4.

91. Report of the Protector of Immigrants for the year ending 1895, 22.

92. Report of the Protector of Immigrants for the year ending 1902, 5.

93. Report of the Protector of Immigrants for the year ending 1901, 6.
94. Report of the Protector of Immigrants for the year ending 1901, 7.
95. Report of the Protector of Immigrants for the year ending 1901, 8.
96. Report of the Protector of Immigrants, 30 June 1895, 59.
97. Report of the Protector of Immigrants (1893, A14).
98. Report of the Protector of Immigrants (1894, A5).
99. Report of the Protector of Immigrants, 30 June 1895, 60.
100. Cited in Lal (2012, 198).
101. Meer (1980, 293).
102. Meer (1980, 295).
103. Meer (1980, 295).
104. Meer (1980, 295).
105. Cited in Hoefte (1987, 57).
106. Report of the Protector of Immigrants for the year ending 1891, BC 1107/500, A91.
107. Report of the Protector of Immigrants for the year ending 1891, BC 1107/500, A91.
108. Carter (1994, 20).
109. Meer (1980, 338).
110. *Indian Opinion*, 30 June 1915.
111. *Indian Opinion*, 30 June 1915; see Lal (1985).
112. IIP, JD Stalker to the Protector of Immigrants, 12 June 1906, 1684/1906, vol. 1/144.
113. Andrews and Pearson (1916).
114. Hoefte (1987, 57).
115. Kumar (2017, 41).
116. *Imperial Gazetteer of India* (1909, 481).
117. *Census of India* (1911, 221).
118. *Indian Opinion*, 25 December 1925.
119. Hiralal (2014, 241–269).

BIBLIOGRAPHY

Andrews, C. F., and W. W. Pearson. 1916. *Report on Indentured Labour in Fiji: An Independent Enquiry*. Calcutta: Star Printing Works. https://nla.gov.au/nla.obj-506079796/view?partId=nla.obj-506085171#page/n36/mode/1up. Accessed 27 September 2020.

Badassy, P. 2005. "'… [A]nd My Blood Became Hot!" Crimes of Passion, Crimes of Reason: An Analysis of the Crimes against Masters and Mistresses by Their Domestic Servants, Natal, 1880–1920'. MA Thesis, University of KwaZulu-Natal.

Bahadur, G. 2014. *Coolie Woman: The Odyssey of Indenture*. Auckland Park: Jacana.

Beall, J. 1990. 'Women under Indentured Labour in Colonial Natal 1860–1911'. In *Women and Gender in Southern Africa to 1945*, edited by C. Walker, 147–167. Cape Town: David Philip.

Bhana, S. 1987. 'Indentured Indians in Natal, 1860–1902: A Study Based on Ship's Lists'. Report Presented to the Human Sciences Research Council (HSRC).

Carter, M. 1994. *Lakshmi's Legacy: The Testimonies of Indian Women in 19th Century Mauritius*. Rose Hill, Mauritius: Éditions de l'Océan Indien.

Census of India. 1911. Vol. 1. Calcutta: Government Printing.

Hiralal, K. 2014. 'Rebellious Sisters: Indentured Women and Resistance in Colonial Natal'. In *Resistance and Indian Indenture Experience: Comparative Perspectives*, edited by Maurits S. Hassankhan, Brij V. Lal and D. Munro, 241–269. New Delhi: Manohar.

Hoefte, R. 1987. 'Female Indentured Labor in Suriname: For Better or for Worse'. *Boletín de Estudios Latinoamericanos y del Caribe*, no. 42 (June): 55–70.

Kumar, A. 2017. *Coolies of the Empire: Indentured Indians in the Sugar Colonies 1830–1920*. New Delhi: Cambridge University Press.

Lal, B. V. 1985. 'Kunti's Cry: Indentured Women on Fiji Plantations'. *Indian Economic and Social History Review* 22 (1): 55–71.

———. 2012. *Chalo Jahaji: On a Journey through Indenture in Fiji*. Canberra: ANU Express.

Meer, Y. S. (ed.). 1980. *Documents of Indentured Labour: Natal 1851–1917*. Durban: Institute of Black Research.

Misir, P. (ed.). 2018. *The Subaltern Indian Woman: Domination and Social Degradation*. Singapore: Palgrave Macmillan.

Pande, A. 2018. *Women in the Indian Diaspora: Historical Narratives and Contemporary Challenges*. Singapore: Springer.

Reddock, R. 1985. 'Freedom Denied: Indian Women and Indentureship in Trinidad and Tobago 1845–1917'. *Economic and Political Weekly* 20 (43): 79–87.

Reports of the Protector of Immigrants. 1880–1909. Gandhi Luthuli Documentation Centre (GLDC), University of KwaZulu-Natal, Bhana Collection (BC), document nos. 1107/428– 448.

Imperial Gazetteer of India. 1909. Vol. 1, *The Indian Empire.* Oxford: Clarendon Press.

Tinker, H. 1974. *A New System of Slavery: The Export of Indian Labour Overseas, 1830–1920.* New York: Oxford University Press, for the Institute of Race Relations.

2

LIFE ON THE PLANTATIONS

INDENTURED INDIANS IN SOUTH AFRICA AND FIJI, 1860–1917

Archana Kumari

This chapter aims to reconstruct life for Indian labourers under the indenture system on the sugar plantations of South Africa and Fiji, examining their everyday experiences, ritual observances and social interactions. The introduction of the indenture system in India in 1834 swiftly followed the 1833 abolition of slavery in the British Empire.[1] Growing protests from anti-slavery society on humanitarian grounds had led the parliament to outlaw slavery, a victory that caused a severe shortage of cheap labour on the sugar plantations of the Caribbean where British capitalists had invested their capital. An industrial depression set in. Two parliamentary committees appointed in 1842 and 1848 reported that 'great distress undoubtedly prevails amongst all who are interested in the production of sugar in the British colonies'.[2] Both attributed the distress to the difficulty in obtaining labour. In the words of the first committee, 'the principal cause of the diminished production [of sugar] and consequent distress is the great difficulty which has been experienced by the planters in obtaining steady and continuous labour ...'. It is no matter of surprise, therefore, that these colonies should have sought out new sources of labour supply, and that India with her teeming population should have appealed to them as a suitable field for recruiting operations.[3] Hence, an alternative labour contract system, officially known as the indenture system, was devised to recruit labourers from India to work on overseas sugar plantations.

Indenture originated in Europe; it was used by European planters in the United States to employ European and Chinese labour. South American planters also followed this practice to obtain Chinese labour from the

Portuguese settlement of Macao in the seventeenth and eighteenth centuries. Under this system, labour was recruited for the planters by agents to work for a certain period of time (usually five years), during which the employer was legally obliged to provide fixed wages, medical attention and other amenities for the labourers. After the designated period had elapsed, the labourer could either renew his term of employment or return to his native land.[4]

The Indian indenture system commenced under the same terms and conditions. Details of work, hours and remuneration per day were included on the agreement form, as was a commitment to provide free accommodation, hospital and ration facilities for the workers. Mauritius in 1834 was the first colony to import Indian indentured labour, followed by British Guyana in 1838 and Trinidad and Jamaica in 1845. The smaller West Indian colonies such as St Kitts, St Lucia, St Vincent and Grenada followed suit in the 1850s, and so did Natal in 1860, Suriname in 1873 and Fiji in 1879.[5]

In the case of South Africa, the colonial office was in favour of a three-year contract, but the planters wanted a longer period of service. In 1862, the five-year period was sanctioned, with the option of a second term of indenture. Employers clearly linked the period of 'industrial residence', the term used to describe the duration of indentured service, with the issue of sponsoring return passages. The first two shiploads of indentured Indians arrived in Natal in November 1860 with the following terms and conditions under the indenture system:

Period of service: Five years from date of arrival in the colony.

Nature of Labour: Work in connection with the cultivation of the soil or the manufacture of the produce on any estate and domestic service.

Number of days on which the emigrant is required to labour in each week: Every day, excepting Sunday and authorised holidays.

Numbers of hours in each day during which he is required to labour without extra remuneration: Nine hours.

Monthly or daily wages or task work rates: When employed at time-work, every able-bodied adult male emigrant above [the] age of fifteen years will be paid not less than one shilling, which is equal to ten annas, and every other emigrant above the age of ten years not less than nine pence, which is equal to seven annas and two pice, for every working day of nine hours; children below the age of ten years will receive wages proportionate to the amount of work done.

When employed at task or ticca-work, every adult emigrant will be paid not less than one shilling for every task which shall be performed. After the emigrant has had practice and experience, he may earn much more than one shilling a day.

Conditions as to return passage: Emigrants may return to India at their own expense after completing five years' service under indenture in the Colony.

After ten years' continuous residence every emigrant who during that period has completed five years' service under indenture and any child of such emigrant, shall be entitled to a free return passage.

Other conditions: Emigrants will receive rations from their employers during the first three months after their arrival in the Colony, according to the scale prescribed by the Government of Trinidad,[6] at a daily cost of five pence, or an anna and three pice, for each person of 15 years of age and upwards.

Each child over one year of age will receive half rations at a daily cost of two pence half-penny or two annas and one and half pice.

Suitable dwellings will be assigned to emigrants under indenture free of rent and will be kept in good repair by the employers. When emigrants under indenture are ill, they will be provided with hospital accommodation, medical attendance, medical comforts and food free of charge.[7]

Throughout the period of indenture, it was the responsibility of the Government of India to curb malpractices within the system. While undertaking this difficult task, the government often collided with the colonial office, which in its turn had to deal with increasing hostility towards Asiatic labourers in the colonies and newly created British dominions in the late nineteenth and early twentieth centuries.

Lal writes that the indenture system was highly organized, which enabled emigration to the various sugar colonies on a large scale. The employers were predominantly the big capitalist sugar planters of Europe (mostly from Britain) who were located in the various British and other

European colonies under imperialism. Among these, the Sugar Refining Company (SRC) was one which won tenders in the colonies.[8] According to Lal, the recruitment of labour under the indenture system was a purely personal venture, undertaken for profit. But later the increase in the demand for labour and the desirability of eliminating competition through efficient recruitment led to the creation of a coordinating agency, both for the purposes of securing supply and for regulating distribution. Recruiters were appointed by these agencies to source labourers in the interior of the country for the colonies.

In the initial years, due to the absence of organized agency for recruitment, there were many problems and abuses in emigration. To reduce these as well as to maintain a continuous supply of labour, an organized agency was developed through emigration legislation and policies. Hence, each Indian labour importing colony appointed an emigration agent in India who oversaw the recruitment of 'coolies' for the colonies. Lal says that the agents were usually former colonial officials, were paid a fixed salary and maintained a large depot to which emigrants were sent before embarkation.[9]

Recruiters may be broadly divided into two classes, licensed and unlicensed. Licensed recruiters were always men; unlicensed recruiters were either men or women. Licenced recruiters may be again subdivided into head recruiters, commonly called sub-agents and ordinary recruiters. Ordinary recruiters were either subordinates to a head recruiter or independent. According to the Grierson report (1883), emigration agents had sub-agents under them, and all the sub-agents up country supervised recruiters. Agents used to hold sub-agent's licences, and sometimes the sub-agent held a recruiter's licence, but very often not. The business of a sub-agent was to collect emigrants brought in by recruiters from all parts of the area over which his operations extended. Sometimes he had outposts, which were under the charge of a subordinate recruiter (Figure 2.1).[10]

The Pitcher report (1883) records that *arkatis*, or unlicensed men, also featured in the system, and used to bring in coolies to the recruiter. *Arkatis* were not employed universally, but rather only in such places where recruiters were few and the chances of obtaining coolies good. The transaction with the *arkatis* was in cash and the recruiter could only afford to engage them when his profit margin was fairly good. Women were also employed as *arkatis*. The *arkatis'* business was limited solely to introducing coolies to recruiters within a few hours of their first meeting with the coolies.

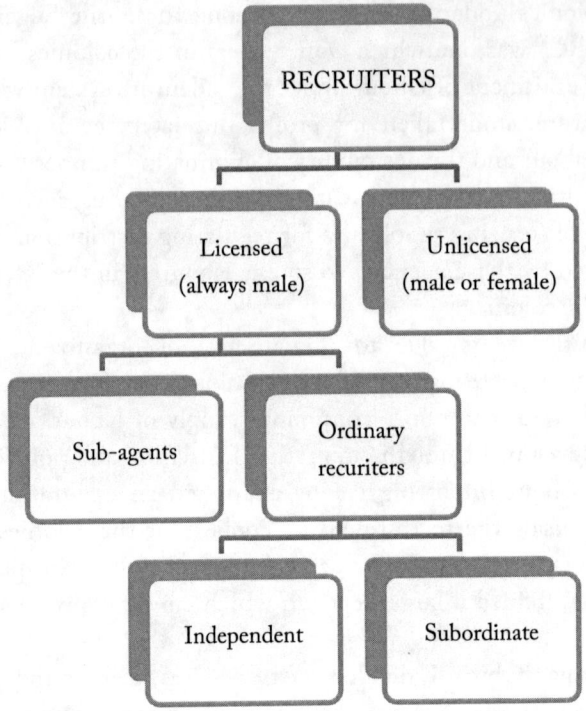

Figure 2.1 Types of recruiters

Source: Grierson (1883, 10).

THE SOCIAL ORIGIN OF INDENTURED
INDIANS IN SOUTH AFRICA

When the indenture system was introduced in the colony of Natal in 1860, the first batch of indentured labourers – 342 people – arrived in Durban harbour on 16 November. Between 1860 and 1866, 6,000 Indians arrived in Natal from Calcutta and Madras. They were from various castes, linguistic groups and religions. As Surendra Bhana has explained, those among Natal's indentured Indians who were recruited from districts in the Madras Presidency and who embarked at Madras city port were referred to as Madras passengers. Those who were recruited in Uttar Pradesh (UP) and Bihar and who embarked at the port of Calcutta were for convenience called Calcutta passengers.[11]

Among the South Indian emigrants to Natal, North Arcot and South Arcot supplied 24 per cent of the total of 59,662 in 1860–1910. The district of

Chingleput was the source of nearly 10 per cent of the Madras passengers to Natal. Madras city was also a large supplier of Natal's indentured immigrants, as was the district of Vishakhapatnam, one of the largest in India, from which 2.7 per cent of all Madras passengers to Natal came between 1860 and 1902. The north-eastern costal Telugu-speaking district of Godavari, consisting of 12 *taluk*s, accounted for 1.2 per cent of Natal's immigrants.[12]

In discussing the places of origin of the Calcutta passengers, it is convenient to separate UP and Bihar. Patterns of geographical and caste distribution can be illustrated more clearly this way. Indentured migrants were recruited overwhelmingly from eastern UP. The reason for this, much as Lal found for Fiji Indians, was that the eastern districts were more densely populated than the western districts.[13] The greater concentration of lower castes and classes with smaller landholdings made the region more vulnerable to economic pressure. It is not surprising, then, that recruitment was easy in the eastern districts. Besides, they were closer to Calcutta, where recruits had to be transported.

The four leading districts were Azamgarh, Basti, Ghazipur and Gonda. In total, they supplied over 27 per cent of the Calcutta passengers between 1860 and 1901. The next group of districts from which Natal's immigrants came lay on a north–south axis in UP, with Gorakhpur to the north and Allahabad to the south. On an average, 2.8 per cent of the Calcutta passengers came from this group of districts, which included Gorakhpur, Faizabad, Sultanpur, Jaunpur, Benares, Pratapgarh, Bareilly and Allahabad. The UP districts from which over 7.7 per cent of the Natal immigrants came were Baliya, Mirzapur, Fatehpur, Kanpur, Unao and Lucknow. These districts surrounded the aforementioned eight districts. The recruitment of indentured Indians was much more intense in these districts. The largest was Kanpur; the smallest was Fatehpur.[14]

Nearly 11 per cent of the Calcutta passengers came from the Bihar region. Here, the most prominent recruitment districts were Shahabad, Patna, Gaya, Saran, Muzaffarpur, Monghyr and Hazaribagh. Why these districts in Bihar and not others? The reason is the same that Lal found for his Fiji sample: these were densely populated, impoverished regions with a long tradition in colonial migration. The population of these seven districts in 1901 was over 14 million. They were comprised of 36 towns and 39,677 villages. In 1901, in the Bengal Presidency, 63.5 per cent of the population was Hindu and 33 per cent was Muslim. However, for Bihar itself, the religious breakdown was 82 per cent Hindu and 18 per cent Muslim. The Magahi dialect of Bihari was spoken among Hindus, and Awadhi was spoken among the Muslims by and large.[15]

SOCIAL AND FAMILY LIFE IN SOUTH AFRICA AND FIJI

CASTE AND SOCIAL NORMS

The social and family life of Indians underwent a drastic change once they signed the contract of indenture. The caste hierarchy and social norms they followed at home were fractured when they entered the depot with their new 'coolie' identity, which was attributed regardless of caste or religion. Munshi Rahman Khan, who was indentured to Suriname, remembers in his autobiography that until reaching the central coolie depot at Calcutta, indentured labourers received raw ingredients and prepared their own food, maintaining all caste and hierarchical differences; once they reached the Calcutta depot, however, they had to forget caste and hierarchy while dining (Figures 2.2–2.3). Khan writes:

> Till we reached here [Calcutta], we were allowed to cook our own meals as we pleased as we were given raw food materials. Everyone followed his own rituals and system. They wore their Janeu (sacred thread), tikka (forehead mark), Kanthi Mala (sacred necklace) etc. according to her/his caste and religion and followed the system of caste and creed … [But in the depot at Calcutta] in order to get food, we had to line up in two separate queues, one for men and the other for women. There was no separation based on caste, religion or class. At this point in time no Brahmin or Kshatriya protested that they would not sit along and eat with Muslims or Chamars [lower castes]. This is because they all had become sudras.[16]

Totaram Sanadhya, a poor, high-caste migrant, who became an indentured worker in Fiji, also writes of the same experience when he entered the depot. He writes:

> Jabardasti chamār, Koli, Brahman ityadi sabko ek jagah baithākar bhojan karāya jāta hai. Lagbhag sabko mitti ke juthe bartanon me bhojan karāya jāta hai aur pāni pilāya gaya.

The Emigrants at their meals.

Figure 2.2 The emigrants at their meals
Source: Kumar (2016, 46).

… that Chamars, Kolis, Brahmans and so forth were all seated in one place and forced to have their meal together. Just about everyone was made to have their meal on re-used plates, and was made to drink water.[17]

These testimonies reveal the discriminating mentality of the Indian brahmanic system, but also how the disruption of this institution in the colonies gave birth to a new society and a community which was forced to be less partisan.

The caste system, which ascribed hierarchy, endogamy, occupational specialization and restrictions on social interaction according to birth, was almost impossible to respect on ship. The sea voyage to the colonies became a site of massive social upheavals. Migrants had to eat, sleep and drink together, and, according to Desai and Vahed, notions of hierarchy and privilege were disbanded by the forced 'closeness'. Further, in the eyes of non-Indians, all Indians became simply 'coolies'.[18]

Sanadhya and Khan's testimonies corroborate Grierson's evidence from Bihar that 'a man can eat anything on board ship, a vessel being like the Temple of Jagannath, without caste restrictions'.[19] The high-caste migrants

Figure 2.3 Food being served to children on an indentured ship
Source: Lubbock (1935, 38).

soon accepted their newfound circumstances; removed from their caste
fellows and traditional social system, they mingled with other castes.[20] As the
poet Sudhesh Mishra eloquently put it:

> many things were lost during that nautical passage, family, caste
> and religion, and yet many things were also found; Chamars found
> Brahmins, Muslims found Hindus, Biharis found Marathis, so that by
> the end of the voyage we were a nation of jahaji bhais ... all for one and
> one for all.[21]

Brij V. Lal asserts that this transformation was the beginning of a new and
powerful ship bond known as *jahaji bhai*.[22]

On the plantations of South Africa, labourers lived in the coolie lines where
indentured workers dwelled together without caste and religious distinctions.
However, this does not mean that caste completely disappeared on the
plantations. Those indentured workers who were economically successful and
became influential tried to re-establish the social and caste practices of India.
Desai and Vahed have provided examples of two indentured workers who
prospered in Natal. Charlie Nulliah became rich after finishing his contract,

eventually becoming leader of a local community in Maritzburg and head of a *panchayat* that decided on matters affecting the Telgus, a religious-cum-caste group.[23] In another case, Boodha Dulel Sing bought a few acres of land in Nonoti and began planting sugar cane, tobacco and vegetables. He soon became one of the wealthiest ex-indentured Indians. His farm, 'Hyde Park', measured over 5,000 acres, and he employed over 100 Indian workers. He had five sons and three daughters, and left each of his sons more than 1,000 acres, while his daughters received a nominal 10 acres each. Boodha Sing's story replicates the patterns of inheritance from 'back-home', where women in north-west India were denied land ownership. This practice persisted in the minds of migrants.[24]

Caste remained an important part of the 'baggage' that Indians carried with them from their villages. But in Natal it did not dominate social interaction, and intermingling became the norm. This was not necessarily borne out of an anti-caste consciousness, but rather the circumstances in which people found themselves.[25] It would have been almost impossible to reposition the caste system in Natal. Recruitment of workers under the indenture system was initiated on an individual basis, and hence it was difficult for worker obligations to be established in line with the caste system. Moreover, although they did not actively ask for it, those emigrants belonging to lower castes enjoyed the opportunity to experience a casteless society and did not want to transplant the traditional system. As Jayawardene has stated, indentured migrants were not visionaries setting out to build a new society:

> [Most] expected to continue to live in the land in accordance with the institutions to which they were accustomed. It is therefore likely that they consciously or unconsciously attempted to maintain in the new setting the cultural pattern they had learned at home and presumably valued … [however] a complete and comprehensive re-creation of the culture of the homeland was clearly impossible.[26]

Hence, one can assume that caste in the new environment was neither abandoned nor duplicated. Employers were more interested in efficient work than in the social status of Indians. Moreover, high-caste workers were not given pre-eminence when identified; they were seen as lazy and less productive. The economic opportunity in South Africa provided mobility among migrants irrespective of caste, and most of them took

advantage of this. The narratives of indentured workers in Natal reveal their
understanding of caste. For example, Ramdeen Ujudha stated to the Wragg
Commission:

> Here I have eaten with different people and broken my caste. My friends
> in India will not even eat with me, so I must come back. When I go
> back I will ask my mother to cook, but I will tell what I have done;
> she will cook and I will eat outside; she will not allow me to eat inside
> where she and my relatives are. No fine could bring me back my caste,
> being a Brahmin. When the coolies come here, they lose all caste, even
> a Brahmins intermarry with the Chamars [sic]. What is to be done? In
> my own country if a Brahmin even goes for a call of nature, he must put
> a thread round his ear.[27]

Some emigrants tried to sustain their caste prejudices and norms even
though they crossed the *kalapani*. They believed that in this way they could
not be called outcastes. Telucksing, a storekeeper and ex-indentured Indian,
told the same commission:

> I have not suffered in my caste in any way by coming across the ocean
> to Natal, because I have observed all my religious ceremonies and I have
> done nothing to debar me from enjoying my caste privileges. I am of a
> Kshatriya caste, which is the caste of fighting men and agriculturists.
> If a Brahmin came here, he would not lose his caste unless he did
> something detrimental to his religion. The Indians here drink to excess
> and do not comply with any of their caste observations.[28]

Totaram Sanadhya, upon his return to India, was interrogated by the
priest of his village. He was asked whether he married a Brahmin girl and
still followed the caste and religious norms in Fiji. The *panchayat* of his village
asked him to give a feast to re-enter his caste, otherwise he would not be
permitted to remain.[29]

MARRIAGE

On the plantations of Natal or elsewhere in the empire, the practice of
marriage was difficult for indentured labourers as colonial governments only
recognized marriages when verified by a certificate from a magistrate. The

struggle for the recognition of religious marriages was a long drawn-out affair. In the context of Fiji, Totaram Sanadhya has a good deal to say about the relationship of women and men under plantation life. Marriages were called *marit*, and very few people invited a priest to perform the ceremony. Widow remarriage was apparently very frequent in Fiji, whereas in India it did not exist.[30] Plantation life also broke long-established rules concerning caste and religion when it came to marriages between Hindus and Muslims. Indian culture does not provide any space for interreligious marriages, but under plantation life, couples were frequently marrying beyond their caste and contravening traditional marriage rules. Sanadhya termed such marriages as *andhadhundh paddhati se vivah* (marriages under an indiscriminate system). According to Sanadhya, 'indiscriminate marriages' were prevalent in all the colonies. Under this system, marriage was performed between a couple from two different religions. The process of marriage was as follows: all the people invited came to the groom's house. On one side of the house, a *vedi* with a banana stump was prepared for the *Satyanarayan Katha* (Story of Satyanarayana), while in the other corner, a *chauki* with a white cloth was put on a mat, and a *lobhan* (*dhup* or *agarbatti*) was lit. Both communities sat facing their own respective priests, the *maulvi* and the *pandit*. Both the bride and the groom wore white *dhoti*s. Now both priests started to call their *devta*s (gods). The Hindu priest started with 'Sri Devayenamah, Sri Ganpatay namah pushpam sarpyami, akshat sarpyami, Sri Navgrah navratnam sarpyami', and the Muslim priest began with 'Bismillah Rahamanorahim, Marhawa-Marhawa Habibullah'.[31]

As in the case of Fiji, mentioned by Totaram Sanadhya, on the plantations of Natal, too, the official registration of a marriage was essential to claim a legal husband or wife. In cases of quarrels between men over a wife, the court always favoured those who had evidence of a registered marriage. For example, in 1887, Muthoora, an indentured migrant, visited the protector of immigrants, Mr Mason, to register his marriage with Tejia, whom he had been living with for two years. However, Mason declined to register Tejia as the wife of Muthoora after discovering that Tejia had already been married to Shewdal in 1882, and there was no divorce between them. According to the marriage law, Mason forced Tejia to stay with Shewdal as their marriage was lawful and 'duly solemnised'. Hence, even though Tejia wanted to live with Muthoora, she had no right to do this.[32]

Emigration from India involved 80 per cent single migrants and only 20 per cent family groups. Among the single migrants, the percentage of men was higher than that of women. The gender disparity created huge problems in the early years for those who wished to establish families. This was compounded by the absence of marriages across the racial divide; the long, hard hours of plantation work; the break-ups of families; houses with no privacy; and the paucity of laws regarding marriage, divorce, adultery, dowry and polygamy. The Government of Natal did not imagine a settled Indian existence there and hence did not bother to frame laws towards securing a stable family life for indentured workers. Despite the various odds, indentured workers formed families, and in many cases, these survived the adversity of bondage. In the initial years, due to a shortage of women, family life was unstable, but as soon as the proportion of women increased, it stabilized. Yet, as Desai and Vahed have indicated, these formative families were more nuclear and differed greatly from the patriarchal joint family prevalent in India at the time.[33]

As marriages solemnized by *pandit*s, or religious leaders, were not recognized by the colonial government in Natal, the status of couples remained unclear. As soon as the numbers of Indians increased, the disputes and complaints related to marriage and divorce also grew. The Natal government set up a commission in 1872, which recommended that the protector of immigrants compile a register of Indian women, whether single, married or concubines, and so on. This commission also recommended that the registration of marriage be made mandatory. This was translated into law, as was the fact that it was now an offence to seduce married women or entice a girl below the age of 16. Those guilty of adultery had to pay a fine of 10 pounds and undergo 30 days of imprisonment. As per data provided by Desai and Vahed, between 1873 and 1886, 4,998 Hindu, Muslim and Christian marriages were registered in Natal. Of these, 115 marriages were registered between Hindus and Muslims, 1 marriage between a Muslim and a Christian, 12 marriages between Christians and Hindus, and 23 marriages between Calcutta and Madrasi Indians.[34] A decade later, the Wragg Commission observed that the registration of marriages not only provided a means to establish the validity of marriage but it also gave married women a proper status and made them respectable. It raised women's self-respect. The colonial reinforcement of registration of marriages was not received well by many Indians. When Gandhi started his *satyagraha* campaign (1906–1914), one of his demands was the recognition of Indian customary marriages. This demand was finally accepted by the South African union government in compromise to end the *satyagraha* in South Africa in 1914.

FESTIVALS, WORSHIP AND RITUALS

Although the plantation regime in South Africa was more interested in the work of Indians than in the observance of their cultural festivals, planters and officials recognized some Indian celebrations. Muharram was one of these. In Natal it was popularly known as 'Coolie Christmas'. Every Indian across religious boundaries participated in Muharram, celebrating the Tazia commemoration. Yet Muharram also became an occasion of confrontation between the police and labourers. Explaining the causes of these clashes between the police and indentured workers, Prabhu Mohapatra argues that the Tazia procession was seen as a big problem for the administration because it brought customary rights into public space and therefore powerfully articulated community aspirations and religious beliefs, challenging the spatial immobility engendered by the indenture system.[35]

In Natal, an annual leave of three days was granted to 'coolie Indians' for the festival of Muharram. During the strike in South Africa in 1913,[36] the *Natal Mercury* reported on Muharram:

The Mohammedan festival of Muharram came at an opportune time this year because it gave 'sunny' and 'May' a chance to show that in the midst of their troubles they still retain their wanted capacity for enjoying themselves. The Indian is a genius at smiling his sorrows away, and yesterday, in spite of the fact that the rain, like the poor was always with us, the Indian community honoured the festival in right royal fashion.[37]

Indentured Indians in Natal also celebrated many Hindu festivals and traditions, including Holi and Diwali. More than 80 per cent of indentured Indians were Hindus, and they did not simply forget their religio-cultural practices upon reaching the Natal plantations. They tried to maintain some aspects of their beliefs and cultural practices, which in most cases required modification to fit their new environment. For example, Hindu priests still played a role in marriage and death ceremonies, as in the case of Matadin Nancoo. When his daughter Tejia got married in 1887, Ganesh Maharaj performed the wedding ceremony.[38] In 1890, Chaita Masan was organized to celebrate Tamil New Year, and Draupadi (fire-walking), the celebration of Kavadi in honour of the god Muruga, was also organized every year by indentured workers.

Rangasammy, an indentured labourer, told the Coolie Commission that he wished for them to protect his cultural and religious life in Natal. C. Behrens, manager of a plantation, stated to the commission that the 'coolies have built a Hindu temple at Riet Valley for worship'.[39] On the sugar estates, too, Indian workers erected temples and shrines for their deities. Some plantations provided land to build temples for worship. For instance, the Lush plantation in Natal gave land to labourers to build a temple near a river. Temples of Shiva, Vishnu and Narayan were erected during the indenture period. In 1888, Chundoo Sing and Baba Talwantsing, who both came to Natal as indentured workers, founded the Gopallal Hindu Temple in Verulam. Places of worship continued to be founded in Natal by indentured Indians until the end of the system.

In later years, Arya Samaj and Sanatan Dharma preachers reached Natal. They formed various societies. Bhai Paramanand was the first to travel to Natal to deliver a lecture on the Hinduism, education and philosophy of India. Later on, discontent began to emerge in Natal between Hindus and Muslims concerning the issue of *shuddhi* (purification), and the issue of cow killing also subsequently reached Natal.[40]

WORK, WAGES AND SAVINGS

Indenture contracts included a written document listing the wages which indentured workers were to receive for their work per day. According to the contracts of Natal workers, they were to work nine hours between sunrise and sunset, from Monday to Saturday. Table 2.1 shows their monthly and daily wages or task-work rates.

It is difficult to find information about the savings of indentured workers in the colonies, but data concerning the savings of those indentured migrants who returned to India following the end of their contract are available. The statement of savings of returned migrants provides a glimpse of their economic status during the indenture period. The following table shows the number of emigrants who returned from the colonies, the amount of their savings and the percentage of mortality on the passage, as exhibited in the subjoined statement for 1876 (Table 2.2).[41]

The data indicate that even though life on the plantations was harsh, migrants were able to save their earnings. Since rations, clothes and medical facilities were provided by the planters during the period of contract, labourers did not have to pay for essential items, allowing them to save

Table 2.1 Monthly and daily wages or task rates (besides free rations)

For men of 15 and upwards minimum rates as follows:	
First year 10 shillings monthly equal to rupees	8 0 0
Second year	9 0 0
Third year	10 0 0
Fourth year	11 0 0
Fifth year	12 0 0

Source: Desai and Vahed (2007, 38).

Note: Adult males working at the mines will receive two shillings extra per month for working on the surface and five shillings extra per month for workers under ground in addition to the aforementioned wages and rations. The women are paid half wages and minors in proportion. Free house to live in and medical attendance.

Rations for an adult as mentioned here:

1½ lbs (4½ ollocks) of rice daily, or for 3 days in the week, in lieu of rice, 2 lbs (5½ ollocks) of maize meal.

Dal	2 lbs (5½ ollocks) per month
Salt	1 lb (2¾ ollocks) per month
Salt fish	2lbs (5½ ollocks) per month
Ghee or oil	2 lbs (5½ ollocks) per month

Immigrants under 12 years of age will receive three fourth of the aforementioned rations.

money. In Natal, there is ample evidence of indentured workers prospering after finishing their contract, as noted in the examples of Boodha Dulel Sing and Charlie Nulliah, in the previous section.

C. F. Andrews and W. W. Pearson, while conducting an independent inquiry into the conditions experienced by Indians in Fiji, found many instances of prosperous Indian ex-indentured labourers. They observed:[42]

> The following are typical cases of prosperous growers of sugar-cane among the Indians in the north of the island:
>
> > Luchman has been three years out of indenture and was able to sell his cane last year for Rs. 1635.
> >
> > Nathu, who has been five years out of indenture, has grown 531 tons of sugar-cane on twenty-three acres of land. He received for his crop Rs. 7,200. This man sold out his interest in the land and its standing crops for Rs. 13,500.

Table 2.2 Savings among returnees and mortality on the passage, 1876

Colonies	No. of ships	No. of souls	Average % of mortality	Savings					
				Aggregate amount			Average amount		
				Rupees	Annas	Pice	Rupees	Annas	Pice
Mauritius	8	1,782	0.84	286,989	0	0	161	0	9
Demerara	1	443	1.35	93,442	3	0	210	14	10
St Vincent		40	12.50	7,026	4	0	175	10	6
Jamaica	1	268	33.20	20,272	0	0	75	10	3
Trinidad	By mail steamer	2	–	5,687	8	0	2,843	12	0
Natal	1	139	2.15	37,703	0	0	271	3	2
Total	11	2,674	4.41	4,51,119	15	0	168	11	3

Source: Annual Report of 1876, Revenue and Agriculture, Emigration, Progs A, 1877.

Ram Singh told us that he had received Rs. 12,000 for his last year's crop. This sum, however, does not present the net profit. An encouraging fact is his cane cultivation by an extensive use of green manure. The small Indian holders, we were told, had not made sufficient use of scientific cultivation, with the inevitable result that their crops are inferior in quality, and the soil is gradually becoming impoverished.

[In 1914 independent Indian growers of cane supplied to the company's mills at Lautaka, on the north of side of the island, a total of 32,328 tons of cane, which realised 2,85,000 rupees, at an average of eleven shillings and eight pence per ton. In 1915 from the same source the estimate was 47,000 tons of cane which would realise 5,40,500 rupees at an average of fifteen shillings and four pence per ton. In this Lautaka district 34% of the total sugar-cane land is already in Indians' hands, and all along the north coast the percentage is ever increasing. In the district of Nadi alone there is a population of 5,000 free Indians and the monthly average applications for leases of land at the magistrate's court was fifty. There are thus a large number of free Indians who are now growing sugar-cane, quite independently, on holdings varying from five to three hundred acres in extent. The large Indian cultivators employ numbers of free Indians to carry on the ploughing, manuring, weeding and cutting of the cane.]

A settlement of free Indians on the border of a small European plantation. These have recently come out of indenture and settled near their old employer. The planter gave to them, at a very low rate, during the last year of their indenture, a piece of ground for growing cane. He now uses their free labour, at the heavy seasons of the year, paying them full wages. In this way, he has been able to reduce the number of coolies under indenture on his estate. The Indians seemed prosperous and contented. The planter was evidently their friend, and they were some distance away from any large coolie 'lines'.

From all this it will be clear that every year the interests of the Indian free settlers will have to be taken into consideration in an increasing measure. For the long run, if the present rate of progress continues, they will be the chief growers and producers of cane in the islands. Indeed, the time may be not far distant, when the European cane grower will give place to the Indian altogether, the organizing work at the centres alone remaining in the Europeans' hands. If the new offer of the colonial sugar refinery company to place pound 100,000 at a low rate of interest at the disposal of the Fiji government for Indians' settlement be accepted and the settlement carried out, this predominance of the Indian cultivator as a grower of sugar-cane for the company's mills will be practically assured.

EVERYDAY LIFE ON THE PLANTATIONS

Various petitions written by indentured workers give us rare insights into everyday life on the plantations. On 6 December 1872, a group of coolies wrote a petition to the town clerk, asking for an increase in their wages:

We, the undersigned Coolies in the service of the Corporation, beg most respectfully to submit the under mentioned pitiful petition for the consideration of the Town Council ... we the undersigned coolies have got large famil[ies] and the wages that we get at present [are] not enough to maintain our poor distressed famil[ies] ... for the period of 9 years of which the corporation is aware [we have] worked hard and tried our endeavours to render the Corporation every satisfaction ... we have received 16 shillings which wages [are] not enough to maintain ourselves … and we also [drove on] the road to draw the cart load of stones, which we feel it very hard and also our strength is broken down, and sometimes we are so badly in want of clothes we are very afraid to go out bare body to the public road, for fear we will be taken to the station. So our extreme need is very great.[43]

The aforementioned petition, negotiating for an improvement in pay and conditions, complains that the wages in the colonies were not always sufficient for a single worker to support a large family and prosper as they might have hoped. Apart from the nominal wages, coolies' complaints also detail assaults by managers of plantations and estates. For example, Hureebhukut's deposition of 10 February 1877 is as follows:

I am an indentured coolie and work for Mr. Thomas Brown, Umgeni Sugar Estate. On Friday … at morning muster I was present, and told the manager Mr. John Brown that I was sick, and went home. Half an hour after, the white man who is in charge of the coolies at the mill, came to me, and said come on, at the same time struck me with a whip which he had in his hand, twice on the legs. Fearing that he would strike me again, I went off to the mill and worked all day. Again at muster on Saturday morning I told the manager and sirdar that I was sick, suffering from loose bowels and was not able to work. So I went to my hut; about an hour after, the same white man came to my hut. I was at that time just entering my hut when he caught me by the neck and struck me three times on the back with a stick after which I snatched away the stick and ran into the cane.[44]

In another complaint lodged by indentured workers with the protector of immigrants concerning ill treatment at the estate of J. Meikle, an indentured labourer, Bhagoo, provided the following testimony dated 19 February 1884:

I am indentured to Mr. Meikle. Five of the men who were assigned with me ran away as they were ill-treated, and about a fortnight ago one of my sons named Augna (25980) about 10 years of age left the estate and has not been heard of since. The circumstances of his leaving were, he had 50 sheep to look after and one evening one did not return with the rest, the boy also through fear stayed away. The missing sheep afterwards returned and the boy also. The next morning Mr. Meikle with Mrs

Meikle's approval tied the boy's hands together with a strap and hung him naked to a rafter in the dining room and thrashed him with a hunting crop. The boy was kept hanging for an hour about two feet from the ground and when breakfast time came he was taken down and sent off with the sheep as usual. He went but as stated never returned.

I am served with (Junari) Kaffir Ammabella one month; and with mealy meal another, I also get salt and dhal but no fish, ghee or rice … I have not received wages for 4 months.[45]

Plantation life was evidently gruelling, whether in Natal, Fiji or elsewhere in the empire. Totaram Sanadhya and Baba Ramchandra, both poor, high-caste indentured migrants to Fiji who subsequently returned to India, discussed the hardships of the plantation in Fiji in accounts based upon their experiences. These figured prominently in the nationalist anti-indenture campaign in India between 1914 and 1917. Sanadhya wrote that coolies were given small rooms to live in, each was 12-feet long and 8-feet wide. If a man was together with his wife, then they were given this room, otherwise he claimed three men or three women were lodged in one room. This was in disregard of the rule that 'employers of Indian labourers must provide at their own expense suitable dwellings for immigrants'.[46] The style and dimension of these buildings were fixed by regulations and insufficient for a coolie working 10 hours a day on the estate. Along with this, for the first six months, the estate provided food and other items, and for this, two shillings and four pence were cut from each week's pay.[47]

According to Sanadhya, women faced more difficulties than men on the plantations, having to labour and also attend to their family's needs. The average woman had to wake up at 3:30 in the morning and prepare food; after that she had to work 10 hours in the field and again prepare food upon returning home. Sanadhya here is at his caustic best:

When women return from work, there is corpse-like shading to their faces. One is so sad to see the dirtiness of their faces at that time that it is indescribable. These women who had never been out of their village in India, who didn't know that there was a country outside of their district, who are soft and tender by nature, who never did hard work at home, these women today, having gone thousands of miles away, to Fiji, Jamaica, Cuba, Honduras, Guyana and so forth have to do hard labour for ten hours a day.[48]

Sanadhya claimed that the women who went to Fiji were not used to hard work and had no knowledge about the world beyond the boundary of their districts. However, this idea contradicts the widespread use of female labour on family farms in north India and also the statistical analyses of Brij V. Lal that about half of the women who reached Fiji were already on the move in search of work.[49]

Sanadhya's account describes the female Indian labourer in Fiji as being in a more vulnerable position than their male counterpart. This was in part, he alleged, because they were subjected to sexual exploitation at the hands of both Indian men and white overseers and agents on the plantations. Ramchandra similarly sensationally claimed:

> Beautiful women are given work at secluded places and both blacks [Indians] and whites sexually exploit their seclusion. Pregnant women are made to work till full term. If they refuse they are tortured so much that it leads to abortion.[50]

These accounts may have been exaggerated, but it was certainly not an easy life. Concerns about the imagined hardships of life on plantations attracted the attention of cartoonists at the time. A Chinese schoolmaster in Georgetown thus gave the following woodcut to Edward Jenkins, who was on a visit to British Guyana to write a book on the condition of coolie labourers (Figure 2.4).

Jenkins explained the cartoon as follows:

> The picture is a tolerably fair representation of a manager's house on its brick pillars. To the left, at the bottom of the picture, is a free Coolie driving his cattle. To the right a rural constable is seizing an unhappy pigtail to convey him to the lock-up, being absent, as we see, from the band just above him, with his arms unbound. This indicates that he is trying to avoid the restraints of his indenture, and for this he is liable – to punishment. Above him, on the right of the picture, is a group of Chinese, and on the left of the steps a group of Indians, represented with their arms bound, an emblem of indentureship. They always speak of themselves as 'bound' when under indenture. At the foot of the steps, on either side, are a Chinaman and a Coolie, from whose breasts two drivers are drawing blood with a knife, the life fluid being caught by boys in the swizzle-glasses of the colony. A boy is carrying the glasses up the steps

Figure 2.4 Life on a sugar plantation as seen through eyes of an indentured labourer

Source: Jenkins (1871, 10).

to the attorney and the manager, who sit on the left of the verandah, and who are obviously fattening at the expense of the bound people below them. A fat wife and children look out of the windows. Behind, through a break in the wall, are represented the happy and healthy owners in England; to the right, under the tree, through a gap in the fence, are aged Chinese, weeping over their unfortunate relatives. In the right-hand corner of the verandah is the pay-table, with the overseers discussing and arranging stoppages of wages. The smoking chimney of the kitchen and the horse eating his provender seem to be intended to contrast with the scene in front. This, then, gives a picturesquely sentimental and satirical aspect of the grievances likely to arise under the Coolie system.[51]

Pitcher and Grierson, two officials in north India, found the rumour of *mimiai ka tel* circulating during their enquiry into the working of the indenture system. Ashutosh Kumar has explained the cartoon as a depiction of *mimiai ka tel* as it was popularly known amongst north Indian peasants. This myth may have arisen due to the demand for young and able bodies for plantation work. Planters instructed the emigration agencies and recruiters in the countryside regarding their needs. Hence, the objection to old or unfit recruits and the publicized desire for the young excited a rumour that an expensive oil was only available in the heads of the young and juvenile.[52] Needless to say, this rumour circulated only in districts unaccustomed to migration.

Apart from the physically exhausting work on the plantations, there were many other problems faced by indentured workers in Natal. Many depositions of indentured workers suggest that the switching of wives was a major source of anxiety among male labourers. The plantation regime provided an unknown freedom for women to choose their partners. Hence, whenever a woman found her husband unsuitable, she left to live with someone else. This independence and assertiveness of women, and the collapse of patriarchal norms, were the reasons sometimes given for the occurrence of male suicides on plantations. In an attempt to redress the situation, male indentured workers often appealed for help to British officials. An example of this is encountered in letter written by Moothen, an indentured migrant, to the protector of Indian immigrants in Natal on 8 February 1875:

I have the honour to humbly to bring to your notice that my wife Chinnamah whom I am married to for upwards of twenty-four years and by whom were born to me five children one of which is deceased and four left with me to look after … is living with another Indian named Theracumny. They are both living together about a mile and half from Pietermaritzburg and my wife is conceived of a child by this Theracumny. I must state how my wife came to live with this man. I having heard that she was living with him, I went to give her advice and told her that she was not doing right towards me. She not heeding me but this Theracumny … deliberately and falsely went and complained to the magistrate of this division and there stated that I threatened to stab her with a knife. Subsequently the case was tried and I was bound to keep the peace towards her for 6 months, which is now over a week … I did not break the peace towards her and she went and lived with this Theracumny and during this 6 months and a week I had to keep my four children which is very hard seeing that I am a poor person.

Now sir, taking all these circumstances contained in this humble petition, I humbly leave it for your judgment and trust that my wife may be sent back to me.

CONCLUSION

Indian labourers who emigrated under the indenture system to South Africa and Fiji had a similar background in India and faced similar problems in their initial years on the plantations; they lacked a familiar family and social life. Yet new sociocultural arrangements developed that differed significantly from their homeland and conservative practices were replaced. Since they were all 'coolies' in the eyes of the planters, despite their varied caste backgrounds, they shared experiences on the plantations and notions of hierarchy and privilege were diluted. During the time of the indenture system, caste practices were not essential to social life in the plantation colonies. Labourers were commonly free to choose their life partners across caste and religious lines and the culture that developed reflected this. And women, if not satisfied with their partner, could leave to marry another. This does not mean that alongside this change indentured Indians did not retain many important religio-cultural practices of their homeland, including festivals such as Holi, Diwali, Muharram and Muruga. These religious practices were a syncretic composite of previous Indian beliefs and practices, that elided what were in India many profound differences. In this way, they formed a distinctive culture in relation to other races in the colonies. Furthermore, indentured and ex-indentured labourers became the backbone of the economy of their respective colonies. Many indentured labourers made their fortunes by saving their incomes under indenture and later opening new businesses, buying farms and going on to participate in mainstream politics. In these matters and many others, Indians in Fiji and Natal were able to avail themselves of opportunities that were not open to them in their homelands.

NOTES

1. In British history, the Slavery Abolition Act of 1833 was a law passed by Parliament that outlawed slavery in the majority of British colonies, liberating more than 800,000 enslaved Africans in the Caribbean, South

Africa, and a small number of people in Canada. On 28 August 1833, it was given royal assent, and on 1 August 1834, it became operative.

2. Rushbrook-Williams (1924, 6).

3. Rushbrook-Williams (1924, 7).

4. Kumar (2017).

5. Kumar (2017).

6. The terms and conditions in Natal were similar elsewhere in South Africa.

7. Register, 5/5. Indian Immigration Department, National Archives Depot, Pietermaritzburg.

8. Lal (1983, 7).

9. Lal (1983, 22).

10. Grierson (1883).

11. Bhana (1991).

12. Bhanan (1991).

13. Lal (1985).

14. Grierson (1883).

15. Grierson (1883).

16. Khan (1943, 138–139).

17. Sanadhya (2012, 5); translation mine.

18. Desai and Vahed (2007).

19. Grierson (1883, 19).

20. Gillion (1962, 162).

21. Mishra (1999, 2).

22. Lal (2005, 2).

23. Desai and Vahed (2007, 167).

24. Desai and Vahed (2007, 169).

25. Desai and Vahed (2007, 170).

26. Jayawardena (1968, 434).

27. Desai and Vahed (2007, 172).

28. Desai and Vahed (2007, 172).

29. Sanadhya (2012).

30. Sanadhya (2012, 79).

31. Sanadhya (2012, 79–81).

32. Desai and Vahed (2007, 190–191).

33. Desai and Vahed (2007, 193).

34. Desai and Vahed (2007, 205).

35. Mohapatra (2006, 173–202).

36. More than 20,000 workers went on strike in October and November 1913. Some workers were murdered by police shooting during the walkout, and other workers were brutally abused by their employer. Baton-wielding mounted police drove hundreds of people back under the custody of their bosses after injuring dozens of them seriously. There had never been a strike of this magnitude among Indian employees. In fact, the majority of people participating were indentured Indian workers.
37. Cited in Desai and Vahed (2007, 227).
38. Desai and Vahed (2007, 229)
39. Desai and Vahed (2007).
40. Desai and Vahed (2007, 242).
41. Annual Report of 1876, Revenue and Agriculture, Emigration, Progs A, 1877.
42. Andrews and Pearson (1916, 44–45).
43. Bhana and Pachai (1984, 4).
44. Bhana and Pachai (1984, 5).
45. Bhana and Pachai (1984, 5–6).
46. Sanadhya (2012).
47. Sanadhya (2012); see also Sanadhya (1974, 10).
48. Sanadhya (1974, 61).
49. Lal (2005).
50. Ramchandra (1937, 10).
51. Jenkins (1871, 10–13).
52. Kumar (2017).

BIBLIOGRAPHY

Andrews, Charles F., and W. W. Pearson. 1916. *Report on Indentured Labour in Fiji: An Independent Enquiry.* Calcutta: Star Printing.

Bhana, S. 1991. *Indentured Indian Emigrants to Natal.* New Delhi: Promila & Co.

Bhana, Surendra, and B. Pachai. 1984. *A Documentary History of Indian South Africans.* Cape Town: David Philip.

Desai, Ashwin, and Goolam Vahed. 2007. *Inside Indian Indenture: A South African Story 1860–1914.* Cape Town: HSRC Press.

Gillion, K. 1962. *Fiji's Indian Migrants: A History to the End of Indenture in 1922.* Melbourne: Oxford University Press.

Grierson, G. A. 1883. *Report on Colonial Emigration from the Bengal Presidency, Calcutta*. Calcutta: Government of Bengal.

Jayawardena, C. 1968. 'Migration and Social Change: A Survey of Indian Communities Overseas'. *Geographical Review* 58 (3): 426–449.

Jenkins, Edward. 1871. *Coolie: His Rights and Wrongs*. New York: George Routledge and Sons.

Khan, Munshi Rahman. 1943. 'Jiwan Prakash'. Unpublished manuscript.

Kumar, Ashutosh. 2015. 'Feeding the Girmitya: Food and Drinks on Indentured Ships to the Colonies'. *Gastronomica: The Journal of Critical Food Studies* 16(1): 39–51.

———. 2016. 'Feeding the Girmitiya: Food and Drink on Indentured Ships to the Sugar Colonies'. *Gastronomica: The Journal of Critical Food Studies* 16 (1): 41–52.

———. 2017. *Coolies of the Empire: Indentured Indians in the Sugar Colonies 1830–1920*. New Delhi: Cambridge University Press.

Lal, B. V. 1983. *Girmitiya: The Origin of Fiji Indians*. Canberra: The Journal of Pacific History.

———. 2005. *Fiji Yatra: Aadhi Raat Se Aage*. India: National Book Trust.

Lubbock, B. 1935. *Coolie Ships and Oil Sailors*. London: Brown, Son & Ferguson.

Mishra, Sudesh. 1999. *Diaspora and the Difficult Art of Dying*. Vol. 10 of *Subaltern Studies*. New Delhi: Oxford University Press.

Mohapatra, Prabhu P. 2006. '"Following Custom"? Representations of Community among Indian Immigrant Labour in the West Indies, 1880–1920'. *International Review of Social History* 51 (Supplement 14): 173–202.

Pitcher, D. G. 1883. *Report on Colonial Emigration from North Western Provinces*. Calcutta.

Ramchandra, Baba. 1937. Unpublished memoir. Ramchandra Private Papers, Nehru Memorial Museum and Library, New Delhi.

Rushbrook-Williams, L. F. 1924. *India of Today*, vol. 5: *Indian Emigration by Emigrants*. London: Oxford University Press.

Sanadhya, Totaram. 1973. *Fijidwip Me Mere Ikkish Varsh* [My Twenty-One Years in the Fiji Islands]. 4th ed. Varanasi: Pandit Banarasidas Chaturvedi. Originally published in 1914 by Rajput Anglo-Oriental Press, Agra.

———. 2012. *Bhootlen Ki Katha: Girmit Ke Anubhav* [in Hindi]. Edited by B. V. Lal, Ashutosh Kumar and Yogendra Yadav. New Delhi: Rajkamal Prakashan.

3

STORIES OF *GIRMITIYAS*

FOLKLORE AND THE SOCIOCULTURAL WORLD OF INDENTURED INDIANS IN THE SUGAR COLONIES

Ashutosh Kumar

The presence of Indian labour across the globe during the nineteenth century not only helped transform the capitalist global economy but also affected the cultural expression, including folklore, of migrant workers. More than 1.3 million Indians signed contracts of indentureship between 1834 and 1916 and shipped out to sugar plantations across the globe under the aegis of European empires.[1] The first colony to bring in Indian indentured work was Mauritius in 1834. British Guyana imported indentured labour next in 1838, Trinidad and Jamaica in 1845, the smaller West Indian colonies of St Kitts, St Lucia, St Vincent and Grenada in the 1850s, Natal in 1860, Suriname in 1873 and Fiji in 1879.[2] Most indentured Indian labourers chose to stay in their new homes after the termination of their contracts and formed a distinct Indian diaspora in their respective host countries. Indentured Indians brought many sociocultural norms and expressions to the host countries which evolved over the succeeding generations. Folklore is one of these traditions.

Folklore is the traditional expression of a society or a particular group of people in which folk tales, songs, ballads, proverbs or jokes are transmitted from one generation to another. In the course of transmission, the folklore changes, depending on the place and cultural context. This is one of the reasons that different versions of the same folk tales exist. The origin and authors of folklore usually remain hidden as the stories and traditions are carried on and spread orally among often illiterate people.

INDENTURED FOLK TALES

When indentured migrants reached plantation colonies, they not only brought Indian religio-cultural norms but also folklore. Most of the folklore of the indentured Indians is in the Bhojpuri language as the majority of migrants were from the Bhojpuri-speaking areas of north India. However, over time, exposure to the languages, places and space of the host countries meant that indentured folklore in Mauritius can be found in both Creole and Bhojpuri. Other folklore in Mauritius is recorded in south Indian languages, such as Tamil, as a significant portion of the indentured there were from south India.[3]

There are broadly five kinds of folk tales prevalent among Indian indentured societies across the globe.[4] These are didactic tales, social stories, religious tales, love stories and entertainment stories. Moralistic tales endeavoured to encourage certain behaviours in children (and adults). A moral education was attempted through such accounts. For instance, in Mauritius, the story of the old man and the crocodile ('Budha aur Magar') teaches that one should not help any creature until one knows its nature. The didactic tales provide advice to safeguard against social evils. In some stories, cautionary narratives describe the separation of a family due to a jealous woman in the home. Family dynamics dominate several stories: 'Gulabkawali' is based on the jealousy of an older brother towards his younger brother; 'Gular ka Phool' (Flower of the Cluster Fig) is about the insensitivity of a woman towards her husband; 'Udane Wala Ghoda' (Flying Horse) details the callousness of a father-in-law and mother-in-law towards their daughter and son-in-law. 'Kauva Hakani' (Crow Driver) describes the destructive attitudes of women, including the ignoring of a younger queen by the older queens (*sautiya darh*). Didactic stories conclude with a happy ending. This is due to the essential actions of human beings, which are based on good intentions. The heroes or central characters of the stories always deal bravely with the crises and problems they face before finally emerging victorious. For example, in 'Char Bahane' (Four Sisters), there is a challenging journey to be completed; in 'Udane Wala Ghoda', there is bravery; and in 'Gulabkawali', there is a terrifying struggle before the protagonist's triumph.

The social stories describe social evils in families and communities. Many indentured folk tales illustrate bickering among family members, but there are also accounts of fraudulent sages and incapable kings who bring sorrow to their kingdoms. The story 'Khargosh aur Ghongha' (Rabbit and Snail) describes the system of sale and purchase of slaves. 'Dhokhebaj Dost' (Deceitful Friend) deals with a break of faith. 'Saas–Bahu' (Mother-in-Law and Daughter-in-Law) is about the bitter relationship between a mother-in-law and daughter-in-law, whereas 'Dulari Bahan' (Adorable Sister) details the strained relationship between a woman and her sister-in-law.

Stories like 'Sahasi Vriddh' (Brave Old Man), 'Raja ke Sir me Singh' (Horns on the King's Head), 'Namak aur Roti' (Salt and Roti) and 'Unbujh Nagari' (Dark Kingdom) see people subjected to a sorrowful state of affairs due to an incompetent or foolish king. 'Kauva Hakani' and 'Gulabkawali' are about polygamy. What is striking in the indentured folklore, especially of Mauritius, is that there is no sign of child marriage, non-marriage and cross-caste marriages. Another important feature of the social stories of the indentured is that in almost all the stories, the central character is female, and male heroes are absent. In many stories, the central character must perform difficult tasks such as crossing vast tracts of forest or pass hard tests before they see the fulfilment of their wishes. The story of Sabur ('Sabur ki Katha') tells how a girl and her four sisters courageously cross a vast jungle. 'Dasi Bani Rani' (The Servant Who Became Queen) is about a queen who, after surmounting several obstacles, wins the love of her husband. In the story 'Kauva Hakani', a wretched queen becomes her husband's most beloved wife on attaining motherhood.

In religious stories, desires are fulfilled through fasting, mysticisms, devotion, worship, prayers or the performance of religious observances. To achieve the wish for a happy life, women especially are depicted as fasting on the occasion of religious festivals and ceremonies. The story of 'Saas–Bahu' (Mother-in-Law and Daughter-in-Law) is an excellent example of such fasting. 'Kauva Hakani' describes a religious ceremony performed by a king. Indian indentured women in overseas colonies fasted for the well-being of their husbands, sons and brothers. Folk tales also seem to reflect the anxiety of indentured women concerning the birth of the requisite male child. In the story of 'Kauva Hakani', all seven queens eat sacred food, hoping that they will be blessed with a male child. However, only a younger queen gives birth to a boy, making her the king's most beloved.

Love is another theme of the folk tales of indentured Indians. In love stories, duty, respect and obedience are recurring threads. The stories depict different kinds of love, such as the love of a mother toward her child, especially her son, a husband's love towards his wife and ideal love between brothers. In the stories 'Gulabkawali', 'Sabur ki Katha', 'Dukh ki Peti' (Box of Sorrows) and 'Dasi Bani Rani', ideal love between husband and wife is depicted. 'Kauva Hakani', 'Dhokhebaj Dost' and 'Sone ka Anda Dene Wali Pakshi' (Bird Which Lays the Golden Egg) represent love between mother and son. 'Dasi Bani Rani' is a fine example of the love of a daughter. 'Dular Bahan' and 'Bajr ka Kiwad' (Strong Door) are examples of true love between brothers and sisters. Indo-Mauritian folklorist Pahlad Ramsurun believes that the love stories of the indentured in Mauritius are influenced by Indian religious epics and stories where the ideal love of Ram–Sita, Savitri–Satyavan, Nal–Damayanti and Sadavrij–Saranga features. These are very popular in Mauritius. 'Sabur ki Katha' and 'Das Bani Rani' are examples of tales where dutiful and virtuous wives save their husbands by taking the utmost care of them.

Entertaining stories among the indentured folk tales primarily seek to amuse their audiences, especially children, whose mental development they also aid. Stories related to dogs, cats, rats, horses and tigers remain attractive to children. These entertaining stories express complicated subjects in the simplest ways. 'Chhipkali aur Girgit' (Lizard and Chameleon), 'Prithvi par Mrityu ka Agaman' (Coming of Death on Earth) and 'Raja aur Bandar' (King and Monkey) are some examples of this.

What is significant about indentured folk tales is that the stories have changed with context, place and time. Sometimes even seven versions of the same story can exist. Common changes include modified versions of the stories with any sexually explicit content removed. This is due to the changing perceptions of Indians regarding pornography and sex. Therefore, stories containing 'indecent' aspects are transformed to maintain propriety. For example, the story 'Sabur ki Katha' is an imitation of a sexually explicit story 'Hazar aur Ek Raten' in which a Muslim woman uses a *sabura* (a wooden or rubber penis used to satisfy sexual desire). Indentured women altered the narrative to fit their requirements of decency. In the indentured version of this story, the *sabura* becomes a *pankha* (hand fan). Similarly, in the story of 'Dasi Bani Rani', a sex toy reference is hidden behind a *kali kathputali* (black puppet). By looking at the structure of these stories, one can perceive the change. In 'Sabur ki Katha', a merchant traveller asks his daughters what gifts he should bring for them. One says jewellery, the second says clothes and the third says a *sabur*. In 'Dasi Bani Rani', likewise, the king asks his fake queen and the original queen (whom he treated as a servant) what gift they would like from foreign lands. The false queen desires *sui–dhaga* (needle and thread), while the original queen asks for a *kali kathputali*. Both things were not available in the local shops, and knowledge of both items was gained through an older woman. Both items were also costly, but the merchant and king had to buy them. In 'Sabur ki Katha', a shopkeeper advises the merchant traveller that his daughter should use this item only when she is alone in a room. Comparatively, in the story of 'Das Bani Rani', the original queen uses the item when everyone sleeps at night. Hence, in both stories, the sexual components are concealed to erase indecency while preserving the knowledge and entertainment contained in the tale.

FOLK CULTURE IN FOLK TALES

Indentured folktales can tell us about three main elements of folk culture: quotidian life, family life and social life. Other specific aspects, such as religious beliefs, festive activities and sources of amusement can also be discerned. References to quotidian features such as dwellings, food habits, clothes and jewellery, make-up, adornments, housekeeping, tools of agriculture and transport are all found in folklore. For example, indentured folk tales mention traditional dwellings as well as modern dwellings.[5] In terms of elite dwellings, we find reference to forts, palaces and castles in stories including 'Dasi Bani Rani', 'Khargosh aur Ghogha' (Rabbit and Snail) and 'Sabur ki Katha'. Simultaneously we can also find public buildings such as churches, banks, hospitals and government schools. In regard to the humbler dwellings of the masses, there are mentions of grass huts, houses, depots and *machan*s (raised seats of bamboo). In 'Mochi ka Duhsahas' (Audacity of the Cobbler) and 'Badnasib Bandar' (Unfortunate Monkey), for instance, there are descriptions of grass huts.

When it comes to food, delicious upper-class food such as milk, curd, *laddu*, *malida*, *kheer* and *puwa* feature, as well as low-class fare such as *daal–roti* (lentils with roti), rice and *sattu* with water. In 'Budhiya ki Jeet' (Victory of the Old Woman), there is mention of *dal–roti*, while in 'Kauva Hakani', *sattu–pani* is featured. Rice is referred to in the story of 'Kachhuwa aur Bandar' (Tortoise and Monkey). Apart from these, there are mentions of butter, fish, sherbet, coffee, soup, honey, alcohol and salt, based on the location.

Before Indians arrived in Mauritius, enslaved Africans predominantly ate *monyok* and Arabic potatoes. Indian migrants introduced rice, and this transformation is depicted in folk tales such as 'Kachhuwa aur Bandar'.

Some stories indirectly describe the master–labourer relationship in Mauritius. For example, 'Khargosh aur Ghogha' portrays the hardships of plantation life; the clever rabbit rules over the snail, but when his self-interests are fulfilled, he sells the snail to a butcher. In this story, the rabbit represents white planters, and the snail the innocent labourers. Similar to indentured labourers, the snail receives six rupees as salary, half a bag of rice, some lentils and salt.

In indentured folktales, there is mention of conventional Indian attire such as the *dhoti* (a cloth wrapped around the waist, taken between the legs and fastened at the back), *achakan* (a long coat with a round collar), *pagadi* (turban), *sehra* (headdress worn by a groom during weddings) and traditional shoes. Women's jewellery in the tales includes the *payal* (anklet), *anguthi* (ring), *ginni* and *mala* (garland), besides gold, silver and diamond necklaces. Make-up includes depictions of vermilion, the 16 bridal adornments (*solah shringar*) and *mehandi* (henna). Reference is also made to upper-class goods such as beds, chairs, *almirah*s, fans, photographs, magazines and books. In contrast to elite items, the *khat* (a kind of bed used in rural areas), mat and *pirha* (a wooden stool to sit on) are seen in relation to subaltern households, as are agricultural tools such as *kudari* (pickaxe), *kunda* (piece of wood) and *kulhadi* (small hatchet). Swords, hammers, cutlery and knives are also seen in the stories.

The introduction by Indian migrants of new items to their host countries sparked references to these in their folk tales. The migrants' exposure to novel things had a similar effect. Since Indians were usually indentured to work on sugar plantations, references to sugar cane production occur. For example, 'Jannat Ki Handi' (Pot of Heaven) centres on crops like sugar cane, barley and corn. Since many indentured colonies were islands, we find mention of ships, boats, *mallah*s and captains. In the story, 'Do Yatri' (Two Travelers), *singh* (lion), dodo (a Mauritian bird, now extinct) and elements of the sea are discussed. Mauritian indentured folk tales have also been impacted by the European, African and Indian folk culture of people who reached Mauritius at different times. Hence, the flora and fauna of these countries or continents can be found in Mauritian tales.

Family folk culture is defined by ties which strengthen or weaken relationships. These bindings include family ideals, behaviours, organization and triumphs or quarrels. They also require obedience – of sons and daughters, women, sisters-in-law and daughters-in-law and in matrimony. 'Gulabkawali', for example, describes an obedient son. His four brothers misuse the property of their father, the king. However, he, the fifth son, protects the property through his cleverness, bravery and conscientiousness. He cures his father's eyes and spreads happiness wherever he goes. He is killed by his brothers, but Gulabkawali, a fairy, revives him, and finally he becomes the king's successor.

In 'Kauva Hakani', six envious queens succeed in destroying the married life of the seventh queen. They force her out of the palace on account of her childlessness and make her a *kauva hakani* (crow driver). However, the youngest (seventh) queen remains patient and gives birth to a baby boy. This is the turning point, and she finally receives the king's love and becomes queen again.

The bitter relationship between a mother-in-law and daughter-in-law is depicted in the story 'Saas–Bahu', where the mother-in-law feels neglected and insulted by her daughter-in-law. Despite this, and even when in peril, she prays for the well-being of her daughter-in-law. However, the daughter-in-law conspires with her husband to burn the mother-in-law alive. Fortunately, an illusion sent by God allows the mother-in-law to escape safely, and the daughter-in-law burns instead.

In indentured colonies, we can see obvious variations in forms of civility and courtesy. In Mauritius, the French say 'bonjour', the English say 'good morning', Muslims use 'salaam', Sanatanies use 'paylagi' and Arya Samajis use 'namaste'. Such civilities are depicted in the folk tales of the indentured in Mauritius. For instance, in the story 'Mochi ka Duhsahas', the characters say 'paylagi'.

Folk culture can be easily seen in the stories of social life. Indentured folk stories contain information about the caste system; brahmanical traditions; the hierarchy of castes; the *ashram* and *varna* system; beliefs related to religion, customs and festivals; folk beliefs and popular proverbs and sayings. In 'Bhagyavan Jyotishi' (Lucky Astrologer), there are descriptions of traditional brahmanical practices such as palm reading, ritual performances during weddings and activities linked to worship in temples. Similarly, Kshatriyas are discussed in 'Udane Wala Ghoda' in the context of rule, administration and war. 'Sabur ki Katha' and 'Do Yatri' inform us about agricultural work undertaken by Vaishyas and business by traders. Remarkably, there are few references to Shudras. We can only find evidence of a cobbler and a washerman in 'Mochi ka Dauhsahas'. Barbers, herdsmen (*gwala*), artisans, *zamindars*, doctors and letter carriers are also mentioned in the folk stories.

Amusing pastimes also find a place in indentured folk tales. These include the game of *gulli–danda*,[6] slave dances, a dance by a fairy and mentions of musical instruments such as a *sarangi* (a stringed instrument), *manjira* (a small pair of cymbals), *veena* (a stringed instrument), *ektara* (a single-stringed instrument), *jhal* (medium-sized pairs of cymbals), *dholak* (a medium-sized two-sided drum), harmonium and flute.

INDENTURED FOLK SONGS

Folk songs are an important and influential component of indentured folklore. They not only illustrate a culture but also became an instrument of resistance against the plantation regime. Indentured labourers in the sugar colonies expressed their grievances and adversities through folk songs. There are a variety of folk songs, and though we cannot ascertain the date of their composition, it is clear that they were sung in the course of migration and in the colonies while working on the plantations. This means that they provide us with a remarkable source for understanding the life of indentured labourers. An important set of folk songs are related to the pain of migration and separation and are a part of Bidesia culture, which consists of songs, poetry, drama, dance and other art narrating the anguish of both the people left behind and those who were leaving for foreign shores.[7] Indentured Indians expressed their experiences in such songs. For instance, an indentured folk song from Fiji reads as follows:

> Kali kothariya me bite nahi ratiya ho
> Kiske batae ham pir re bidesia
> Din rat biti hamari dukh me umariya ho
> Sukha sab naunuwa ke nir re bidesia[8]

> The night is difficult to pass in the dark rooms
> To whom I should confide my pain
> My days and nights are passing in grief
> The water of my eyes is dry now.

Many indentured labourers felt that they were tricked into recruitment under the indenture system and blamed the colonial government. They expressed this in their folk songs. The following is an example:

Khun pasina se siche ham bagiya
Baitha baitha hukum chalaye re bidesia
Firangiya ke rajua me chhuta mora desua
Gori Sarkar chali chal re bidesia[9]

We irrigated the plantation with our sweat and blood
They sit and command us, O migrant
In the British rule, I was forced to leave my country
The White government does trickery, O migrant

Along with male migrants, many women also went to overseas sugar colonies under the indenture system. Indentured folk songs depict how these women were deceived through false promises made by recruiters. They signed contracts which they could not understand the terms of. This is expressed in the following song:

Bholi bhali dekh arkati bharmaya ho
Kalkatta par jao pach sal re bidesiya
Dipuwa ma laye pakadayo kagaduwa ho
Angutha lagay din hay re bidesiya
Pal ke jahajuwa me roye dhoye baithi ho
Kaise hoi kalapani par re bidesia
Jiura daraye ghat kyo nahi aaye ho
Bite kai din bhaye mas re bidesiya
Aayi ghat dekhe jab fijiya ke tapua ho
Bhaya man hamara udas re bidesia[10]

Seeing innocent me, an arkati/recruiter misled me,
Go beyond Calcutta for five years O migrant.
Brought into the depot to makeover the [contract] paper,
Took fingerprint on it O migrant.
In the sailing ship I sit crying,
How did I cross the black-water O migrant …
In the dark room, the night was not passing,
How do I express my pain O migrant?

On the plantations, Indian labourers worked in the fields all day, in sun or rain, with spades and pickaxes. Any mistakes were met with a whipping from the manager. The pain and also happiness of the indentured were expressed in their traditional folk style. Since most of them were from the Bhojpuri-speaking areas of north India, the folk songs of indentured Indians are usually in the language and style of that region. They also conveyed the realities of their conditions in satirical ways. The following describes their rooms on the plantations:

Sab sukh khan C. S. R. ki kothariya
Chhar foot chaudi, aath foot lambi
Usi me dhari hai kamani ki kudariya
Usi me sil aur usi me chulha
Usi me dhari hai jalane ki lakadiya
Usi me mahal, usi me dumahla
Usi me bani hai sone ki atariya[11]

The rooms of C. S. R. contain all luxuries,
Four foot wide and eight foot long
There is a spade inside the room
There is a grinding stone and make-shift stove
There is also wood for firing inside
This is a palace and double palace inside
There is also a slab for sleeping inside

In the aforementioned song, indentured labourers in Fiji describe the plantation quarters satirically as a place of heaven. However, a different version of the same song was also sung by them:

Sab dukhkhan C. S. R. ki kothariya
Yahi me khana yahi me sona, yahi me bahat panariya
Pas khada sardarwa dekhe sir par hardam hanat kudariya
Mud fatah hai, deh dukhat hai, tuti jawai sabki kamariya[12]

There is every sorrow in the rooms of C. S. R.
One has to eat and sleep in this, there is a drain also inside
A sirdar is always watchful, one has to work continuously with a spade
The head aches and body pains, everyone's back is broken.

Through the folk songs, the migrants themselves agree with the complaints of the Bhojpuri people that they left their homeland in search of money. This is brought out in a Mauritian Bhojpuri folk song:

Sonwa karan aili ram, ehire marich des
Segati bhaile sonwa sarir, ehi re marich des

We came to this Mauritius land because of money
This money is the cause of the torture of our bodies in this Mauritius land.

The Bidesias themselves say that they did not want to leave their homeland, but their compulsions led them to do so. One song sung in Suriname depicts the misery of the migrants in their destinations:

Ab se khabardar raho bhai
Teri bigri baat banjai
Kalkatte mein bharti karke bhej diye jab bhai
laye utare surinam mein dipu mein bhat khawai
Teen mahine jalyan safar mein lakh jhapere khai
Shri ram nagar ki charcha karke surinam giye pahunchai
Hot savera nam bulakar bakara ne baat sunai
Paanch saal contrak kat lo fir bharat dev pahunchai
chautis hazar bharati aae the bara hazar gaye lautai
1873 se 1926 tak chausat jalyan yaha bhai
jahaji bankar aye the, sab bankar rahe jahaji bhai[13]

Be careful and your bad fortune will come to an end.
From Calcutta, we were sent to a depot in Suriname where we were fed rice.
After a three month long difficult journey by ship,
we reached Suriname, which we had earlier taken to be Shri Ram's land.
As soon as it is morning, the *bakara* (white owner),
called us and promised to send us back to India after completing the five-year contract.
34,000 Indians came here and only 12,000 have gone back.
Between 1873 and 1926, 64 ships came here.
We came here as *jahaji*, and remained as *jahaji* brothers.

CONCLUSION

The hundreds of thousands of Indian labourers who travelled overseas under indenture contracts to work on sugar plantations across the globe in the nineteenth and early twentieth centuries carried diverse traditions and folklore with them. However, their folk tales evolved with their experiences; narratives grew and altered following interactions with new people, environments, flora and fauna. The stories serve as receptacles of sociocultural practices, family dynamics and culture in a new land. Sometimes they played an educational role but they also helped migrants to mitigate their hardships through togetherness and entertainment.

Significantly, indentured Indians brought a homegrown culture of expressive folk songs with them. They conveyed their sorrow and happiness through these songs. Most of them are in the *bidesia* style, which had been prevalent in the Bhojpuri-speaking areas of north India where many of them originated.

While striving to create a new life in the plantation colonies, the Indian indentured labourers consolidated their cultural presence with their folklore and songs. They imbued the complex fabric of the host countries with the potent influence of their cultural heritage and have left us with a rich source of insights into their lives.

NOTES

1. For a general historiography on indenture, see Gangulee (1947); Nath (1950); Kondapi (1951); Cumpston (1953); Gillian (1962); Weller (1968); Saha (1970); Tinker (1974); Lal (1983); Kale (1998); Kumar (2017).

2. See Northrup (1995).

3. For the folklore of Mauritius, see Ramsuran (1974).

4. All the folk tales mentioned in this chapter are from the following sources: Ramsuran (1974); Parmasad (1984); Mahabir (2005).

5. Ramsuran (1990).

6. Indian subcontinent-born *gulli-danda* is a sport that is popular in small towns and rural areas. Two sticks are used in the game: a huge one called a *danda* and a smaller one called a *gulli*.

7. For a deeper analysis of the songs of indentured Indians, see Kumar (2013, 2015).

8. Cited from Varma (2000); translation mine.

9. Varma (2000); translation mine.
10. Varma (2000); translation mine.
11. Varma (2000); translation mine.
12. Varma (2000); translation mine.
13. Cited from Mazumdar (2008); translation mine.

BIBLIOGRAPHY

Cumpston, I. M. 1953. *Indians Overseas in British Territories, 1834–1854*. Oxford: Oxford University Press.

Gangulee, N. 1947. *Indians in the Empire Overseas*. London: New India Publishing House.

Gillian, K. L. 1962. *Fiji's Indian Migrants: A History to the End of Indenture in 1920*. Melbourne: Oxford University Press.

Kale, Madhavi. 1998. *Fragments of Empire: Capital, Slavery, and Indian Indentured Labour in the British Caribbean*. Pennsylvania: University of Pennsylvania Press.

Kondapi, C. 1951. *Indians Overseas*. Madras: Oxford University Press.

Kumar, Ashutosh. 2013. 'Anti-Indenture Bhojpuri Folk Songs and Poems from North India'. *Man in India: An International Journal of Anthropology* 93(4): 509–519.

———. 2015. 'Songs of Abolition: The Anti-Indenture Campaign in Early Twentieth Century India'. In *Indian Diaspora: Socio-Cultural and Religious Worlds*, edited by P. Pratap Kumar, 38–51. Amsterdam: Brill.

———. 2017. *Coolies of the Empire: Indentured Indians in the Sugar Colonies, 1830–1920*. New Delhi: Cambridge University Press.

Lal, Brij V. 1983. *Girmitiyas: The Origin of the Fiji Indians*. Canberra: The Journal of Pacific History.

Mahabir, Kumar. 2005. *Caribbean Indian Folktales*. San Juan: Chakra Publishing House.

Mazumdar, Mausami. 2008. *Kahe Gaile Bides, Why Did You Go Overseas*. Allahabad: G. B. Pant Social Science Institute.

Nath, Dwarka. 1950. *A History of Indians in British Guiana*. London: Nelson.

Northrup, David. 1995. *Indentured Labour in the Age of Imperialism, 1834–1922*. New York: Cambridge University Press.

Parmasad, Kenneth Vidia. 1984. *Salt and Roti: Indian Folktales of the Caribbean*. Charlieville: Sankh Productions.

Ramsuran, Pahlad. 1974. *Mauritius Ki Lok Kathayen*. New Delhi: Rajpal and Sons.

———. 1990. *Mauritius: Lok Sahitya Aur Sanskriti*. New Delhi: Rajesh Prakashan.

Saha, Panchanand. 1970. *Emigration of Indian Labour, 1834–1900*. Delhi: People's Publishing House.

Tinker, H. 1974. *A New System of Slavery: The Export of Indian Labour Overseas, 1830–1920*. London: Oxford University Press.

Varma, Dhira. 2000. 'Fiji Ke Hindi Lok Geet: Girmitiyayon Ke Maukhik Dastavej'. *Gagananchal* (April): 204–215.

Weller, Judith Ann. 1968. *The East Indian Indenture in Trinidad*. Rio Piedras: Institute of Caribbean Studies.

4

TRACES OF FEMALE BHOJPURI MIGRANTS IN SURINAME

Sarojini Lewis

This chapter explores the portrayal of Bhojpuri indentured female migrants and their identity formation in Surinamese photographs. By examining several archival photographs, I connect visual traces to various contemporaneous cultural developments described by Tejaswini Niranjana, Roshini Kempadoo, Marina Carter, Anouk de Kooning and Patricia Mohammed.[1] Analysing the photographs, considering the social circumstances that must have influenced identity formation, it is possible to reconstruct the social roles that were imposed on women migrants. As noted by Bhikhu Parekh, I attempt to understand the journey of these women and how they were transformed by diasporic experiences.[2] Since Bhojpuri females belonged to villages characterized by diverse Indian traditions, how did the latter remain or change within this process leading to multiple identities? These photographs can be mined not just for their archival and historical value but also for what they aesthetically communicate and the way they have been staged. The photographs have been archived in various collections, including the National Archives, the Tropenmuseum and the Rijksmuseum collection in the Netherlands.

There is a lack of academic scholarship on female indentured labourers in archival photographs. The images selected from Suriname feature individuals from Chinese, Indian and Indonesian indentured labour communities that were shipped there and lived alongside the descendants of enslaved Africans. Women have been documented in the actual landscape of the places they lived in Suriname, becoming agents of reinvention and cultural innovation. This chapter seeks to address and discuss this, in particular the ethnic mixture and diverse cultural influences that are visually unavoidable in these images. I argue that by viewing the cultural and ethnic diversity apparent in these photos, we can analyse visual traces that may indicate the emancipation of female Bhojpuri migrants from gender norms based in the rural settings in India.

THE ARRIVAL OF BHOJPURI MIGRANTS

After the abolition of slavery by the Dutch government in 1863, indentured labourers were required in Suriname to maintain the plantation economy.[3] Most of the recruited labourers came from the region covering the western part of Bihar and eastern Uttar Pradesh (UP).[4] The present generation of diasporic Indians living in Suriname and the Netherlands have their migrant roots mostly in these Bhojpuri- and Awadhi-speaking regions.

When the first ships with Indian indentured migrants from Calcutta arrived in Suriname in 1873, only a small proportion of the inhabitants were Dutch. The majority of the population were of African, Chinese, Portuguese and Brazilian Jewish or of multi-ethnic descent and possessed a variety of migration backgrounds. The original inhabitants of Suriname come from various indigenous communities, such as, Kaliña (Carib), Lokono (Arawak), Trio (Tirio, Tareno) and Wayana. Colonizers had initially tried to force the native population to work for them.[5] Their efforts were in vain, and they had come to rely upon importing labour over the course of several centuries, starting with the transportation of enslaved Africans for labour on the plantations until about 1826.

Generations before the indentured labourers arrived, Creole[6] communities lived together with the Dutch colonists, and Creoles had been admitted into civil service positions. They predominantly lived in cities where their children had access to education. The dominance of Creole and European cultures in Suriname meant that Indian indentured labourers had to reconstruct their identity, amending social habits and adapting to their new environment. The construction of the Indian migrants' transformed identities was influenced by their past and what they had left behind in India, as well as completely new social conditions in Suriname. Reprising the work of Khal Torabully, Veronique Bragard has argued that 'the experience of descendants of indentured labourers from India testifies to a similar limbo consciousness as they are no longer Indians and have to construct new identities for themselves'.[7]

Johan Dirk Speckmann, C. J. M. de Klerk and Chan Choenni, among others, have explored the plural nature of Surinamese society at the time, divided between rural and urban areas.[8] Already a multicultural society before the arrival of South Asian migrants, Suriname presented a complex environment for newcomers to blend into. As Choenni has observed, Suriname still consists of four major ethnic groups – Creoles, Hindustanis, Javanese people and Maroons – as well as a number of smaller groups such as Chinese inhabitants, Burus (descendants of Dutch peasants), various indigenous communities and the Lebanese.[9]

The 'multicultural' society that the Indian migrants had entered was one in which each ethnic group was hired by the Dutch for specific duties within the plantation. S. van Lierop, the colonial administrator working for the Dutch East India Company, made some interesting observations regarding the Mariënburg plantation in Suriname, which can be considered an early microcosm of 'multiculturalism'. In order to create and maintain a well-functioning plantation, the administrators had to incorporate previous experiences setting up sugar cane factories in the Dutch colony of Indonesia.

The Dutch colonizers, in pursuing their business interests, depended on indentured labour migrants working in Mariënburg (Figure 4.1), who had arrived during earlier waves of migration, as well as on the formerly enslaved to work their plantations. They had a number of Creole workers and free migrants. Among the indentured workers were Indonesian and British Indian labourers.[10] A multicultural society thus emerged with a division of labour, and specific duties for each ethnic group within the plantation. Speckmann draws attention to the discriminatory assignment of work to different communities: 'The Indians were assigned, first and foremost to the weeding gangs, while Creoles were used predominantly for arduous fieldwork'.[11]

van Lierop recommended in 1905 that a certain number of Indians be kept in the sugar factory and the Mariënburg plantation as they were considered hardworking, but they were also considered troublemakers who had rioted in previous years:

> The British Indians have a great insatiable greed for more money that motivates them to work without needing instructions at all times. With Javanese this factor is unfortunately absent. Moreover, they are people recruited from cities, for them agriculture is a new profession that requires special strict supervision on their labour. It is recommended to not exclusively work with them but to keep a certain number of

Figure 4.1 Plantage Mariënburg 1947 (photographed by Willem van de Poll)
Source: Nationaal Archief Nederland, Photocollection Van De Poll.

British Indians in the company. They need to be in minority to avoid a repetition of earlier situation where the English protector of Emigration needs to interfere.[12]

The Indian indentured labourers were thus compared to the Javanese migrants and their ability to function in the plantation. The colonial administrator expressed his prejudice by stereotyping the Indians as greedy, but also viewed this as a quality that would earn him profits.

Documents pertaining to Colonial Act Number 9615-9615 for 1873 and 1875 obtained from the National Archives of the Netherlands (Figure 4.2) show the amount of money spent on salaries, divided by Chinese and Indian

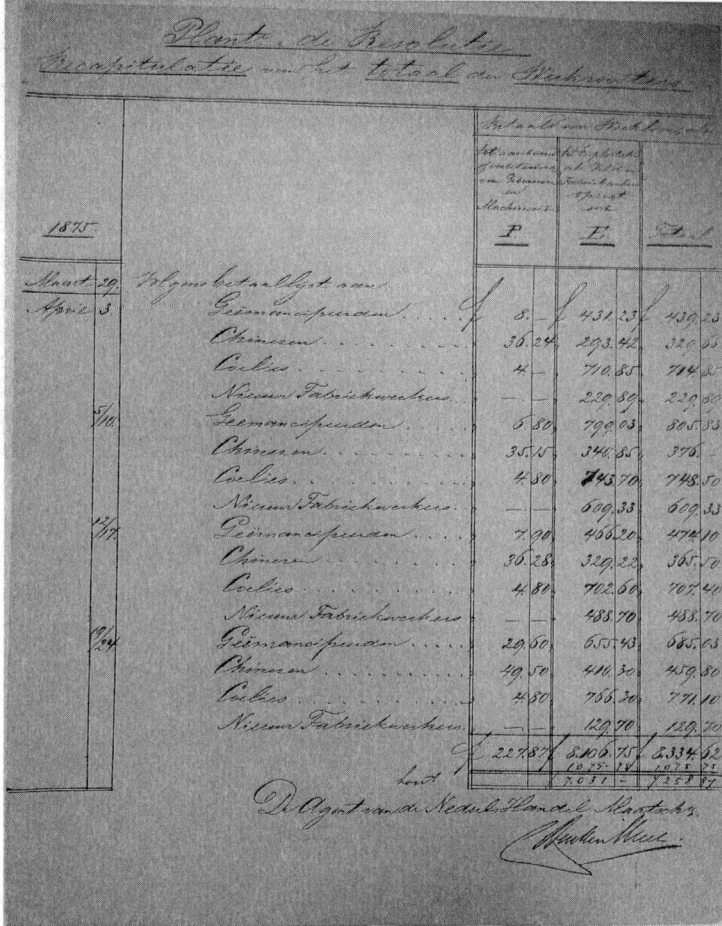

Figure 4.2 Document showing the amount of money spent on salaries, divided by ethnicity

Source: National Archives of the Netherlands, file number 2.20.01, Cultuurzaken Suriname, Colonial Act Number 9615-9615.

ethnicity. Besides Chinese and Indians, there are two more categories to be found in the act without any ethnic description or gender: 'the emancipated' and 'newcomers'. The document also demonstrates the segregation of living quarters by ethnic origin. The Chinese (Chinezen) and Indians (Coelies) on the plantation at Resolutie were spatially divided.

Indentured labourers were introduced to other ethnic migrant groups for the first time on the plantations, where European and Creole staff supervised. Furthermore, they were required to live with these groups. The 'forced' living conditions gave them a chance to communicate with each other, and they developed a new language, Sranan Tongo.[13] Housing was also often segregated as can be seen from the map with the *Immigrantenwyk* of plantation *de Resolutie* from the Dutch National Archives (Figure 4.4). Although this map seems to divide people by strict boundaries, they still lived in close proximity under the same conditions. There were also spaces used by all ethnicities, such as the streets that joined their quarters and the factories. We can imagine that there were enough opportunities to converse and compare experiences after work (Figures 4.3a and 4.3b).

The segregation present in the housing plans is made visible in the construction of photographs that documented migrants as embodiments of a collective group identity. These group photographs are made in several surroundings and use different compositions as discussed later in this chapter.

Speckmann observed the development of a 'multicultural' society and the position of Indian migrants in Suriname, drawing attention to the spatial divisions that migrant communities developed. Some settled in cities and

Figure 4.3a *Drie Hindoestaanse mannen op een veld met kippen, op de achtergrond sluis* (Three Hindustani men on the field with chickens, with a lock in the background), c. 1900–1940 (photographer unknown)

Source: Tropenmuseum Collection, object number TM-10030415.

Figure 4.3b *Een groep Javaanse en Hindoestaanse contractarbeiders* (A group of Javanese and Hindustani contract labourers), c. 1900–1940 (photographer unknown)

Source: Tropenmuseum Collection, object number TM-10019007

some in rural districts, leading to different social patterns. He also reflected on the social interactions of Creoles and Indian indentured labourers:

> One has a strong impression that each of the two ethnic groups led a life of their own, and that contacts between them were superficial. The Indians learnt to use Negro English, and took over from the Creoles, here and there, certain customs regarding plantation life: but social intercourse remained largely restricted to their own group.[14]

Speckmann claims that the aversion of Indians to Creoles was caused by their racist response to 'black skins', which dated back to Vedic times and mirrored colonial attitudes towards race. For this reason, women purportedly had an aversion to 'Creole' men, although some did have relationships with them.

Speckmann remarks that the groups led lives of their own, a view that was clearly held by colonizers. However, this conflicts with the common

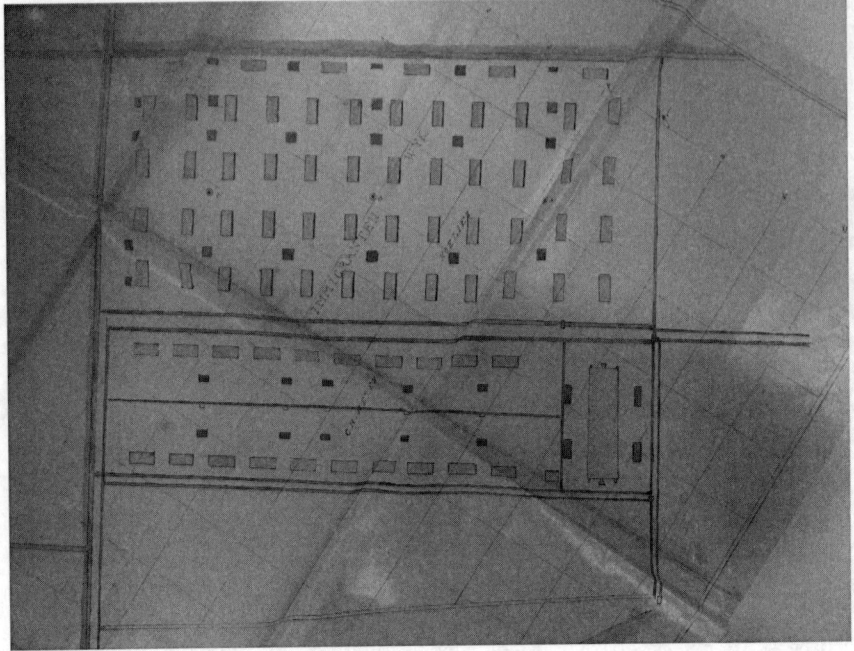

Figure 4.4 Map of Plantation de Resolutie

Source: National Archives of the Netherlands, file number 2.20.01, Cultuurzaken Suriname, Colonial Act Number 9615-9615.

knowledge that Indians learned Sranan Tongo to communicate in daily life, a practice that continues even today. Sranan Tongo as a language could only have developed because of social interaction. Although there were differences between the two ethnicities, they worked together on the plantations and must have had some sort of mutual understanding. I argue that despite the social division, there were still spaces of interaction as evidenced by new forms of linguistic developments. For instance, the Indian Bhojpuri speakers absorbed words from, for example, African languages, to develop Sarnami.[15] Tejaswini Niranjana[16] argues that Africans and Indians were of the same class in the Caribbean. Indians had to inhabit and change through a series of complex negotiations with other racial groups, significantly Africans. This social intercourse was of great importance for Suriname and its inhabitants who, despite racism, had to break through the isolation of their own community.

Understanding Suriname merely through its ethnicities is criticized by Anouk de Kooning. She states, 'People's diverse historical origins and trajectories could be read from their skin, making ethnic difference seem natural, and pluralism a merely common way of conceiving history. Ethnicity was, moreover, a guiding principle in the organization of the colony'.[17] Her statement criticizes how Speckmann analyses Indian indentured labourers, which does not differ much from the colonial classification system. This perspective did not acknowledge 'social mixing' and certain collective memories. Uncritical adoption of this mode of analysis, according to de Kooning, implies that 'one's ethnic identity is' categorized with one's character, life course and social environment, and this leads to stereotypical ideas of people.[18]

Stereotypical definitions of Surinamese ethnicities imply that one no longer questions what it means to be from a certain ethnic group and how identity is constructed on the basis of individual experience. Without the voices and specific stories of these people, we cannot understand the identities of the Surinamese people. After conducting an interview with a Surinamese woman, Mrs A, de Kooning clarifies:

> Traumatic experiences of the past lived on inside the former plantation grounds in the form of ghosts that came to haunt even an indentured labourer's family. These nocturnal apparitions are suggestive of how people like Mrs. A and her family tried to appropriate an already marked landscape and make it their own.[19]

Exploring the personal narrative of Mrs A allows de Kooning to speculate upon the reconstruction of identities among indentured labourers. de Kooning argues that the formation of identities is not based upon ethnicity and colonial hierarchy but rather on experience itself.

From a gendered perspective, Patricia Mohammed argues that one cannot understand the reconfiguration of identity without describing the different ways men and women dealt with the daily lived experience of indentured labour. Her observations are made in the context of women in the Caribbean:

> Ethnicity is a collective word that in its political appeal to a group, forgets sexual differences within culture. Recognizing the different ways in which men and women within any cultural group experience enslavement, indentureship or migration is integral to understanding the ethnic identity.[20]

With this observation Mohammed argues that identity is not a static process but one determined by external influences and internal changes specific to place and time. Identities are constructions in relation to the 'other' in society. Self-awareness among women in the Caribbean was influenced by interaction between women of diverse ethnicities forming communities together. Ethnicity needs to be understood by defining more clearly the role of women and their agency compared to the opposite gender. Mohammed furthermore notices that markers for these reconfigurations include dress and hairstyles. She thus, like de Kooning and Carter, draws her conclusions by observing the everyday lived experience of migrants. As Roshini Kempadoo[21] notes, we can connect feminist approaches to the visual analysis of photographs. Kemapdoo uses autobiographic and personal notes to specify the position of knowledge production. She thus shows how she analyses historical imagery having inside knowledge as a person of the Caribbean diaspora. Kemapadoo further argues that we can analyse women in colonial photographs in order to acknowledge the predominance of a male gaze in the construction of images of women. In constructing gendered perspectives, it is therefore worthwhile to understand the origin of the production and gender-specific influences that were involved in creating the photographs.[22]

INTERPRETING THE ARCHIVAL PHOTOGRAPHS

The social construction of identity that emerged from multicultural Suriname, built upon imposed differences and expressions of agency against a background of hierarchal control, can be evidenced through the photographic lens.

As has been remarked by Elisabeth Edwards:

> Photographs provide glimpses of a prior reality, the indexical traces of which were chemically inscribed on to a sensitised film or plate. They transfer to viewers 'a fragment of time and space'. As fragments of the past they may come to stand for whole, rectifying culturally formed images as observed realities.[23]

This notion can be applied to the photographs presented in this chapter to further explore how collective memories can be accessed through photographs.

The first and oldest photograph taken in Suriname, held in the collection of the Rijksmuseum in Amsterdam, portrays a couple from a mixed background. It dates to 1846. The woman, Maria Louise de Hart (born 1826), and the man, Johannes Ellis (born 1812), were photographed seven years after the medium of photography was invented, using the daguerreotype technique (Figure 4.5a). de Hart, daughter of a freed ex-slave and a Jewish plantation owner, had a mixed background. Johannes Ellis was the mixed-race son of Abraham de Veer, the governor of the Dutch Gold Coast (now Ghana) and a Ghanaian woman, Fanny Ellis. This early photograph symbolizes the multicultural society that Suriname had become by this time. J. L. Riker and Warren Thomson were Americans who travelled through Suriname to make a series of daguerreotypes, of which the portrait of this iconic couple has become a celebrated example. Despite their multicultural origin, the couple wears Western clothing in the style of the colonizers. They would later migrate to the Netherlands, and their clothing in the daguerreotype signifies a total cultural adjustment, which enabled them to live in Dutch society. In mimicking portraits of Westerners, the photographers are not defining the couple as part of a separate category or ethnic system. The portrait of the couple reveals a very different attitude towards ethnicity. This might well have been due to the status of their Dutch ancestors.

Figure 4.5a Portrait of a couple in Suriname 1846 (photographed by J. L. Riker and Warren Thomson)

Source: Rijksmuseum Collection, file number RP-F-BR-2009-1.

The photograph shown in Figure 4.5b, titled *Britisch Indische Koeliemeisjes Calcutta* (British Kuli girls from Calcutta), is an example of one of the oldest photographs of female Bhojpuri migrants in the Rijksmuseum collection. The photograph was taken in Calcutta, the city of departure for Bhojpuri migrants who journeyed to Suriname.

Photography was introduced to India in 1868, when 73 album prints were taken that were published over successive years under the title *The People of India*.[24] They showcased individuals and groups of Indians. The method of photographing people at this time was mostly with the intention of creating systematic order using plain backdrops and props. Furthermore, certain artefacts were used to symbolize different occupational categories. *The People of India* was primarily a documentation of race and class across different Indian states. Christopher Pinney says with reference to the women in these images, 'This quest for difference tended to make the woman of a group of more interest, since their costume and material culture were identified as being more resistant to change'.[25] Indian women in conjunction with their caste affiliation were thus perceived as the anchors of cultural groups, most immutable in the hierarchy of natives, and fixed as such in the photographic survey of the country.[26] In addition to Pinney's observation, Suryanandini Narain[27] gives a realistic idea of the cultural representation of women and their caste since they were photographed and picked out for their 'exotic' looks and therefore might not be representative examples of their community or caste. The colonial images of their 'subjects' were clearly filtered through the imaginations of the colonial photographers, which may nullify any claim that the women presented are images of individuals resistant to change.

In this chapter, I will discuss how some photographs that were taken in Suriname claim the opposite and highlight a sense of multi-ethnic mixing. These images paint a different picture of inter-ethnic relations altogether. Before I get to this, I briefly mention the different indentured labour communities that arrived in Suriname and the stereotypical image that has been made of female indentured labourers.

The photograph (Figure 4.5b) taken in an earlier time frame as compared to the photographs in Suriname seems to foreground femininity, purity and maintenance of tradition. Niranjana[28] suggests that often the differences between agricultural labourers in Bihar and those in Trinidad have been erased in order to victimize the indentured labourer in the eyes of the nationalist discourse in India. The immorality and depravity of indentured

Figure 4.5b *Britisch Indische Koeliemeisjes Calcutta* (British Kuli girls from Calcutta), c. 1870–1900 (photographer unknown)

Source: Rijksmuseum Collection, file number RP-F-F01154-K.

women were in contrast with the virtuous and chaste Indian woman at home. The depiction of this kind of Indian women seems to co-relate with Figure 4.5b taken in Calcutta; the idea that these heavily decorated females could be from agricultural communities in Bihar or UP seems erased in their visual representation.

Some of the following group photographs depict 'multicultural society'; they were made in diverse surroundings and based on different compositions. The depot pictures show the diversity of cultures; nevertheless ethnicities are strictly segregated to ensure colonial control.

Figure 4.6 shows a photograph of a group of women and men at the 'coolie depot', having just arrived from India. Some of them look weary after a three-month boat journey. Posed before the depot where they would reside for the time being, the uncertainty of the moment is visible in their facial expressions. They did not yet know which plantation they were going to work for, under what conditions; knowing their status of temporariness and perhaps the dawning awareness of the difference of their lives left behind in the Bhojpuri and Awadhi belt in India. Could they have been aware during this photograph of their forthcoming experience that would craft new identities to suit their new lives as indentured labourers in Suriname? Munshi Rahman Khan[29] writes in his diary how Indian people who already worked

Figure 4.6 *In Het Koeliedepot* (The Kuli depot), c. 1906–1913 (photographed by Hendrik Dooyer)

Source: Rijksmuseum Collection, file number NG-1994-65-5-28-4.

on plantations came to visit and searched for people who came from their village or district to hear news from home. 'When they did so, they started talking continuously'.

de Klerk mentions that male migrants who were residing for a longer period in the colony would go to the depot to find unmarried women against payment of three-fifths of the transportation costs of the female migrant.[30] The depot was filled with feelings of happiness and nostalgia for their places of origin. The procedure of allocating the migrants to their plantation took about four weeks, during which people were divided in groups.

The process of transformation, starting from the first migratory experience of transition from north Indian customs and habits into Surinamese daily life, developed over generations into settled diasporic identities. During their emotional labour, they recreated new traditions and a space and value of Indianness. This kind of process has been highlighted by Stuart Hall, who states, 'Diaspora identities are those which are constantly producing themselves anew, through transformation and difference, leading to the idea of "no fixed" identity'.[31]

The Javanese migrants (Figure 4.7) came to Suriname in the period between 1890 and 1930, 17 years later than the Indian indentured labourers. They are photographed in a similar way to the Indian indentured labourers and at around the same time of arrival. Their postures are photographed from a greater distance, and this could be the result of different photographic approaches taken by the respective photographers, Hendrik Dooyer (Figure 4.6) and Julius Muller (Figure 4.7). The Javanese have assumed or been arranged in several different postures; they appear more 'composed' before the depot.

The Chinese indentured labourers of Suriname arrived from 1858 until 1874 (Figure 4.8), thus serving as the first replacement labour force following the abolition of slavery in Suriname in 1863. As Lisa Lowe states, they presented the first 'free labourers' and were named 'coolies' (a term used for Asian labourers in general, including Indian and Javanese indentured labourers).[32] Their indentured migration stopped one year after the initiation of Indian indentured labour in 1873. The work of Chinese and Indian labourers was widely compared by the colonial administration. The photographer Julius Muller created a series of images in his own garden with different backdrops for each migrant community. In his photograph entitled *Een Chineesche Familie* (Figure 4.9), we see the interior of a house rather than the Dutch agricultural landscape visible in the photograph presented in Figure 4.10. Since the time frame of arrival of indentured labour migrants was different,

Figure 4.7 *Groepsportret van Javanen* (Group Portrait of Javanese), c. 1895–1900 (photographed by Julius Muller)

Source: Rijksmuseum Collection, file number NG-1994-65-3-31.

one can assume that the variety in the depictions was inspired by the sitter's main occupation.

It is important to understand that there was almost no migration of female Chinese indentured labourers, although some Chinese women did migrate in a later time frame as free migrants to unite with family and as so called 'import-brides'.[33] Despite this absence, Lowe has described how the image of Chinese women played an important role during the indentured migration of Chinese male labourers as a 'trope for colonial imagination in the capacity of the colonized to develop into a reproductive, family community'.[34] Chinese men instead started relationships with Creole women and later with Javanese and Indian indentured labourers (Figures 4.10 and 4.11). Although visually presented as separate groups, over time, ethnic groups did mix in Suriname. Carter and Torabully remark in regard to Mauritius, 'The process of creolization is the process of mixing

Figure 4.8 *Ingang Wanicastraat Chineesch Begraafplaats* (Entrance of the Wanicastraat Chinese Cemetery), c. 1906–1913 (photographed by Hendrik Doijer)

Source: Rijksmuseum Collection, filenumberNG-1994-65-2-3-1.

of a number of ethnic groups. This process has a plural character in which "complexity and not clarity is the key"'.[35]

In the nineteenth century, the indentured diaspora of the Caribbean islands, Fiji, Mauritius, Réunion and South Africa introduced a multiplicity of subjects who could be 'exoticized' for tourist postcards. Figure 4.11 is a postcard depicting exoticism as well as the agency of the couple to choose their mixed marriage that was photographed by Julius Muller in Suriname. Niranjana[36] has noted that the East Indian woman in post-slavery society had to be imagined differently than the African woman, and thus Indian tradition was invoked. The postcard of the mixed couple differs thematically from those depicting Indian women. Gaiutra Bahadur points out that the female indentured labourers had to attract white men and tourists:

[I]n the late nineteenth and early twentieth century, Indian women were photographed in Jamaica, Trinidad, and British Guiana for a thriving postcard industry built on marketing the Caribbean as a

Figure 4.9 *Een Chineesche Familie* (A Chinese family), c. 1898–1902 (photographed by Julius Muller)

Source: Rijksmuseum Collection, file number NG-2015-4-1-78.

holiday destination for Western tourists. During the colonial period, the Caribbean islands had developed a reputation as hothouses of hard drink and yellow fever, virtual graveyards for white men. Determined to change this perception, colonial administrators launched a concerted campaign to sell the Caribbean as an 'exotic but safe' destination, a message well represented by images of beautiful women who were once among the British empire's most denigrated labourers.[37]

Apart from producing postcards, Muller was working together with emigration officers. The following photograph made by Muller, part of the Tropenmuseum archive, is particularly striking, especially when one observes the combination of cultural layers that are depicted (Figure 4.12). First of all, the clothing of the Indian–Creole Surinamese woman is remarkable since it is a mix between *kotomisi* style[38] and traditional Dutch costume. Displaying the woman in clothing destined for Dutch housekeepers gives the viewer a

Figure 4.10 *Chinees–Creoolse Familie* (Chinese and Creole family), c. 1910 (photographed by R. Del Castielo)

Source: Surinaams Museum Collection.

feeling of displacement. In her book *Spiegelrefelex*, Susan Legêne observed regarding another photograph of the same woman that she is a 'kotomisi of intermixed blood of Indian and Creole descendance'.[39] The time frame of the photograph is 1880–1900, and by her costume we can understand that the woman had a higher position as housekeeper than women who would work as field labourers.

In the photograph in Figure 4.12, items denoting the subjects' cultural identity are missing except for the thick bracelets worn by the woman. The staged 'Dutch identity' creates a feeling of alienation. The symbolic presentational aspect of the photograph becomes even more apparent when one observes the children. They may have been chosen to represent 'multicultural' Surinamese society. The taller child has perhaps Chinese roots, and the smaller child could be of Creole descent as is described in the Tropenmuseum photo catalogue. The figures all stand close to each other but remarkably have no physical contact. Their bodily position communicates a

Een gemengd Huwelijk (Chinees met Zijn Kleurling Echtgenoote)
Suriname

Figure 4.11 Postcard from Suriname, *Chinees Met Zijn Kleurling Echtgenoote* (Chinese with the coloured wife), c. 1900 (photographed by Julius Muller)

Source: Collection Jean Jaques Vrij.

rather uncomfortable feeling. The hands of the boy with the striped t-shirt are stiffly placed on either side of his body. The gaze of the children and the woman are a little odd. None of them are facing the photographer directly. The boy on the left looks at the camera, but his gaze is diffused. The woman and the child on the right are staring at something in the corner, avoiding the eyes of the photographer. It is not clear why these three are selected for Muller's photograph, compared with Figure 4.9 where we can clearly see his purpose of showing a Chinese family as is apparent in the title. The title that Muller uses for the photograph here (Figure 4.12) *Suriname, Hindoestaanse Koelievrouw met een Chinese zoon en een Creoolse zoon* (Suriname, Hindustani coolie woman with a Chinese son and a Creole son) suggests that the woman is of Indian descent, and that she has a Chinese son as well as a Creole son. One can compare this title to the same woman photographed alone with another background titled *Portret Van Een Vrouw Met Gemengde Brits Indische Afkomst, Gefotografeerd Voor Een Fantasiedecor In De Tuin Van De Fotograaf*

Figure 4.12 *Suriname, Hindoestaanse Koelievrouw Met Een Chinese Zoon En Een Creoolse Zoon* (Surinamese, Hindustani Kuli woman with a Chinese and a Creole son), c. 1880–1900 (photographed by J. E. Muller)

Source: Tropenmuseum Collection, object number TM-60008921.

(Portrait of a woman of mixed British Indian descent, photographed in front of the fantasy decor in the garden of the photographer). In this case, Muller has chosen to mention mixed British Indian descent instead of Hindustani[40] descent as he did in Figure 4.12, pointing to the diverse colonial fantasies about ethnic categories that the same woman can portray. We can understand through the research of Legène pointing to the mixed Creole and Indian background that the woman in both photographs became a central figure for Muller and his fascination for ethnic diversity.

The painting in the photograph shows an idealized agricultural landscape in the Netherlands. In front of and to the left behind the painting we can see the tropical vegetation of Suriname. Plants painted into the foreground of the backdrop suggest a visual continuity in the landscape. We can see a stream of water meandering through the depicted landscape, and in the background we see typical Dutch houses. Is the background intended to symbolize or evoke the future for the people in the foreground? Instead of the real Suriname landscape with tropical palm trees and the wooden houses of their daily existence, the solid Dutch houses betray the mindset of the colonizer who seeks to embed these migrant people into an ideal 'Dutch' life.

The photograph reminds us of what Bahadur has observed regarding 'coolie' women: 'They did not leave behind diaries or letters. The relative silence of coolie women could be a strategy for women who had secrets to keep'.[41] This acute observation is made in relation to the lack of documented female voices: we can track written traces of their experiences through official testimonies. However, the gaze of this particular woman may be a visual manifestation of the gulf between 'subject' and colonizer. Female voices may be passed on as secrets and stories through other avenues, in oral communications and songs. This photograph, in a way, portrays a silent gap between the woman and photographer.

As Bahadur has remarked, 'These images don't simply document, they enact a struggle – between the imaginations of colonial-era photographers and the real lives of the women behind the portraits. In doing so, they suggest a radically different perspective on imperial history'.[42] The gaze of the women in these colonial-era photographs gives us a strong sense of the 'struggle' they faced in a colonial setting. In this photograph (Figure 4.12), we see the woman confronted with the colonizer, and a sense of her 'real life' and 'struggle' slips into the frame by the action of directing her eyes away from the viewer as if challenging the onlooker not to be seduced by her exotic appearance. By examining seemingly small details, we see how colonial photographic subjects succeeded in 'speaking for themselves' without leaving textual, archival records of their feelings. The gaze in this way tells us more and intensifies our actual understanding of indentured women and their bodies.

The background and composition of the photograph here in Figure 4.13 has a different method of staging. The way the logs over the water are angled towards the vanishing point immediately draws attention to the 'staged' frame. The scenery resembles a village, and some of the people in the picture may well live in the house in the background. It is interesting to note the figure on the very left side of the photograph, visible in the slightly overexposed edge. One wonders if he is in the frame to show his surveillance of a *kulidorf* (coolie village). This over-exposed figure of whiteness appears to wear a sola topee, the pith helmet used commonly by Europeans in the tropics. He also appears to be wearing long trousers and carries an umbrella. Is he a Dutchman posing and aware of the fact that somebody is taking a photograph? He certainly appears to be looking at the camera, rather than being a passive subject of representation.

The man and woman at the centre of the photograph are presumably the inhabitants of the hut. It is difficult to read their facial expressions, but their stance looks static. Indeed, there is a slight blurring around the figure of the woman suggesting that she may have begun to move while the photograph was taken. She is placed in the foreground of the image with the man further behind, something that is quite unusual when one thinks about the relative position of Indian indentured women and men in Surinamese society and also when compared to the conventional positioning of male and female subjects at this time. The impression is that the woman feels embarrassed to stand in front of her husband: she has protectively positioned her hands in front of her chest, in an air of modesty. Perhaps the photographer positioned the couple so that the Indian man was in the middle of the composition, with the women on either side. This also places the man standing directly in front of the hut. However, his legs are obscured. Is he standing on a pile of leaves?

His 'incompleteness' is disquieting. One is tempted to view him as emasculated – his pride in his status as husband and head of household is illusory – he is not complete in his authority, subjected to the power of the colonizer, the plantation owner or other employers. His freedom, his mobility appears cropped by the fallen leaves. He is disembodied and cut adrift in an alien society and culture where his ancestral traditions are tolerated at best and where his authority is marginalized. Of the three figures who are the subjects proper of the photograph, the woman on the left also appears

Figure 4.13 A coolie village in Paramaribo (photographer unknown)

Source: Utrecht Archive, file number 422, Fotoafdrukken Suriname.

as an 'outsider' to the 'coolie' village. She appears to be observing the Indian figures, who may well be the inhabitants of the hut pictured in the centre of the image. Her dress is similar to the working clothes of the Afro-Creoles on Surinamese plantations. Her headwear as well as her physiognomy suggests that she is of Afro-Creole ethnicity. Her pose, looking at the Indian female figure as an observer, suggests that she is not a resident of the house, but has been placed there as a counterpoint to the 'coolie couple', perhaps by the photographer. Her gaze suggesting distance between the Indian woman and herself is enforced by her reflection in the water. Nevertheless, there is a symbolic connection between the two females through their bodily engagement. She is a single female figure standing before the more fragile looking Indian female and her posture suggests self-awareness and sternness while at the same time being aware of her role of posing before the photographer. Kempadoo remarks in regard to African photographed females, that they were not feminine, not fragile and sexually knowing and available.[43] The awareness that the woman in Figure 4.13 bodily represents, could be a process of the Surinamese encounter of cultural diversity and 'mixing'. The sexual availability is an insidious colonial fantasy, but you also see a redemptive and emancipatory potential of their identity influenced by their diverse surrounding.

Symbolically the position of the Indian female between the two figures seems also to relate to a daily migratory experience between the traditional role of a wife for the Indian man and newly explored relationships as independent women created between the Afro-American diaspora and Indian diaspora.

In Figure 4.14, one can see an example of a photograph of a female indentured labourer. The staged position of her body seems to express a certain seduction to the viewer; her gaze is challenging the photographer. These types of photographs are aligned with the 'exoticized' postcard series that Bahadur writes about and I mentioned earlier. Analysing a similar photograph with a woman wearing similar jewellery, Bahadur states, '"Coolie belles" gaze back with pain or melancholy as often as with mischief or play'.[44] As stated before, the gaze of the woman sits in contradiction to her staged body position as a sign of her interior life and mitigates the possible exploitation present in the photograph. Her expression is certainly not melancholic or full of pain. If anything, it is defiant. The final image combines the photographer's desire for the portrait and her own powerful ability to look back at him unapologetically.

Figure 4.14 A British Indian woman in Suriname

Source: Moravian Archive.

The identity of indentured women must have undergone modifications from the time of their recruitment to their period of settlement in Suriname. An emigration officer wrote in 1877–1878 about the recruits for Suriname gathered in the depots prior to departure, 'Their number was considerably augmented by a batch of dancing girls and women of similar description with their male attendants. These people laughed at the idea of labouring as agriculturalists.'[45] The idea of this 'type' of women being prostitutes is mentioned in different colonial reports. For some women, once they were in the colonies, they could indeed use sex as a tool of power and status. According to Niranjana, the women had 'great freedom of intercourse'. Compared to male labourers, their female counterparts received half the amount of wages or less. They were therefore dependent on men in the colony for support and additional income. This financial dependency in combination with the unequal sex ratio provided a motive for women to break through traditional patterns of behaviour; in some cases this led to relationships with multiple men that caused a counter-act from their husbands. Carter has observed that the statistics reveal that the overseas Indian populations were committing a greater number of wife-murders and suicides than other ethnic groups in their various territories. As a consequence of the unequal sex ratios, besides

Figure 4.15 Cropped image from a postcard of a 'coolie belle' taken in Port of Spain, Trinidad, c. 1890 (photographed by Felix Morin)

Source: Michael Goldberg Collection, University of the West Indies, St Augustine, Trinidad; found in Bahadur (2015).

the harassment of women by colonial officers, jealous men would murder or physically attack women, leading to a double struggle with their husbands and a colonial authority.

Refiguring identity among females must have led to diverse realities beyond the idea of 'lower castes having low morals and higher castes having higher ones'. With the freedom of a new life, the first generation of indentured women could choose their own partners regardless of caste and furthermore became sexually liberated. The women in Figures 4.14 and 4.15 exude a sense of confidence. However, sexual liberation cannot be evidenced solely through projecting agency into their images, which were taken within a studio context where liberation could be 'staged'. In these photographs, the colonial construction of 'lower caste' women as prostitutes or decorative objects can be imposed. Besides the idea of being sexually independent through various factors within their own community, Afro-Surinamese women had been sexually independent for generations as they lived in disrupted family structures and, during the time frame of slavery, marriage was forbidden. These women might have set an example in creating awareness of alternative family structures among Indian-Surinamese women.

An expression of having multiple modes of identification is seen in the photographs of clothing styles that change into a more 'Western' style in the left photograph and the traditional 'Indian' style in the right photograph in Figure 4.16. The set of photographs belongs to the Moravian archive of German missionaries and shows the same couple who have set an example of a 'Christian couple' and a 'Hindu couple' within the same time frame. This

Figure 4.16 *Paramaribo* (photographed by Augusta Curiel)

Source: Moravian Archive.

Note: Augusta Curiel was born in Paramaribo in 1873. She took her mother's surname as her father abandoned them. She and her sister Anna were together known as the Ladies Curiel or the Curiel Sisters. Augusta took pictures, and Anna acted as her assistant. In 1929, Queen Wilhelmina granted her the title of *hofleverancier*. She was the first photographer of Suriname for the royal house. The Sisters Curiel were the owners of one of the most famous photography studios in Suriname: *Augusta Curiel*. Photographs by Augusta Curiel and the former overseer of plantation Zoelen, Frederik Oudschans Dentz (1876–1961), among others, were employed to analyse how Hindustani residents bridged and broadened differences of class, caste, gender and race through dress.

altogether points to the multiple ways in which identification processes took place among indentured labourers. This also clarifies that missionaries did have a strong influence, since education for first-generation female migrants was provided by Evangelic missionary schools. Mitrasingh recounts in his autobiography how his mother was attracted to work for the wife of the missionary P. M. Legêne, because she was interested in being educated. She was introduced by the same missionary couple to his father, and they had a Christian marriage in 1920.[46] Nevertheless, Mitrasingh recounts how he learned Hindi when he was seven years old because his father was 'Hindustani by blood' and preferred Hindi Sarnami to be spoken at home.

In addition, Parekh notes that Hindu parents sometimes gave their children both a Hindu name and a Christian name because of bureaucratic administrations.[47] The clothing style that the Indian couple is wearing on the left side is similar to the clothing Afro-Surinamese women would wear when they attended formal occasions such as travelling by boat with the missionaries in Figure 4.17. One can criticize the missionaries who caused a cultural transformation that distanced Indian migrants from the Hindu religion that they originally practised. Furthermore, one can question if

Figure 4.17 *Bruder Scholze mit dem Von Claire, Schwesters Scholze, Weiß* (Brother Scholz with Von Claire and Sister Scholze, Weiss)

Source: Moravian Archive.

emancipation of Bhojpuri females through Christian education distanced them from their traditional religion. In case of the family of Mitrasingh, they tried to stay loyal to their cultural affinity with India through their language and use of Hindi and Sarnami (a Surinamese mixture of Bhojpuri and Awadhi) (Figures 4.16 and 4.17).

CONCLUSION: MULTIPLE CONNECTIONS

In Suriname, diverse migrants influenced each other and common languages developed, Sarnami among the Bhojpuri migrants and Sranan Tongo as the *lingua franca*. Cultures adapted, as is evident in food and musical traditions. This demonstrates that the process of migration is not a single event. Between the country of origin and colonial destinations, multiple connections evolved beyond conventional distances and political borders.

As Parekh has noted, 'The diasporic Hindu was no longer a Hindu happening to live abroad, but one deeply transformed by his diasporic experiences. The Hindu diaspora then contains multiple identities, all sharing some common features but relating them differently and additionally having distinct features of their own.'[48] Transformation of identity is a long continuous process that lasted throughout multiple generations of Indians. The initial transition to new identities already took place on the sea journeys to colonies, when people were placed in groups, and caste hierarchy was ignored while new relationships were formed. The emotional and psychological process of change often must have begun with grief and the pain of separation from family members.

Recent studies of colonial archival photography vary from the examination of personal photographs from the albums of colonizers and missionaries to new analyses of material in the public domain.[49] In most visual presentations on indentured Indians, the perspective no longer focuses on their villages of origin in India and what the migrants left behind, but on photographic depictions in destination colonies found in collections outside of India. Indentured labourers were primarily photographically documented in their destination colonies rather than in India owing to the strict colonial observation systems abroad. Dividing ethnicity through photographic representation, actual daily labour and living situations resulted in the maintenance of hierarchy among the ex-slaves and indentured labourers and secured the continuation of colonial power. The photographic print on the

Figure 4.18 Postcard titled *Suriname Onze Jeugd* (Suriname, our youth),
c. 1907–1908 (photographer unknown)

Source: Carl Haarnack Archive, Buku Bibliotheca Surinamica postcard.

postcard in Figure 4.18 titled *Onze Jeugd* (Our youth) also depicts this ideal
imaginary of the Surinamese population through the projection of diverse
ethnicity and clothes that are worn by the children in 1907–1908 when the
image was taken.

The female indentured labourers having a position of sexual independence
as compared to their situation in India has been mainly clarified from their
unequal gender equations allowing them more freedom in their choice of
male partners.[50] The gender inequality is not directly visible in photographic
material. However, the photographic material contains a mix of imposed
identity formations and sometimes reflects aspects of agency among migrants
concerning their identities. Further understanding of identity formation in
colonies such as Suriname is made possible through the comparative analysis
of photographic studies of the Indian diaspora, including images that record
their connection with other ethnicities. In the photographs presented in
this chapter, one can thus find some examples of female Bhojpuri migrants
intermixed with other ethnicities. One may draw several conclusions from
this, but it suggests at least an emancipation from cultural norms that would
not be found in India.

NOTES

1. Niranjana (1999); Kempadoo (2013); Carter (2000 [1996]); de Kooning (2011); Mohammed (2002).
2. Parekh (1994).
3. Majumder (2010).
4. Of the indentured labourers, 82.5 per cent came from the United Provinces and 12 per cent from Bihar in 1873–1874. See de Klerk (1953).
5. Kruijer (1953, 64).
6. Reddock (1998, 65). Creole is a Surinamese description for a person descending from Africa. The Creole culture has influences from Africa, Europe and India. It is also commonly used to refer to skin colour and people descending from ex-slaves. It has a certain sensitive layer when used because of the relation to slavery. Furthermore, it refers to the language Creole. Originally the term 'creole' was used to refer to all persons born within the region with an external origin. Today in Trinidad and Tobago for example, it is used in three senses: (*a*) to refer to an amalgam of descendants of Europeans who still dominate the local economy, known locally as French creoles, (*b*) primarily by Indians to refer to persons of African descent, also referred to by a Hindi derivative 'kirwal' and (*c*) to refer to cultural artefacts of the dominant culture, namely, creole food, creole bacch, and so on. The term 'creole' therefore for Indians is strongly identified with Afro-Creole culture, and Creolization is seen by many as a process of cultural domination.
7. Bragard (2005).
8. Speckmann (1965); de Klerk (1953); Choenni (2011).
9. Choenni (2011, 8).
10. Reddock (1998, 65).
11. Speckman (1965, 35).
12. National Archives of the Netherlands, file number 2.20.01, Cultuurzaken Suriname, Colonial Act Number 9615-9615.
13. Sranan Tongo was named Creole English or Negro English in the colonial period. This Creole language is shared between the Dutch-, Javanese-, Hindustani- and Chinese-speaking communities. Most Surinamese speak it as a lingua franca in Suriname and as migrants in the Netherlands.
14. Speckmann (1965, 36).
15. The Hindi Sarnami people speak their own version of Bhojpuri, a language spoken in northern India. Their language changed over time and words were borrowed from Dutch and local languages like Sranan Tongo.

16. Niranjana (1999, 238).

17. de Kooning (2011, 261).

18. de Kooning (2011, 266).

19. de Kooning (2011, 270).

20. Mohammed (1998, 8).

21. Kempadoo (2013, 3).

22. Kempadoo (2013, 6).

23. Edwards (2001); Ryan (1997, 19).

24. Pinney (2011).

25. Pinney (1997, 24).

26. Narain (2013).

27. Narain (2013).

28. Niranjana (1999, 231).

29. Hira (2003, 142).

30. de Klerk (1953, 88).

31. Hall (1994, 396).

32. Lowe (2015, 30).

33. Bol and Vrij (2009).

34. Lowe (2015, 30).

35. Carter and Torabully (2002).

36. Niranjana (1999, 236).

37. Bahadur (2015, 52).

38. The *koto* is a traditional garment of the Creoles in Suriname. Women wearing a *koto* are called *kotomisi* (*misi* meaning 'madam'). The *koto* is still worn on traditional or modern form on festive occasions such as birthdays, weddings or *koto-dansi* (a dance party). There are *koto*s for different occasions, including the birthday *koto*, work *koto*, mourning *koto* and wedding *koto*. The accompanying headscarf, the *angisa* (sometimes *anisa*), has a special significance. The way the headscarf is folded expresses a message. The folding of these headscarves is a special art, which is passed on orally and is still taught today. The wearing of the *koto* itself can also express a message. The development of the *koto* as a garment continues to lead to changes.

39. Legêne (2010, 93).

40. Hindustani is a term used in Suriname and the Netherlands to denote people of Indian descent who live in or trace ancestry back to Suriname, and furthermore India and this is an ethnic marker.

41. Bahadur (2015, 52).

42. Bahadur (2015, 50).

43. Kempadoo (2013, 5).
44. Bahadur (2015, 54).
45. Niranjana (2006, 62).
46. Mitrasingh (1996, 12).
47. Parekh (1994, 617).
48. Parekh (1995, 617).
49. Bahadur (2011, 48–61); Carter (2017, 85–104); Mohammed (2004, 52–62);
    Kempadoo (2013, 1–14); Legêne (2007); Mohabir (2017, 112–122).
50. Carter (2000 [1996], 54).

BIBLIOGRAPHY

Bahadur, G. 2011. 'Coolie Women Are in Demand Here'. *Virginia Quarterly Review* 87 (2): 48–61.

―――. 'Postcards From Empire'. *Dissent Magazine*, 50–52.

Bol, P., and J. J. Vrij. 2009. *Sranan Famiri*. Den Haag: Centraal Bureau voor Genealogie.

Bragard, V. 2005. 'Transoceanic Echoes: Coolitude and the Work of the Mauritian Poet Khal Torabully'. *International Journal of Francophone Studies* 8 (2): 219–233.

Carter, M., and D. Flynn. 2017. 'Pulled through Time: Art and the Indian Labour Migrant'. *South Asian Studies* 33 (1): 85–104.

Carter, Marina. 2000 (1996). *The Bihari Presence in Mauritius*. Port Louis and London: Centre For Research on Indian Ocean Societies.

Carter, Marina, and Khal Torabully. 2002. *Coolitude*. London: Anthem Publications.

Choenni, E. S. 2011. *Integration Hindustani Style? On the Migration, History and Diaspora of the Hindustanis*. Amsterdam: Vrije University.

de Klerk, J. C. M. 1953. *De Immigratie der Hindostanen in Suriname*. Amsterdam: Urbi et Orbi.

de Kooning, Anouk. 2011. 'Beyond Ethnicity: Writing Caribbean History Though Social Spaces'. *Latin American Ethnic Studies* 6 (3): 259–282.

Edwards, E. 2001. *Raw Histories: Photographs, Anthropology and Museums*. Oxford: Berg.

Hall, S. 1994. 'Cultural Identity and Diaspora'. In *Colonial Discourse and Post-Colonial Theory*, edited by P. Williams and L. Chrisman, 396. London: Routledge.

Hira, Sandew 2003. *Het Dagboek van Munshi Rahman Khan*. Den Haag; Paramaribo: Amrit; NSHI.

Kempadoo, Roshini. 2013. 'Defining Women Subjects: Photographs in Trinidad (1860s–1960s)'. *Caribbean Review of Gender Studies* 7: 1–14.

Kruijer, G. J. 1953. *Suriname en zijn Buurlanden*. Meppel: J. A. Boom & Zoon.

Légene, S. 2007. *From India to Suriname: A Journey into the Future Narrated by Two Photograph Albums (1913–1930)*. Allahabad: Manav Vikas Sangrahalaya, G. B. Pant Institute.

———. 2010. *Spiegelreflex*. Amsterdam: Uitgeverij Bert Bakker.

Lowe, L. 2015. *Intimacies between Four Continents*. Durham: Duke University Press.

Majumder, Mousumi. 2010. *Kahe Gaile Bides* [*Why Did You Go Overseas?*]. Allahabad: G. B. Pant Social Science Institute.

Mitrasingh, F. E. M. 1996. *Zijn Leven En Zijn Werken En Wat Anderen Zeiden*. Paramaribo: Vaco Press.

Mohabir, Nalini. 2017. 'Picturing an Afterlife of Indenture'. *Small Axe* 21.2 (53): 81–93.

Mohammed, Patricia. 1998. 'Towards Indigenous Feminist Theorizing in the Caribbean'. *Feminist Review: Rethinking Caribbean Difference* 59 (1): 6–33.

———. 2002. *Gender Negotiations among Indians in Trinidad, 1917–1947*. London: Palgrave Macmillan.

———. 2004. 'Haiti I'm Sorry'. *Caribbean Quarterly* 50 (4): 52–62. DOI:10.1080/00086495.2004.11672250.

Narain, Suryanandini. 2013. 'The Intercepted Photograph: Photography and Marriage in Contemporary Delhi'. PhD Thesis, Jawaharlal Nehru University, New Delhi.

Niranjana, T. 1999. '"Left to the Imagination": Indian Nationalisms and Female Sexuality in Trinidad'. *Public Culture* 11 (1): 223–243.

———. 2006. *Mobilizing India: Women, Music, and Migration between India and Trinidad*. Hyderabad: Duke University Press.

Parekh, B. 1994. 'Some Reflections on the Hindu Diaspora'. *Journal of Ethnic and Migration Studies* 20 (4): 603–620. DOI:10.1080/1369183x.1994.9976456.

Pinney, Christopher. 1997. *Camera Indica: The Social Life of Indian Photographs*. Chicago: University of Chicago.

———. 2011. *Photography and Anthropology*. 1st ed. London: Reaktion Books.

Reddock, Rhoda. 1998. 'Contestations Over Culture, Class, Gender and Identity in Trinidad and Tobago: "The Little Tradition"'. *Caribbean Quarterly* 44 (1–2): 62–80.

Ryan, James R. 1997. *Picturing Empire: Photography and the Visualization of the British Empire*. Chicago: University of Chicago Press.

Speckmann, Johan Dirk. 1965. *Marriage and Kinship Among Indians in Surinam*. Leiden: Proefschrift Social Science University.

5

AGEING *GIRMITIYAS* AND THE STORY OF SALT BEHIND THE SUGAR

Bobby Luthra Sinha

Old age and ageing are categories that can ground anthropological reflection on ways of living. Anthropological inquiries into old age have also contributed to ethnographic practice: participant observation, the use of biographies, individual trajectories and audio-visual narratives form part of the research legacy of anthropological literature on old age.[1] Evolving forms of social and spiritual care for geriatric needs reflect complex and diverse transformations in any era.[2] This chapter points out that the existing literature on plantation-based indentured Indians is yet to feature detailed studies on ageing and the factors that may have accelerated the process. Additionally, there is a dearth of studies on the social-care networks that came into being to provide for the elderly once the indenture system was abolished and/or free living outside of the plantations started.[3] While striving to fill this gap, this chapter endeavours to open up themes for further research.

RETHINKING 'AGEING' AMONG THE *GIRMITIYAS*

In the nineteenth to early twentieth centuries, the indenture system was used to recruit Asian workers for employment elsewhere in the European colonies. Despite the end of slavery, the British Empire's quest to make sugar and keep it profitable continued. It was a major source of governmental revenue, and consumer demand increased as the masses developed a taste for this labour-intensive commodity, using it to sweeten tea and coffee all over Europe.[4] As a layered, divisive and discriminatory process, indenture steadily revealed the global division of labour as well as the scale of exploitation of the body that went along with it. The physical sweat and toil accompanied by regimes of bodily control not only became the salt behind the success story of sugar production, but, I argue, these factors also hold the key to understanding the problems of ageing among the indentured and ex-indentured population.

Ageing in an era when longevity (as we know it now) was yet to be established as a fairly probable norm, provides us with a compelling context. The colonial perception of 'ageing' under indenture was shaped by economic needs: in the plantation system, older workers were a burden or a liability. Able-bodied individuals likely to perform well under harsh tropical conditions were preferred. Thirty-five was considered too old to re-migrate.[5] Many aspiring migrants were rejected on 'account of old age or some bodily infirmity'.[6] By the standards of the time, those who were indentured twice or stayed on already faced 'old-age' if they reached the age of 35. Life beyond this age therefore would be a continuation of the process of ageing.

Our temporal distance from the process and implications of ageing among first-generation indentured Indian communities brings forth many challenges. In order to do justice to the issues of old age tackled by first-generation *girmitiyas*, ageing needs to be freed from the assumption of it being a linear process. Ageing among the indentured should be examined through a nuanced appraisal of the challenges faced on the plantation fields under the aegis of restrictive contracts and controls. Just as in other highly perilous, abusive and stressful situations, exposure to ageing factors was unavoidable for indentured Indians.[7] Considering that people in their mid-30s were perceived as too old to toil, ageing cannot be seen as simply an innate biological process defined by movement towards the 'end of life'.

The contracts of indentured labourers – referred to as *girmit*s – required them to work in destinations such as Fiji, Trinidad and Natal for a certain period of time. During their tenures, a few immigrants were able to keep up ties with India. After five years under their *girmit*, the *girmitiya*s were free to return to India at their own expense. If a labourer opted for re-indenture, the colonial government was compelled to provide free passage back to India for the migrant and their children after ten years (which it did its best to resist).[8] Around 40 per cent of migrants opted to return. Many immigrants stayed and settled on the land as farmers; some prospered after much toil, but some also failed and remained impoverished. Indian workers were initially extolled for their docility, industriousness, familiarity with agriculture, strong family life, respect for authority and respect for the sanctity of contract.[9] These positive characterizations of Indian labour presented a better alternative to ex-slave workers over whom planters struggled to reassert authority.[10] Over time, as India and China emerged as major sources of 'coolie'[11] labour, negative stereotypes emerged: (*a*) the Indians were themselves to blame for their ill-health, mental instability and medical suffering; (*b*) only government (colonizer, empire, planter) intervention could save the Indian and (*c*) the non-compliant Indian should be 'disciplined' and intimidated to remain in the field, be imprisoned or be hospitalized at the behest of the masters.[12]

Indian nationalists retaliated, describing indenture as a system based on an unfair contract, the safeguards in which were ineffective and illusory and which entailed conditions of appalling human misery.[13] On 4 March 1912, Gopal Krishna Gokhale moved a resolution in the Imperial Legislative Council, recommending the prohibition of the recruitment of Indian indentured labour. He was particularly concerned by the heavy mortality rates of overseas workers.[14] This issue was examined from time to time by commissions of inquiry. Forms of control such as bio-medicinal claims, hospital ordinances and imprisonment laws that extolled the virtues of colonial power and made judgments concerning the indentured body and mind increased the negative impact of the system.[15] The indenture system which often led to the separation of families and community groups (before newer relations of kinship and ties came into being) added to the baggage of an isolated, neglected and alienated existence overseas.

By 1920 the imperial government had largely ended the system of indentured labour owing to the exigencies of the First World War, growing Indian nationalist protests and pressure on the British 'Government of India' as well as its declining profitability.[16] However, the bodily woes of those who were already indentured or those 'freed' and trying to settle amidst poverty and deprivation did not come to an end. They faced newer challenges including confronting the ageing and debilitating effects of labour. From this grew the search for social welfare and care.[17]

POWER AND CONTROL OF THE BODY: THE SALT BEHIND THE SUGAR

The British Empire oversaw the institution of regulations to procure young, robust workers with fit minds and bodies to serve on the plantations. As its bio-medicinal knowledge of diseases and the then prevalent cures grew, the empire furthered its remedial hold on the physical and mental lives of indentured labourers. Laws intended to 'safeguard the public health' were enacted to ensure control over what their subjects could and could not do. Medical science was used to create a more comprehensive understanding – and hold – over the lives and labour of the colonized. To know the subject was to rule the subject. In the past this had meant amassing state knowledge about language, culture and religion. The science of public health transformed this inclination into empirical data regarding disease and good health. Medicine and public health were directly related to the political, commercial and militaristic aspects of colonial power.[18]

The first generation of ageing *girmitiya*s faced ever-intensifying racism that marginalized them further. Survivors of indenture had been selected and had served with their once 'healthy bodies', but now they were 'free' to manage their ageing bodies alone. In a highly racist context when little social security was available, how did indentured and ex-indentured Indians come to terms with the crucial realities of the twilight of life?

Alongside honing their skills in foreign working conditions, difficult and painful journeys of survival amidst death and disease defined the everyday of indentured workers. *Girmitiya*s had to contend with the ever-present danger of hookworm infection, leprosy and sexually transmitted infections (STIs) which caused the mortality rate to rocket.[19] Dysentery and ulceration of the lower extremities were frequently listed in earlier reports. Yellow fever, typhoid and malignant and comatose fevers were reported as causes of death by 1869. In the 1870s, anaemia, debility and exhaustion were most frequently listed. By the 1880s, malaria had become the number one killer and cause of illness.[20] In the early 1900s, ankylostomiasis,[21] a kind of hookworm disease, had become second to malaria. Near the close of the indenture system, diseases treated in the colonial hospitals in Trinidad were 3,176 cases of malaria, 1,613 cases of ankylostomiasis, 1,018 cases of skin diseases and 836 cases of digestive diseases.[22] Leprosy[23] was also hugely problematic. Aside from its immediate implications for the body owing to the dearth of treatment options,[24] many of its ramifications were long-term and debilitating. Highly painful, uncomfortable and deformative, leprosy was not only crippling but also highly contagious. Stigmatized as a result of its visible manifestations such as scaly lesions on the skin and blisters, leprosy presented multiple problems for indentured labourers. Directly related to undernourishment and crowded living conditions, leprosy added to the list of dreaded challenges for the migrants.

Certain practices such as *ganja*-smoking and excessive rum or toddy drinking were treated as health as well as moral concerns. The prevalence of diseases and the desire to control and treat the patients had a multi-layered significance within the indenture system, including leading to accelerated ageing of the body. Not surprisingly, mental illness was a common feature of indenture, and one that initially tended to be ignored by plantation and colonial officials. In order to look into these uncomfortable issues, the colonists and planters would have to have reflected upon and reconsidered the system they were implementing. Instead, they preferred to devise newer arguments and mechanisms to endorse the system and to keep resistance to it under check.[25]

It is important to note that hospitals, under these narratives, although no replacements for prisons, were another way to exert granular control over the lives of the indentured. While some vagrants could be sent to jail, others could be directly hospitalized without much ado. Once the weaning out was accomplished, the rest could be confined to work long hours in the field. All these methods served to keep indentured workers bound to their plantations. Ironically, the ordinances and laws of control governing indentured life, whilst minutely controlling the worker, eventually also became the reason that the system faced growing adversity, as workers learned how to use them to sue for their rights.[26]

Day-to-day life was filled with disease and illness for the *girmitiya*, and these elements kept him from his work. Some planters chose to see disease and infection as an ethnographic anomaly of the indentured subject. Sick bodies were therefore dragged from one punishment to the next. It was the very experience of indenture that exposed him to myriad illnesses (ankylostomiasis, malaria, STIs, mental trauma, and so on), and yet the system was rarely accused. In the late-nineteenth-century understanding of disease and public health, infected indentured workers were seen as a potent threat to the viability of agricultural production. Hence, various measures of control were enacted to remove infected and mentally unwell individuals from the plantation so that others would not be affected. In a world defined by fields, barracks, hospitals, courthouses, reform homes and prisons, the empire slowly reduced the *girmitiya*'s humanity into a labouring, ageing body.

When indenture ended, the first generation of labourers faced a strange paradox, one of those situations for which they needed to process newer realities in newer ways. Having left their homeland, many still yearned for it culturally. However, fewer returned than remained in their adopted homelands. In the hope of pursuing economic opportunities in the colonies, decisions were taken to stay back and be 'free'. Those who stayed back were now left to their own resources.[27] Knowing this, a spirit of self-sufficiency was necessary.

Could the indentured Indians uphold the dignity of their 'debilitated' and ageing bodies? By calling forth humanitarian, philanthropic and spiritual energies, the Indian inhabitants of South Africa experimented with a successful model of healing and care. Their efforts, it can be argued, were grounded interventions which showed that old age was not just found in visible changes to the body.

SELF-HELP IN SOUTH AFRICA: TOWARDS A HEALING TOUCH

Arriving in the port city of Durban in South Africa to work on the coastal belt of the province of KwaZulu-Natal, indentured labourers began their economic journeys by processing raw material for the sugar industry. While some 'migrants' travelled alone, others brought their families to settle in the colonies where they worked. Indians also came to South Africa as 'free' or 'passenger' Indians who were able to maintain closer links with their communities back home.[28] Whereas the indentured came to South Africa as a result of a triangular pact between three governments, the passengers were mainly traders exploring new opportunities.[29]

The evolution of people of Indian origin in South Africa has been a dynamic transnational process, incorporating changing and complex identities that reflect the agency of the migrants.[30] Although in terms of global flows, Indian migration continued to peak elsewhere,[31] in the context of India and South Africa, the system of indentured labour came to an end in 1911. When the formerly indentured labourers were 'freed' from their contacts, many quickly established themselves as part of the important general labour force in Natal, particularly as industrial and railway workers. Others began to engage in market gardening, growing most of the vegetables consumed by the white population.[32]

The initial decades following abolition were fraught with inequality, injustices and poverty as well as job insecurities as indenture contracts ceased. Indian migrants in South Africa were ageing and the social and economic demands on the men to support their families increased tremendously. At the same time, the South African legislature had no governance in place which officially gave labour rights to these migrants. During the 1920s and 1930s, the low wages of Indian workers resulted in widespread poverty. This was exacerbated by the attempts of the South African government to maintain the hierarchy of racial privilege and prevent poverty spreading amongst the white population in South Africa. The Pact government decided to implement segregation legislation that prioritized the uplifting of poor whites and limited the access of other race groups to employment.[33]

In the case of South Africa, it is evident that the inherent suffering of indenture contributed several factors towards ageing and self-care needs even after its demise. First, it led to bodily stress and distress, both faced by the first generation of indentured after the end of the system and inherited by their descendants. Aside from low incomes and resources, the post-indenture populations were also exposed to the repercussions of the first and second world wars with an intermittent disaster in the shape of the economic depression of the 1920s and 1930s. Second, although the brutality of working conditions changed for the better post-indenture, labourers continued to be mired in negligence by the state. Poverty and other forms of non-plantation related terror came in the wake of the ascendency of apartheid. Finally, ageing for the poorest, most isolated and lonely elders in the post-indenture world of Indian South Africans was accelerated and remained harsh.

In order to fully understand the situation of ageing indentured Indians at the end of *girmit*-based labour in South Africa, the following factors are important to consider: First, when immigration from India was ended, the majority of the Indians were living in stringent poverty.[34] Although there was an emerging Indian petty bourgeoisie, comprised of free passengers and ex-indentured labourers, 95 per cent remained working class, out of which 70 per cent were desperately poor.[35] Second, social welfare and dignity of life for the marginalized non-European remained a challenging theme in terms of state interest. While there were old age homes for the European homeless and destitute, there were none for people from other races.[36] Additionally, Indians formed a vulnerable ethnic minority who were not even considered citizens for more than a century after their arrival and were regarded as aliens in the country of their choice or birth by both the ruling whites and the discriminated black natives.[37] Although the Indians and Asians were 'better off' than the black population, their use as a racial, spatial, political and economic boundary or, buffer zone was far from pleasant and served to compound their socio-political burdens.[38] Moreover, unlike the native

Africans, Indians could not always count on extended family support systems, as such structures were often fragmented as a result of their migration.

The political encumbrances and discrimination surrounding migration were further compounded by continued poor housing and dearth of infrastructure to tackle overcrowding and negligence of sanitation and health.[39] In such a climate, the essential question is, who catered to the new needs of the ageing and the sick or the destitute and the homeless, and how was it possible to ameliorate their social suffering?

According to Arthur Klienmann, Veena Das and Margaret Lock, 'Social suffering results from what political, economic and institutional power does to people and, reciprocally, from how these forms of power themselves influence responses to social problems'.[40] The conditions spawning the origin and growth of the Aryan Benevolent Home (ABH), a first of its kind in community driven social and geriatric care in Durban, KwaZulu-Natal, bring to light one such example. While eradication of social suffering would not have been possible, the ABH invested its resources, time and money in saving and providing for the destitute, the old and the abused, including food and education for needy children.[41]

The precursor of the self-help model undertaken by the ABH was a collective social-uplift platform that catered to the religious, spiritual as well as educational needs of the community, known as the Arya Yuvak Sabha (AYS). At the time Hinduism was being reformed in India at a grassroots level by showing the community ways to demystify oppressive religious practices such as the caste system, untouchability and child marriages. One of the most important of these reforming organizations was the Arya Samaj – led by Swami Dayanand Saraswati. An Arya Samaj missionary, Swami Shankaranand, gave his support and guidance to young Indians, who established the AYS in 1912, adopted Arya Samaj principles and began to work amongst the community. This wing of the Arya Samaj engaged in upliftment of the community through various endeavours such as the provision of education.[42] Three years later, the first home, a small wood and iron house in Cato Manor, opened its doors to three homeless beggars. It soon became a refuge for elderly, disabled and chronically ill people in need. The ABH was finally opened in 1921 by an eminent scholar, journalist and humanitarian, D. G. Satyadeva, who had dedicated his life to spreading the religious ideas of Saraswati and resisting social and political injustice.

The ABH has a special mixed history; it started out as a movement that echoed beneficent frameworks used in the ancestral homeland. Despite all odds, it succeeded in enacting a community vision that provided homes, care and nursing for aged and needy Indians, when scant attention was paid to such humanitarian needs elsewhere. Amongst its many goals were the establishment of the rights of women and children, the education of girls and a reinforcement of the pride of being an Indian. At a time when there were places of shelter for the homeless and destitute of 'European' origin, and the government made no provision for the same category of people from other races, this formation of the ABH reflected a collective recognition of the burgeoning crisis among people of Indian origin and their firm resolve to cater to it institutionally.[43]

The conception of the ABH is linked to an unusually cold day in 1918. D. G. Satyadeva witnessed a policeman mercilessly assaulting a homeless old Indian man for taking shelter overnight in a public toilet in Durban. Deeply distressed by this incident and inspired by the teachings of the Arya Samaj of India, whose ninth principle states that everyone must see his or her own welfare in the welfare of others (a parallel to the African idea of *ubuntu*), Satyadeva and his colleagues, Nayanah Rajh and K. Singh, resolved to provide an alternative home for the city's neediest. The first generation of poor Indian migrants, indentured or otherwise, faced many harsh circumstances in coming to terms with an ageing body. Nonetheless, they managed to engender community welfare through an old age home such as the ABH, demonstrating the vitality and strength of the society they had developed.[44]

The ABH depended on support from within the community. Money was raised for it through drama productions, concerts and musical evenings organized by the cultural arm of the AYS. Gradually, as it collected funds, it expanded and acquired property for bigger premises. The British protector of Indian immigrants, the police and hospitals soon took full advantage of the situation and the ABH became occupied with humanitarian services beyond its capacity.[45]

By 1926, the home had also admitted two children as there were no existing provisions for 'non-European' children in need of care. This created a further problem as admitting children led to a corresponding necessity for a school in the vicinity. The dearth of formal schools for Indians in Cato Manor and its surrounding areas led to the ABH opening a private school with one hall and one teacher. Although it began as a very basic facility for children in the area, it functioned in a climate of keen cooperation between local inhabitants. Refusing to be bogged down by government failings over humanitarian issues, the ABH made provisions for the education of the Indian 'homeless', whether the old, the poor or needy children. From very early on, the ABH learned to function as a non-governmental organization devoted to care, education, generating awareness and other humanitarian work.[46]

Extensive poverty dominated the lives of Indian people during this time. According to Goolam Vahed, a stranger who visited Durban was appalled at the living conditions of the majority of Indians.[47] They were malnourished and housed in hovels without any sanitation. In addition, he made reference to the half-starved Indians with whom he interacted. He indicated that full families were ill-nourished and that their daily diets consisted of dals or lentils and rice and excluded any meats or other variations of protein. Some aged developed medical conditions because of the malnutrition, whereas others simply died. Many similar observations have been documented by historians.[48] Poverty and unemployment continued even after the industrial expansion of Durban from 1934. Poverty manifested itself in diseases and early deaths within the Indian community at the time and it was reported by Dr G. H. Gunn that Indians suffered higher disease and death rates due to defective nutrition and slum housing.[49] These trends continued with minimal medical support from South African authorities. Even after the 1930s, the government did not provide Indians with proper sanitation and electricity in Durban. They perceived Indians to be uneducated and therefore unaware of how to use or appreciate these resources.[50] In such circumstances, the ABH became the first Indian-sustained effort to provide shelter and care for its old and ageing community members in Durban. It continues to function in South Africa today.

CONCLUSION

A central aim of this chapter has been to engage in an empathetic reconsideration of ageing and avenues of social welfare under indenture and during the post-abolition period. Historians in South Africa have described the poverty-stricken lives of this community in detail, yet specific information on the lifespan, retirement, testimonies and experiences of the first generation of indentured immigrants is scarce. This study has highlighted the fact that there were no welfare systems in place between the late 1800s and early 1900s to care for ageing indentured communities. There was little political will for devising even minimal care for the frail, the physically dependent and the aged. Globally this was not unusual, but many migrants lacked the kith and kin whom they could rely upon for support. With no state support structure, the geriatric care of a migrant generation was a challenge for the community. The advent of formal homes for the aged and the needy such as the ABH came to fruition slowly yet steadily. Positive interventions such as the ABH evolved to include nursing facilities and became spaces that articulated a people's right to age with dignity.[51] Further research on the themes tackled in this chapter to build on the insights should include (*a*) examination of the ageing body of indentured labourers with non-linear perspectives on longevity, (*b*) exploration of personal histories for a more grounded, ethnographic understanding of ageing and humanitarian responses that chart both the successes and failures of that era, and (*c*) the undertaking of comparative studies, across indentured labour contexts, on old age care homes, philosophies and institutions that catered to the geriatric care of the elderly migrant who survived in the new worlds of the Global South.

NOTES

1. Cohen (1994); Buch (2015).
2. See Luthra Sinha (2017, 2018).
3. See Vahed (1995); Chetty and Luthra Sinha (2013); Luthra Sinha (2014, 2017, 2018).
4. Mintz (1985).
5. Parliamentary Papers (PP), 1910, XXVII (Cd. 5192–5194), Part II.
6. Comins (1893, 9).
7. See Selwyn (1972); Rothschild (1973); Twaddle (1975); Payne and Sutton (1993); Clarke, Peach and Vertovec (1990); Kempadoo (2017).
8. Ibid.
9. Alatas (1977). Indians, for their part had been eyed, even before indenture, to be perfectly industrious and obedient workers for hard labour. Trinidad Duplicate Despatches (1814, 4).
10. Mahmud (2012, 17–21); Kempadoo (2017, 48); Alatas (1977).
11. In contrast to 'coolies', a term used by the British for Indians throughout the indentured world, Indian indentured labourers often referred to themselves as *girmitiya*s. This was a term derived from the English word 'agreement' – a direct reference to the contract under which they laboured. The number of

'girmityas' that left Asia for colonies in the British Empire was estimated to be around 1.5 million. Hoerder (2002, 366–405).

12. Mahmud (2012, 17–21); Batsha (2017).

13. Gokhale (1912, 351–358).

14. Speaking about the 'appalling human misery of indenture', Gokhale (1912) brought to notice the fact that heavy mortality, which prevailed in the past in all colonies under the system, was examined from time to time by Commissions of Inquiry. It had been established beyond doubt that such a mortality existed, and whether in few instances or more, as Lord Curzon also said in 1901, 'even if such cases have occurred only in a few instances, the very fact that such cases can occur under the system constitutes a severe condemnation of the system' (356). See Gokhale (1912) recommending the prohibition of the recruitment of Indian indentured labour on 4 March 1912.

15. Trinidad Duplicate Despatches (1814, 4); Parliamentary Paper (1910, 3).

16. *The Economist* (2017).

17. Vahed and Desai (2010, 196).

18. Arnold (1988); Foucault (1973).

19. Perry (1969, 11).

20. Agent General of Immigrants Report (1869); Council Paper No. 64, 1876, p. 127.

21. The disease is commonly known as ancylostomiasis in contemporary medicine. This chapter uses 'ankylostomiasis' in congruence with its spelling in the colonial archive.

22. Perry (1969, 148–150); Council Paper No. 32, 1884, and Council Paper No. 29, 1885; *Trinidad Royal Gazette* XXIII, No. 22, 3 June 1857; see also Nanhu (2012); Brereton (2005); Laurence (1996).

23. The first effective treatment of leprosy surfaced in the 1940s. Further developments in the 1960s and 1970s led to the production of more effective anti-leprosy drugs.

24. Perry (1969, 148–150); Council Paper No. 32, 1884 and Council Paper No. 29, 1885; *Trinidad Royal Gazette* XXIII, No. 22, 3 June 1857.

25. Batsha (2017).

26. Sturman (2014).

27. There was a crucial difference between those that chose to remain during indenture and after: When the 5-year indenture period or 10-year residence period expired, the labourer was offered inducements in the form of land or bonuses so that they would remain in Trinidad or South Africa. Few Indians accepted either the inducements or the option to return to India;

most took their savings from the plantation years and went into a business of some sort on their own. See Perry (1969, 11).

28. Ginwala (1977).
29. Arkin, Magyar and Pillay (1989); Ramamurthy (1995).
30. Marin (1999); Lal (2010).
31. See Mckeown (2008, 48).
32. Vahed and Desai (2010).
33. Seekings (2007).
34. Ginwala (1977, 9).
35. Maharaj (2009, 69–82).
36. Singh (2000, 16); Chetty and Luthra Sinha (2013); Luthra Sinha (2015, 2018).
37. Moodley (1975, 256).
38. Lemon (1995); Davies (1981).
39. Chetty and Luthra Sinha (2013).
40. Klienmann, Das and Lock (2017, introduction).
41. Luthra Sinha (2017, 2018).
42. For a more detailed account of the inspirations that culminated in the establishment of the ABH in 1921, such as a community consciousness and the enthusiasm for providing relief to the old, the sick and the homeless among the Durban-based South African Indians, see chapter 2, 'The World of a Child' in Singh (2000, 5–21).
43. Luthra Sinha (2017, 2018).
44. Singh (2000); Chetty and Luthra Sinha (2013); Luthra Sinha (2017, 2018).
45. Singh (2000); Chetty and Luthra Sinha (2013); Luthra Sinha (2018).
46. Singh (2000); Chetty and Luthra Sinha (2013).
47. Vahed (1995).
48. Vahed (2019); Seekings (2007); Jain (2009).
49. Vahed (1995).
50. Vahed (1995).
51. www.abh.org.za (accessed 19 June 2023); Chetty and Luthra Sinha (2013).

BIBLIOGRAPHY

Alatas, Syed Hussein. 1977. *The Myth of the Lazy Native: A Study of the Image of the Malays, Filipinos and Javanese from the 16th to the 20th Century and Its Function in the Ideology of Colonial Capitalism*. London: Frank Cass & Co.

Andrews, Charles F., and W. W. Pearson. 1916. *Report on Indentured Labour in Fiji: An Independent Enquiry*. Calcutta: Star Printing.

Arkin, A. J., K. P. Magyar and G. J. Pillay. 1989. *The Indian South Africans: A Contemporary Profile*. Pinetown, South Africa: Owen Burgess Publishers.

Arnold, David. 1988. 'Introduction: Disease, Medicine and Empire'. In *Imperial Medicine and Indigenous Societies*, edited by David Arnold, 1–26. Manchester: Manchester University Press.

Batsha, Nishant. 2017. 'The Currents of Restless Toil: Colonial Rule and Indian Indentured Labor in Trinidad and Fiji'. PhD thesis, Graduate School of Arts and Sciences, Columbia University, New York.

Bowen, Richard L., and Craig. S. Atwood. 2004. 'Living and Dying for Sex'. *Gerontology* 50 (5): 265–290.

Brereton, Bridget. 2005a. 'Family Strategies, Gender, and the Shift to Wage Labor in the British Caribbean'. In *Gender and Slave Emancipation in the Atlantic World*, edited by Scully, Pamela and Diana Paton. USA: Duke University Press.

———. 2005b. 'The Experience of Indentureship 1845–1917'. In *Calcutta to Caroni and the Indian Diaspora*, edited by La Guerre and Bissessar, 3rd revised edition.

Buch, Elana D. 2015. 'Anthropology of Aging and Care'. *Annual Review of Anthropology* 44 (1): 277–293.

Cashman, Richard. 1982. 'White Mutiny: The Ilbert Bill Crisis in India and Genesis of the Indian National Congress'. *Pacific Affairs* 55 (3): 514–515.

Chetty, Suryakanthie, and Bobby Luthra Sinha. 2013. 'Aryan Benevolent Home (ABH): A Peoples' Movement for Upholding the Dignity of Life'. In *Chatsworth: Making of a South African Township*, edited by A. Desai and Goolam Vahed, 381–391. Durban: University of KwaZulu-Natal Press.

Clarke, Colin, Ceri Peach and Steven Vertovec (eds.). 1990. *South Asians Overseas: Migration and Ethnicity*. Comparative Ethnic and Race Relations Series. Cambridge: Cambridge University Press.

Cohen, Lawrence. 1994. 'Old Age: Cultural and Critical Perspectives'. *Annual Review of Anthropology* 23 (October): 137–158. https://doi.org/10.1146/annurev.an.23.100194.001033.

Comins, D. W. D. 1893. *Note on the Abolition of Return Passages to East Indian Immigrants from the Colonies of Trinidad and British Guiana*. Calcutta: Bengal Secretariat.

Davies, R. J. 1981. 'The Spatial Formation of the South African City'. *Geo Journal* 2 (suppl. 2): 59–72.

de Barros, Myriam Moraes Lins, Clarice Ehlers Peixoto and Andrea Moraes Alves. 2016. 'Ageing and Anthropology'. *Vibrant, Virtual Brazilian Anthropology* 13 (1): 52–54.

Drescher, Seymour. 2002. *The Mighty Experiment: Free Labor Versus Slavery in British Emancipation*. New York: Oxford University Press.

Feltes, Bruno César, Joice de Faria Poloni and D. Bonatto. 2015. 'Development and Aging: Two Opposite but Complementary Phenomena'. *Interdisciplinary Topics in Gerontology* 40: 74–84.

Foucault, Michel. 1973. *The Birth of the Clinic: An Archaeology of Medical Perception*, translated by A. M. Sheridan. New York: Vintage Books.

Ginwala, Frene. 1974. 'Class, Consciousness and Control: Indian South Africans, 1860–1946'. D. Phil dissertation, Oxford University.

———. 1977. *Indian South Africans*. Report No. 34, Minority Rights Group (MRG) International, London, UK.

Gokhale, Gopal Krishna. 1912. 'Prohibition of Indentured Labour'. Resolution in the Imperial Legislative Council, 4 March. https://www.coolitude. shca.ed.ac.uk/sites/default/files/Speeches%20and%20Writings%20of%20 Gopal%20Krishna%20Gokhale%20Vol.%201%20Economic.pdf. Accessed 3 July 2020.

Hoerder, Dirk. 2002. 'The Asian Contract Labor System (1830s to 1920s) and Transpacific Migration'. In *Cultures in Contact: World Migrations in the Second Millennium*, 366–405. Durham: Duke University Press.

Jain, R. 2009. 'Reflexivity and the Diaspora: Indian Women in Post-indenture Caribbean, Fiji, Mauritius and South Africa'. *South Asian Diaspora* 1(2): 167–179.

Jamal, Vali. 1975. 'Expulsion of a Minority: Essays on Ugandan Asians edited by Michael Twaddle London, Athlone Press, 1975, pp. 240. £4.50'. *Journal of Modern African Studies* 14(2): 357–361. DOI:10.1017/S0022278X000 53404.

Jones, A. Creech. 1953. 'Indians Overseas, 1838–1949, by C. Kondapi'. *Pacific Affairs* 26 (3): 278–279. DOI:10.2307/2753313.

Jones, Kenneth W. 1976. *Arya Dharm: Hindu Consciousness in 19th-Century Punjab*. Berkeley: University of California Press.

Kempadoo, K. 2017. '"Bound Coolies" and Other Indentured Workers in the Caribbean: Implications for Debates about Human Trafficking and Modern Slavery'. *Anti-Trafficking Review* (9): 48–63.

Klienmann, Arthur, Veena Das and Margaret Lock. 1997. *Social Suffering*. Berkeley: University of California Press.

Lal, Brij. 2010. *In the Eye of the Storm: Jai Ram Reddy and the Politics of Postcolonial Fiji*. Canberra: ANU E Press.

Laurence, K. O. 1996. 'The Development of Medical Services in British Guiana and Trinidad 1841–1873'. In *Caribbean Freedom: Economy and Society from Emancipation to the Present: A Student Reader*, edited by H. Beckles and V. Shepherd, 269–273. London: Hames Curry Publishers.

Lemon, A. (ed.). 1995. *The Geography of Change in South Africa*. New York: J. Wiley.

Luthra Sinha, Bobby. 2014. 'Social Movements of the Historical Indian Diaspora in South Africa: Binding the "Home" and "Homeland" Creatively?' *Journal of Diaspora Studies* 7 (1): 1–17.

———. 2015. 'The Ubuntu Democracy and an Anti-Drug Movement of the Indian South Africans in Durban'. Colleccion Uni-Com Facultad de Ciencias Sociales, Universidad Nacional de Lomas de Zamora 3, no. 5 (April), ISSN 2346-8647. http://www.sociales.unlz.edu.ar/unicom/ ColecionUniCom/A3N5-TheUbunto.pdf. Accessed 19 June 2023.

———. 2017. 'Of Social Change Cloaked in Geriatric Care: How the First Generation of Indentured Indian Migrants in Durban Confronted Ageing'. *Indian Anthropologist* 47 (1): 19–34.

———. 2018. 'Diaspora Memories and the "Common Social" as Benchmarks for Collective Action: Indian South Africans Articulate Against Substance Abuse in Durban'. In *Through the Diasporic Lens*, vol. 2, edited by Nandini C. Sen, 222–237. New Delhi: Authors Press.

Maharaj, B. 2009. 'Ethnicity, Class, State and Conflict: The "Indian Question" in Natal, South Africa'. In *The Indian Diaspora: Historical and Contemporary Context*, edited by L. N. Kadekar, A. K. Sahoo and G. Bhattacharya, 68–96. New Delhi: Rawat.

Mahmud, Tayyab. 2012. 'Cheaper than a Slave: Indentured Labor, Colonialism and Capitalism'. Seattle University School of Law Research Paper No. 12-34. SSRN: https://ssrn.com/abstract=2155088.

Marin, Louis. 1999. *Sublime Poussin*. Translated by Catherine Porter. Stanford: Stanford University Press.

McKeown, Adam. 2008. *Melancholy Order: Asian Migration and the Globalization of Borders*. New York: Columbia University Press.

Mintz, Sidney W. 1985. *Sweetness and Power: The Place of Sugar in Modern History*. New York: Penguin.

Moodley, K. A. 1975. 'South African Indians: The Wavering Minority'. In *Changes in Contemporary South Africa*, edited by L. Thompson and J. Butler, 250–279. Berkeley: University of California Press.

Nanhu, K. 2012. 'Health and Medicine during Indian Indentureship in Trinidad 1910 to 1920'. Unpublished MPhil Thesis, University of Oxford.

Parliamentary Paper. 1910. 'Report of the Committee on Emigration from India to the Crown Colonies and Protectorates (Sanderson Committee Report)'. XXVII, 5192–5194.

Payne, A., and P. Sutton (eds.). 1993. *Size and Survival: The Politics of Security in the Caribbean and the Pacific.* 1st ed. London: Routledge. https://doi. org/10.4324/9781315037325.

Perry, John Allen. 1969. 'A History of the East Indian Indentured Plantation Worker in Trinidad, 1845–1917'. LSU Historical Dissertations and Theses 1612, Louisiana State University. https://digitalcommons.lsu.edu/ gradschool_disstheses/1612. Accessed 20 June 2020.

Ramamurthy, T. J. 1995. *Apartheid and Indian South Africans: A Study of the Role of Ethnic Indians in the Struggle Against Apartheid in South Africa.* New Delhi. Reliance Publishing House.

Rothchild, Donald. 1973. *Racial Bargaining in Independent Kenya: A Study of Minorities and Decolonization.* New York: Oxford University Press.

Seekings, J. 2007. '"Not a Single White Person Should Be Allowed to Go Under": Swartgevaar and the Origins of South Africa's Welfare State, 1924–1929'. *Journal of African History* 48 (3): 375–394.

Selwyn, Ryan D. 1972. *Race and Nationalism in Trinidad and Tobago: A Study of Decolonization in a Multiracial Society.* Toronto: University of Toronto Press.

Singh, K. 2000. *A Labour of Love: The Biography of Dr Shishupal Rambharos.* Durban: Atlas Printers.

Sturman, Rachel. 2014. 'Indian Indentured Labor and the History of International Rights Regimes'. *American Historical Review* 119 (5): 1439–1467.

The Economist. 2017. 'The Legacy of Indian Migration to European Colonies'. 2 September.

Trinidad Dispatch No. 263, 30 August 1917.

Trinidad Dispatch No. 390, 13 November 1914.

Trinidad Duplicate Despatches. 1814. Woodford to Bathurst, 3 October 1814, Pub. No. 126 of the Trinidad Historical Society.

Twaddle, Michael (ed.). 1975. *Expulsion of a Minority: Essays on Ugandan Asians.* London: Institute of Commonwealth Studies, Athlone Press.

United Nations Population Fund (UNFPA). 2002. *Population Ageing and Development: Operational Challenges in Developing Countries.* New York: United Nations Population Fund.

Vahed, Goolam. 1995. 'The Making of Indian Identity in Durban, 1914–1949'. Doctoral thesis, Department of History, Indiana University, Bloomington.

———. 2019. '"An Evil Thing": Gandhi and Indian Indentured Labour in South Africa, 1893–1914'. *Journal of South Asian Studies* 42 (4): 654–674.

Vahed, Goolam, and Ashwin Desai. 2010. 'Identity and Belonging in Post-Apartheid South Africa: The Case of Indian South Africans'. *Journal of Social Sciences* 25 (1–3): 1–12, DOI: 10.1080/09718923.2010.11892861.

Young, Hershini Bhana. 2017. *Illegible Will: Coercive Spectacles of Labor in South Africa and the Diaspora*. Durham; London: Duke University Press.

PART II

AFTERLIVES

6

SANCTIONS FOR CITIZENSHIP

INDIANS OVERSEAS AND IMPERIAL RECIPROCITY

Heena Mistry

On 4 November 1944, the home department of the Government of India ordered a notice to be placed in the *Gazette of India* announcing the enforcement of the Indian Reciprocity Act against South Africa. Because persons of Indian origin in the Union of South Africa faced restrictions in entering, residing in, and trading, the central government directed that similar restrictions be imposed on South Africans of non-Indian origin in British India. In addition, the home department distributed an office memorandum explaining that the Government of India had decided to enforce the Indian Reciprocity Act and take retaliatory measures against the union government. The memorandum declared that the decision to finally implement the Indian Reciprocity Act against the Union of South Africa was a reaction to proposed legislation, such as proposed legislation that was colloquially known as the Pegging Bill. The proposed bill, which would later be passed as the Trading and Occupation of Land (Transvaal and Natal) Restriction Act in 1943, was referred to as the 'Pegging Act' because it 'pegged' a racial pattern of land ownership in the Durban municipal area.[1] Sir Shafa'at Ahmad Khan, the agent of the Government of India in South Africa at the time, had also recommended that the Government of India consider more drastic retaliatory measures towards the union government, advising that the bill be made immediately applicable.[2] The floor of the legislature, Indian public opinion and the press were all insistent in demands for retaliatory measures against South Africa.

The Government of India decided to give effect to all measures of the Reciprocity Act. One of these measures was to refrain from employing any more South African nationals of non-Indian origin in the various services in India, as Indians in South Africa were not employed in any but the 'most subordinate and menial posts'. Only approximately 200 white South Africans were employed in India.[3] Specifically, the Home Department requested that South Africans of non-Indian origin not, in future, be appointed to posts in the Indian Civil Service and the Indian Police and other services at the provincial or federal levels. Despite putting these measures in place, the memorandum admitted that they were 'not likely to be of any considerable magnitude' because so far, no South African had been employed in the Secretary of States or Provincial Services and the number of those who held technical posts was negligible. Regardless, the Government of India felt that implementing the Reciprocity Rules would 'have a considerable moral effect' both on public opinion in India, on the South African government, and on Indians domiciled in South Africa.[4]

The *Gazette* announcement and the office memorandum were both steps in the enforcement of the Reciprocity Act of 1943. This act was a retaliatory measure which allowed the Government of India to mirror the legal and citizenship restrictions which Indian settlers faced in white settler and other colonies and apply them to the nationals of those states in India. This chapter will contextualize the implementation of the Reciprocity Act within the culmination of several failed attempts by Indian moderates to reform empire and the position of Indians within it to extend the civil and political rights of white settlers to British Indians. It will then outline the concept of imperial reciprocity, and the notions of imperial citizenship that supporters and formulators of the act employed to push for the equal treatment of Indian settlers to white settlers. Finally, I will detail how the implementation of this act and the expression of dissatisfaction with the position of Indians overseas as subordinate to white settlers during the Second World War were means of putting pressure on the Colonial Office.

A DRAMATIC TURN FROM MODERATE MEASURES

The Reciprocity Act was a drastic step taken after failed attempts to improve the position of Indians overseas in relation to white settlers, through negotiation. The Government of India repeatedly tried to improve the status of Indians settled in South Africa before the passing of the Reciprocity Act. The Cape Town Conference of 1927, the Cape Town Agreement, the appointment of an agent for the Government of India and the Cape Town

Conference of 1932 were efforts to introduce 'unobtrusive and unoffending' measures to better the condition of Indians in South Africa and argue for their right to settle in the union as well as in other dominions.[5] During the Cape Town Conference of 1927, delegations from the Government of India and the Government of the Union of South Africa worked to renegotiate the terms of the Indian Relief Act of 1914, which M. K. Gandhi had made with Jan Smuts. It was the most well-known product of his Satyagraha campaigns in South Africa. Both parties who participated in the Cape Town Conference of 1927 shared the understanding that the Indian Relief Act was a failed agreement that no longer served either Indian or white interests in South Africa. The South African delegation insisted that the Indian Relief Act did not adequately reduce or stabilize the Indian population in South Africa, nor did it reduce the perceived threat of Indian penetration into white areas and economic competition with whites.[6] Leaders of the Indian community in South Africa found that the clause in the Indian Relief Act that provided Indians with easier access to repatriation was instead used to justify attempts at large-scale incentivized emigration of Indians from the union. Legislation that Gandhi had initially intended as a means of allowing indentured Indians who faced barriers to repatriation to return to India became a means of disrupting Indian claims to settler citizenship in South Africa.[7]

The 1927 Cape Town Conference led to the Cape Town Agreement. The Cape Town Agreement outlined a plan to assimilate, uplift and integrate Indians who could be expected to conform to what white South African officials referred to as 'western standards'. It also outlined a plan to incentivize the repatriation of all Indians who both white and Indian delegates deemed undesirable. Officially known as the Assisted Emigration Scheme, it provided a bonus of 20 pounds to voluntary emigrants and free transportation back to India with additional transport to whichever areas in India they wished to travel to. It was also agreed that the Government of India would, if repatriates expressed a desire to do so, assist them in finding employment as well as help them manage their bonus by depositing it in bank accounts upon arrival. Another difference between the Cape Town Agreement's incentivized Assisted Emigration Scheme and the Indian Relief Act's provision for Indian repatriation was that those who took advantage of the scheme were not required to give up their right to domicile in South Africa immediately, although those who took advantage of the Assisted Emigration bonus and then wished to return to South Africa had to do so in under three years, return the bonus and repay the costs of the passage that had brought them to India. To assist in upholding the terms of the Cape Town Agreement, the Colonial Office appointed an agent of the Government of India in South Africa. V. S. Srinivasa Sastri was the first agent, appointed in 1927, followed by Sir Kurma Venkata Reddi, Sir Kunwar Maharaj Singh, Sir Syed Raza Ali, Sir Benegal Rama Rau, Sir Shafa'at Ahmad Khan and R. M. Deshmukh, who ended his tenure in 1946.

In 1932, following the end of Sastri's first term as agent of the Government of India came a second Cape Town conference. During the 1932 conference, leaders of white interests in South Africa argued that the Cape Town Agreement needed to be renegotiated as it did not adequately contribute to the reduction of the Indian population in the union, since numbers of Indians taking advantage of the Assisted Emigration Scheme every year were dwindling. Indians in South Africa at the time had largely rejected the Assisted Emigration Scheme as unsettling to their claim to equal citizenship in the union, as it cast them as an alien element in the population that needed to be dealt with. After the 1932 Cape Town Conference, the Government of the Union of South Africa passed more restrictive legislation targeted towards Indians, including the Pegging Act in 1943. The work of the agents of the government of India was meant to assuage the attitude of white settlers towards Indians in the union, but often it did more to symbolically improve relations between Indians and whites than it did to achieve practical improvements in the restrictions Indians in the union faced.[8]

Throughout all four of these attempts, the Government of the Union of South Africa stubbornly kept trying to find avenues to enlist the Government of India's cooperation in implementing strategies to reduce the Indian population in the union. They argued that a large Indian population was a threat to 'Western civilization' and 'western standards of living' in South Africa.[9] In response, during the negotiations for the first of the Cape Town conferences in 1927, the Indian delegation kept suggesting that they were also interested in maintaining Western standards of living in the union. They pointed out that many Indians were willing and able to conform to 'western standards', but for those who were not, the Government of India would advise the union 'in any scheme to assist the emigration of such Indians to India or to some other country where western standards are not required'.[10] V. S. Srinivasa Sastri explicitly made the distinction between Indians who were capable under sympathetic treatment of 'becoming used to western standards of life' and who should remain in South Africa and those who were in South Africa 'as a burden' and should therefore receive assistance in returning to

India.[11] Those whom Sastri considered unassimilable, even with the help of upliftment efforts, tended to be indentured Indians and their descendants. Sastri's desire for these overseas Indians to leave for India is perhaps best encapsulated in John Kelly and Martha Kaplan's study of the relationship between Indian diaspora and Swaraj, which expressed that 'being coolies anywhere was a threat to Indians everywhere, in prospects of cosmopolitan respect and full citizenship however defined'.[12] Thus, what seemed to underlie the Government of India's decision to push for the rights of certain groups of Indians overseas was their capability to project a respectable image of India abroad,[13] one that maintained Indians' proximity to both whiteness and settler citizenship as opposed to being associated with racialized labourers.[14]

However, after Sastri's tenure as agent of the Government of India ended in 1929, he began to argue against incentivized repatriation schemes. During the Cape Town Conference of 1932, he argued that repatriates would only serve to burden the Indian economy, and insisted that villages in India could not absorb repatriates.[15] He stated that although both the Government of Madras and the officers concerned had done everything under the agreement that was possible, and even did more than the law required them to do to ensure the well-being of South African repatriates upon arrival, the global economic depression was so severe that India could hardly feed the mouths that it had. The addition of even a few hundred in the respective villages was a burden that India was unable to bear. He explained that returned emigrants had difficulty finding work in India in addition to facing social and other difficulties. Towards the end of the 1920s, for many who worked to improve the rights of Indians overseas within the empire, including C. F. Andrews, M. K. Gandhi, V. S. Srinivasa Sastri and others, it became clearer that even the repatriates who were not ideal representatives of India abroad were better off overseas than in India.[16] Sukanya Banerjee argues that while 'passenger Indians' – those who did not come to South Africa under indenture – wanted to extricate themselves from the generic label of 'coolie', they and their advocates eventually realized that the figure of the indentured labourer became crucial to forwarding the claims of imperial citizenship.[17]

ASPIRATIONS OF THE RECIPROCITY ACT

The Reciprocity Act of 1943 and the various drafts of the Indians Overseas Reciprocity Bill which circulated in the preceding years encapsulated how

Indians, both in India and in the colonies, made the claim to imperial citizenship. The statement of objects and reasons in the numerous drafts of the bill were a window to the different purposes it served. Govind Ballabh Pant, who was at the time the chief minister of the United Provinces, first proposed a draft of an 'Overseas Indians Reciprocity Bill' to the Indian Legislative Assembly early in 1937.[18] Later in the same year, Mohan Lal Saksena, then president of the United Provinces Pradesh Congress Committee (PCC), wrote up another identical draft of the bill.[19] The statement of objects and reasons in Saksena's draft expressed frustration at the failure of patient attempts to improve the situation through 'unobtrusive and unoffending' means, such as negotiations and representations to the Colonial Office and to the Government of the Union of South Africa, as well as to the governments of Fiji, Kenya, Zanzibar, Malaya, Iraq, British Guiana and other places, addressing claims of Indian subjects in those areas to equal treatment to white settlers and to citizenship rights. A later draft from 1939 by Saksena and 12 other members of the Indian Legislative Assembly made it clearer that the creation of the bill was in large part due to 'His Majesty's Government [not wishing] to interfere or [being impotent] to interfere in spite of ... strong protests against discriminatory legislation' towards Indians settled overseas.[20] Drafts of the bill clarified that it was intended as a more dramatic measure to protest against the position of Indians overseas than the government had previously taken.

In another later draft of the bill by Govind V. Deshmukh, the 'Statement of Objects and Reasons' was more explicit in holding the Colonial Office accountable to promises made during the Imperial War Conferences of 1917–1918 and the Imperial Conference of 1921 to give 'early consideration' to the removal of disabilities on Indians residing in other parts of the empire. Deshmukh's 1939 draft acknowledged that although dominions had the right to restrict immigration and control their populations, 'there [was] an incongruity between the position of India as an equal member of the British Empire and the existence of such disabilities upon British Indians lawfully domiciled in some parts of the empire'.[21] Saksena's early draft of the bill also tried to hold settler governments accountable by pointing out that 'the progressive deterioration of [Indians'] civic status [was] similarly due to the growth of European interest with the full backing of their dominant political power'.[22] Deshmukh and Saksena stated that the bill was also intended as a measure for holding the empire to Britain's articulation of the purpose of their own citizenship. British Empire citizenship, as articulated by the

British government and British colonial officials, merited equal citizenship privileges, equal access to these privileges and equality of treatment among all British Empire citizens. Deshmukh and Saksena pointed out that the discrepancies in access to the full benefits of British citizenship were characteristically un-British.[23]

Running through the various drafts of the Reciprocity Bill were also different expressions of the claim to equal citizenship for Indians within the empire. Most of the drafts did this by highlighting Indian contributions to expanding the British Empire's frontiers in the various areas Indians had settled. Saksena's early draft highlighted the role of Indians overseas in building up large interests abroad, mostly in countries which formed part of the British Empire. He pointed out that 'Indian subjects migrated to [the colonies] at their instance, and on their invitation', and that the colonies 'owe their progress and prosperity to Indian industry and enterprise in large measure'.[24] In the Indian Legislative Assembly debates preceding the passing of the Reciprocity Act in 1943, N. B. Khare, who was at the time head of the department of Indians overseas, tried to make the case that Indians in South Africa had at least earned equal treatment to whites by quoting a 1907 Commission in South Africa, which stated that 'Indians are industrious, law abiding ... that their presence has no injurious effect on the morals of the "whites" or the "natives"'.[25] He even alluded to Leige Hukett, a speaker in the Natal Parliament, describing the colony before the importation of Indian labour as 'one of gloom'. In the Council of State Debates (29 July 1943), Saiyed Mohamed Padsha Sahib Bahadur put forward a claim to Indian entitlement to British imperial citizenship by emphasizing the contributions of Indians under indenture or voluntary migration, stating that 'the Indian has always tried to help and improve the country ... by making proper use and developing the natural resources of the country'.[26] It was clear that the bill was intended to highlight the entitlement of Indians to the same imperial citizenship privileges as whites, a claim they could make via the contributions made through their labour, which made them equally proficient settlers to whites in the colonies.

The implementation of the Indian Reciprocity Act was also motivated by a resistance against affronts to Indian 'national self-respect' that arose when disabilities facing Indians settled legally in other parts of the empire were not sufficiently challenged by the Colonial Office or the Government of India. Saksena's early draft complained that the grievances of Indians overseas had been 'a constant source of embarrassment and concern to the people of

India, having aroused intense public feeling [...] on many occasion[s]', and that the 'treatment meted out to Indians [was] hardly fair anywhere, while in the British Colonies it [was] particularly galling and irritating'.[27] Saksena made it clear that the 'ceaseless inroads on legitimate interests of Indian settlers', constant 'impudent challenge[s] to the national self-respect of the people of India' and the futility of methods adhered to so far 'in spite of grave provocation', made a retaliatory Reciprocity Bill the only effective option left for Indian nationalists to defend the national self-respect of India overseas. Saksena employed the concept of imperial reciprocity to highlight the right of Indians to settle in the union as allies to South Africa and the British Empire during wartime, and Indian public opinion both in India and in South Africa complained of the offence taken when Japanese settlers in South Africa, who, unlike Indians, were not British subjects, and were enemies to the British Empire during wartime, faced fewer restrictions in the colony than Indian settlers.[28]

Complaints against the unequal treatment of Indian settlers in comparison to white settlers in the British Empire, which highlighted how this unequal treatment was an affront to Indian national-self-respect, also reveal an understanding of Indian nationalism and Indian citizenship as inseparable from belonging in the empire. During the council of state debates following the passing of the Indian Reciprocity Act, when members were considering the application of the Act's sanctions against the Union of South Africa, Prakash Narain Sapru explicitly stated that the necessity of the Act lay in the fact that '[i]t is not a question of Indian Independence. It is not a question of Indian self-government. This is a question of Indian *izzat*'.[29] Sapru spoke explicitly to white settlers and colonial administrators, warning that if they treated 'the Indian in any part of the British Commonwealth or the British Empire as unequal to you in status, then you destroy the very foundations of that Empire; you sap the very foundations of that Empire. You do something which will affect our allegiance to the Commonwealth ideal.'[30]

It was also clear that the Reciprocity Act was meant to protect the more respectable classes who could emigrate through official channels. It did not claim to protect those who were forced to circumvent discriminatory restrictions on their mobility which made movement through official channels inaccessible to them. The Indian Reciprocity Act of 1943 claimed to safeguard the *legitimate* rights of Indians overseas, including Indians *settled* or *domiciled* in a state. This was not the first time that the Government of India had employed the notion of *izzat*, or 'honour', to justify legislation that intervened in the affairs of Indians overseas, or to be selective about which Indians should have the right to emigrate without disruption. The Indian Emigration Act of 1922 criminalized all emigration from India for the purpose of unskilled labour except to Malaya, Ceylon and the Straits Settlement colonies in an attempt to ensure the 'maintenance of self-respect of India in foreign countries' which Pyari Lal argued was compromised when Indian labouring classes went abroad.[31] However, by the time the Indian Reciprocity Act was passed, many who were concerned with the position of India within the British Empire especially as reflected in the treatment of Indians overseas, realized that the claim to citizenship rights for Indians within the empire must be tied to a claim for even the labouring classes to those same privileges. The Reciprocity Act of 1943 very clearly defined which people of Indian descent settled overseas legitimately merited the protection of the Government of India and what kind of help they could expect. It still fell short of asserting a right to unrestricted mobility throughout the empire for Indians of *all* classes.

DEBATING THE RECIPROCITY RULES

The debates surrounding the passing of the act reflected competing understandings of the function of empire, the privileges merited by British subjecthood and the aspiration towards British Imperial citizenship. In the Indian Legislative Assembly debates preceding the passing of the bill, G. V. Deshmukh asserted that for so many years, the 'Viceroy down to the Government officers were lying supine on their backs; they did not take things seriously and they did not move in the matter ... this Government was helpless'.[32] For Deshmukh, membership in the British Empire merited the proactive protection and intervention by Britain in instances where Indians faced discrimination in British colonies and in the Dominions. Similarly, Hosseinbhoy A. Lalljee, another member, expressed frustration at the government of India's concern with displeasing the South African government and their decision to take less drastic measures to object against the treatment of Indians overseas, even when Indian public opinion was actively denouncing such mistreatment.[33]

Some saw reciprocity measures as a logical and necessary step to ensure that the empire was working in the interest of Indians and not at their expense. An article by G. A. Natesan in *Indian Review* described it as a measure which was 'primarily intended to safeguard the legitimate rights and interests of Indians in countries outside India; and only urges reciprocity against such of those States as are proved to act against the interests and honour of our nationals abroad'.[34] Natesan described G. B. Pant's bill as 'a modest measure and quite unexceptional', asserting that it was 'common knowledge that Indians suffer from various disabilities and indignities abroad, and it is but proper that we should possess some means of expressing our resentment'.[35] The bill was well received in the Indian press.

The fact that the act was passed during wartime was used both to justify and condemn it. Those who condemned the act framed it as an unpatriotic exacerbation of intra-imperial tensions during desperate times. Despite the multiple failed attempts at less severe measures, colonial administrators like Frederick Earnest James criticized the bill as too drastic. James lamented that 'it is a sad commentary on the position in the Empire today that a Bill of this nature should be considered necessary by this House'.[36] He felt it tragic that the house should enact a bill with the sole intention 'to apply in a retaliatory manner those measures of discrimination in this country which are unfortunately imposed upon Indians in other parts of the Empire'. He did not believe the act would ever produce a lasting solution to 'imperial racial problems' arguing that a more effective solution lay not in 'provocation and subsequent retaliation', but instead in 'consultation and conciliation'. No doubt his resistance to the bill came in no small part because of the difficulties that retaliation, especially through trade sanctions, would place on the war effort. James understood empire as 'an association, a free association of peoples of different races ...', and he saw the Reciprocity Act as a threat to this ideal. Whereas James emphasized the importance of empire as a framework that enabled trade and other interactions between the different comprising members, Indian participants in the legislative assembly debates underlined that if empire was to legitimately hold its different parts together, 'free association' between different members of the empire should not come at the benefit of some and the expense of others.

Many Indian members of the Indian Legislative Assembly protested against F. E. James' claim that the passing of the Reciprocity Act would be an unpatriotic move during wartime. Lalchand Navalrai also pointed out his frustration with 'conciliatory methods' suggested by F. E. James. Although he agreed that such methods 'would be best', India had 'tried the method of conciliation, and when we fail in that we are forced to adopt this retaliatory measure'.[37] It became clear that negotiations and moderate protest under the supervision of the India Office and the Colonial Office were no longer effective at implementing permanent changes in the position of Indians overseas. Indians in support of the bill framed it as a retaliation of necessity which helped uphold Indian dignity as India contributed heavily to the war effort, yet Indians in the empire continued to face discrimination. In responding to James, Cowasjee Jehangir asserted that the issue of disabilities faced by Indians overseas had agitated public opinion in India for the last 35 years, and that while the Colonial Office might criticize the Government of India for taking up sanctions against the Government of South Africa in particular during wartime, it was 'unpatriotic to the commonwealth of nations' for the South African government to put in place discriminatory legislation against Indians in South Africa during wartime in the first place.[38]

Others pushed for the implementation of the act's sanctions for their symbolic value, especially seeing as their effects would not be as drastic once the war was over. During the council of state debates immediately following the passing of the act, M. N. Dalal of Bombay argued that it would be

> futile to enforce retaliation after the war for after the war South Africa will no longer be dependent for its essential requirements, like foodgrains, jute and jute products and textiles. After the war search for substitutes and alternative sources of supply will be so great that no nation will be dependent upon another.[39]

He pointed out the irony of 'talk of international and inter-racial amity and unity in peace and war ... when negotiation, reconciliation and representation fails', asserting that retaliation was the only way to secure the place of Indians settled in South Africa as justly settled in the dominion.[40]

Other members complained of attempts to use wartime as an excuse to minimize the urgency of the Pegging Act on Indians domiciled in South Africa. Govind V. Deshmukh pointed out that after the Pegging Act was passed in South Africa, and agitation there started, Indians were advised to 'sit quiet in terms of war' and not 'alienate' the feelings of the colonies that Indian troops and resources were actually assisting.[41] For Deshmukh, the bill was a necessary step towards consistency and effectiveness of interventions made by the Government of India and the Colonial Office when dealing with grievances regarding Indians overseas.

Despite there being support for the Reciprocity Act in the Indian Legislative Assembly, members still expressed uneasiness at the effectiveness of such measures in improving the conditions of Indians overseas, especially in South Africa. Although he supported the act and its implementation against South Africa, Jehangir pointed out that while India had thousands of her people in South Africa, only about 100 South Africans were in India, and if South Africa retaliated against the sanctions enforced through the Reciprocity Act, the damage would potentially be much greater for India than for South Africa. Jehangir's opinion was that trade retaliation would be a more effective sanction than the application of the same disabilities faced by Indians in South Africa to South Africans in India.[42] Jehangir's assessment was quite perceptive, as India did have more leverage with South Africa if it applied trade sanctions, especially since South Africa relied on India for jute, which was used to make the gunny bags required for packing South African manufactured and agricultural products.[43] Members of the European group of the Indian Legislative Assembly also warned of the potential consequences of retaliatory legislation, agreeing with many of the Indian members that India could not allow the matter to 'stand as it is', but that retaliatory measures risked prejudicing the case of Indians overseas and having a 'boomerang effect'.[44]

The passing of the Reciprocity Act was not the first time that the Government of India had employed the concept of imperial reciprocity in an attempt to reform empire. Indian delegates to the Imperial War Cabinet of 1917–1918 and the Imperial Conferences of 1921 and 1923 had put forward a set of reciprocity resolutions which the self-governing Dominions, except South Africa, accepted. These reciprocity resolutions declared that the inherent function of the governments of the British Commonwealth, including India, was that each should enjoy complete control over the composition of its own population by means of restriction on immigration from any of the other communities; that British citizens domiciled in any British country, including India, should be admitted into any other British territory for visits, commerce, temporary residence, or education, except with temporary residence for the purpose of labour or permanent settlement; that Indians already domiciled in the other British countries should be allowed to bring one 'lawfully certified' wife and their minor children.[45]

The Indian delegation's frustrations with imperial reciprocity reflected a shift in India's understanding of empire from a benevolent paternalistic humanitarian organization to an infrastructure through which member states could build a framework for navigating international relations. This latter understanding of empire placed it in the same vein as the League of Nations.

I argue that for Indians who saw reform of empire as the ideal avenue for change, reformed empire would be an association of states that worked together to advocate for benefits for all members on the international stage and would be advantageous when India attained dominion status.

CONCLUSION

Nawabzada Muhammad Liaquat Ali Khan described the Pegging Act as 'the last straw on the camel's back' in 30 years of tense relations between the governments of India and the Union, and the Government of India's failure to effectively address the union government's unwillingness to include Indians within white settler citizenship.[46] The Indian Reciprocity Act of 1943, especially in its implementation towards the Union of South Africa in 1946, was one of the final attempts to put pressure on the Colonial Office to take more drastic measures in protecting the citizenship rights of Indians overseas before independence in 1947. The Reciprocity Act was not meant to legislate against British rule but was instead meant as a prompt to reform it. It was one of the final attempts before independence to put pressure on the Colonial Office to take more drastic measures for protecting the citizenship rights of Indians overseas. Overall, as far as the Reciprocity Act was a retaliatory measure meant to improve the conditions of Indians overseas, it served in more of a symbolic sense than a practical one. The trade sanctions applied were much more effective as an ultimatum than the mirrored application of Indian disadvantages in South Africa to South Africans in India.[47] The Reciprocity Act also reflected a step away from negotiation as an effective avenue for improving the position of Indians overseas. For those who supported the act, empire was meant to be a framework in which member states benefitted equally from their interactions with other members of the empire. Those who reproached it saw the legislation as a measure that symbolized the opposite of what empire was meant to achieve, which was the facilitation of uninhibited relations between the member states of the empire. During the 1932 Imperial Conference in Ottawa, Canada, imperial reciprocity was an alternative to 'imperial preference', a concept which justified advantageous tariffs for British manufactured goods at the expense of the colonies. The Reciprocity Act was one of the last attempts of India to make the case for the rights of Indians overseas as a member of the British Empire. The next major incident in which India intervened on behalf of Indians overseas was in 1949, when the

Government of India brought the issue of discriminatory treatment towards Indians in South Africa to the United Nations.

NOTES

1. Maharaj (2003).
2. Dhupelia-Mesthrie (1987, 250).
3. Rao (1947).
4. Excerpt from Home Department Office Memorandum No. 23/3/43, 1945, in NAI: Home Department, Establishment Proceedings, File No. 533. 45-Ests, 1945.
5. For more on the Cape Town conferences of 1927 and 1932, the Cape Town Agreement and the agents of the Government of India in South Africa, see Hofmeyr (2014); Naidoo and Bramdaw (1931); Rao (1963); Dhupelia-Mesthrie (2004); Tinker (1976).
6. Proceedings, 17 December 1926. See also Dhupelia-Mesthrie (1985) and Hofmeyr (2014).
7. Mistry (2021).
8. See Mistry (2021); Mesthrie (1985, 1987).
9. Precedence of Government of India's representative, 1927–1932.
10. Mahommed Habibullah in Proceedings, 21 December 1926. See also Mohapatra (1998).
11. Proceedings, 5 January 1927.
12. Kelly and Kaplan (2007, 231).
13. See Seecharan (2011, introduction).
14. See Hofmeyr (2010, 2013).
15. Proceedings, 15 January 1932.
16. Gandhi (1926); Sannyasi and Chaturvedi (1931); Kelly and Kaplan (2007).
17. Banerjee (2010, 92–93).
18. Confidential Letter, 28 July 1937. For a copy of Govind Ballabh Pant's draft of the Overseas Indians Reciprocity Act see India Office Records (IOR)/ L/PJ/8/309 COLL 108-33L. Also see National Archives India: Foreign/ Ministry of External Affairs Department, South Africa Papers, South Africa Serial No. 23, 01-OR/36: Overseas Reciprocity Bill by Pandit GB Pant.
19. Enclosure in Confidential Letter, 28 July 1937.

20. Saksena et al. (1939).
21. Govind V. Deshmukh, Draft of the Overseas Indian Reciprocity Bill, in IOR/L/PJ/8/309 COLL 108-33L.
22. Enclosure in Confidential Letter, 28 July 1937.
23. See also Banerjee (2005).
24. Enclosure in Confidential Letter, 28 July 1937.
25. Indian Legislative Assembly Debates, 29 July 1943.
26. Council of State Debates, 29 July 1943.
27. Enclosure in Confidential Letter, 28 July 1937.
28. *Indian Views*, 10 September 1943.
29. Council of State Debates, 4 August 1943.
30. Prakash Narain Sapru, Excerpt from Council of State Debates, 4 August 1943, in IOR/L/PJ/8/309 Coll. 108.
31. Indian Legislative Assembly Debates, 6 February 1922.
32. Indian Legislative Assembly Debates, 29 July 1943.
33. Indian Legislative Assembly Debates, 29 July 1943.
34. Natesan (1936).
35. Natesan (1936).
36. Indian Legislative Assembly Debates, 29 July 1943.
37. Indian Legislative Assembly Debates, 29 July 1943.
38. Indian Legislative Assembly Debates, 29 July 1943.
39. Council of State Debates, 4 August 1943.
40. Council of State Debates, 4 August 1943.
41. Govind V. Deshmukh, Indian Legislative Assembly Debates, 29 July 1943, in IOR/L/PJ/8/309 Coll. 108.
42. Indian Legislative Assembly Debates, 29 July 1943.
43. Dhupelia-Mesthrie (1987, 251–252).
44. Sir Henry Richardson, Indian Legislative Assembly Debates, 30 July 1943.
45. Outlined in a pamphlet circulated to the Members of the Indian Legislative Assembly in 1941 during the discussions surrounding the Indians Department, Paper No. III, *Opinions on the Reciprocity Bill* (Introduced by Mr Govind V. Deshmukh, MLA), Opinion no. 13, 22, in IOR/L/PJ/8/309 Coll. 108. Overseas Reciprocity Bill, Government of India, Legislative Assembly.
46. Nawabzada Muhammad Liaquat Ali Khan, Indian Legislative Assembly Debates, 2 August 1943, in IOR/L/PJ/8/309 Coll. 108.
47. Dhupelia-Mesthrie (1987, 251–252).

BIBLIOGRAPHY

Banerjee, Sukanya. 2005. 'Political Economy, Gothic, and the Question of Imperial Citizenship'. *Victorian Studies* 47 (2): 260–271.

———. 2010. *Becoming Imperial Citizens: Indians in the Late-Victorian Empire*. Durham: Duke University Press.

Confidential Letter from the Secretary to the Government of India in the External Affairs Department to the Under Secretary of State for India, Public and Judicial Department. 1937. In National Archives UK (NAUK), Colonial Office (CO)/323/1520/17, 28 July 1937.

Council of State Debates. 1943. In India Office Records (IOR)/L/PJ/8/309 Coll. 108, 4 August.

Deshmukh, Govind V. 1943. Draft of the Overseas Indians Reciprocity Act. In IOR/L/PJ/8/309 Coll. 108-33L.

Dhupelia-Mesthrie, Uma. 1985. 'Reducing the Indian Population to a "Manageable Compass": A Study of the South African Assisted Emigration Scheme of 1927'. *Natalia* 15: 36–56.

———. 1987. 'From Sastri to Deshmukh: A Story of the Role of the Government of India's Representatives in South Africa, 1927 to 1946'. PhD dissertation, University of Natal.

———. 2004. *Gandhi's Prisoner? The Life of Gandhi's Son Manilal*. Cape Town: Kwela Books.

Gandhi, M. K. 1926. 'Out of the Frying Pan'. *Young India*, 9 September.

Hofmeyr, Isabel. 2010. 'Universalizing the Indian Ocean'. *Publications of the Modern Languages Association of America* 125 (3): 721–729.

———. 2013. *Gandhi's Printing Press*. Cambridge, MA: Harvard University Press.

———. 2014. 'Seeking Empire, Finding Nation: Gandhi and Indianness in South Africa'. In *Routledge Handbook of the South Asian Diaspora*, edited by J. Chatterjee and D. Washbrook, 153–165. London: Routledge.

Home Department Office Memorandum No. 23/3/43. 1945. In National Archives of India (NAI): Home Department, Establishment Proceedings, File No. 533.

Indian Legislative Assembly Debates. 1922. In IOR/L/PJ/6/1744 file 2396, 6 February.

———. 1943. In IOR/L/PJ/8/309 Coll 108, 29 July, 30 July and 2 August.

Kelly, John D., and Martha Kaplan. 2007. 'Diaspora and Swaraj, Swaraj and Diaspora'. In *From the Colonial to the Postcolonial: India and Pakistan in*

Transition, edited by Dipesh Chakrabarty, Rochona Majumdar and Andrew Sartori, 311–331. Oxford: Oxford University Press.

Maharaj, Brij. 2003. "'Co-Operation, Consultation and Consent": The Failure of Voluntary Residential Segregation in Durban (1920–1945)'. *South African Geographical Journal* 85 (2): 134–143.

Mesthrie, Uma. 1985. 'Reducing the Indian Population to a "Manageable Compass": A Study of the South African Assisted Emigration Scheme of 1927'. *Natalia* 15: 36–56.

———. 1987. 'From Sastri to Deshmukh: A Study of the Role of the Government of India's Representatives in South Africa, 1927 to 1946'. Unpublished PhD diss., University of Natal.

Mistry, Heena. 2021. 'The Repatriation Debate after the Abolition of Indenture'. *Journal of Indian Ocean World Studies* 5 (1): 114–138.

Mohapatra, Prabhu P. 1998. *Longing and Belonging: The Dilemma of Return Among Indian Immigrants in the West Indies 1850–1950*. New Delhi: Centre for Contemporary Studies, Nehru Memorial Museum and Library.

Naidoo, S. R., and Dhanee Bramdaw (eds.). 1931. *Sastri Speaks: Being a Collection of the Speeches and Writings of the Right Honourable VS Srinivasa Sastri in South Africa during His Term of Office as Agent of the Government of India in South Africa*. Pietermaritzburg: The Natal Press.

Natesan, G. A. 1936. 'Overseas Indians Reciprocity Bill'. *Indian Review* 37 (9): 541.

Precedence of Government of India's Representative in the Union of South Africa. 1927–1932. India Office Records (IOR)/L/E/7/1520, File 6847, April 1927–11 August 1932.

Proceedings of Conference Between Representatives of the Government of India and Representatives of the Government of South Africa, Cape Town. 1926–1932. In NAI, Ministry of External Affairs, South Africa Section, South Africa Papers, File No. 26-A/H/C/SA/1926.

Rao, P. Kodanda. 1963. *The Right Honourable VS Srinivasa Sastri: A Political Biography*. London: Asia Publishing House.

———. 1947. 'Sanctions against South Africa: A Critique'. In *Papers of P. Kodanda Rao*, Installment 1, 'Speeches and Writings by Him', no. 15, NMML Manuscripts.

Saksena, M. L., B. D. Pande, S. Satyamurti, Sri Prakasa, Kailash Behari Lal, M. Thirumala Rao et al. 1939. Draft of the Overseas Indians Reciprocity Act. In IOR/L/PJ/8/309 Coll. 108-33L.

Sannyasi, Bhawani Dayal, and Benarsidas Chaturvedi. 1931. *A Report on the Emigrants Repatriated to India Under the Assisted Emigration Scheme from*

South Africa and On the Problem of Returned Emigrants from All Colonies (An Independent Enquiry). 15 May. Bihar: Pravasi Bhavan.

Seecharan, Clem. 2011. *Mother India's Shadow Over El Dorado: Indo-Guyanese Politics and Identity 1890s–1930s*. Kingston: Ian Randle Publishers.

The Ottawa Agreement. 1932. Report of the Indian Delegation to the Imperial Conference at Ottawa. In IOR/L/I/1/151 File 20.

Tinker, Hugh. 1976. *Separate and Unequal: India and the Indians in the British Commonwealth 1920–1950*. Vancouver: University of British Columbia Press.

7

100 YEARS AFTER INDENTURE

THE PRESENT GENERATION OF INDO-TRINIDADIANS AND THEIR CULTURAL ENVIRONMENTS

Satnarine Balkaransingh

TRINIDAD AND TOBAGO TODAY

Trinidad and Tobago is a twin-island republic located at the southern tip of the Caribbean archipelago. Approximately 10 kilometres from the northern coast of Venezuela, the islands are collectively comprised of around 2,000 square miles of land. Tobago is the smaller of the two with a wealth of natural scenic beauty. Trinidad is the agricultural, industrial and service hub of the nation. Both islands have separate and interesting histories. While Tobago has a predominantly homogeneous racial grouping, Trinidad reflects a mosaic of races and cultures, the result of its separate and distinct historical antecedents and heritages (built and natural). This multicultural mix is reflected in existing population statistics, in its philosophical, social, economic, religious and physical landscape and in its artistic expressions. It is manifested in its performative traditions: its fasts, feasts, rituals and festivals. Within this cultural dynamo the Indo-Trinidadian contribution is noteworthy, adding significantly to the rhythm of daily life. This chapter explores what has been, and what continues to be, the role of the Indo-Trinidadian in shaping this dynamic, syncretic culture.

Addressing this question requires a definition of the term 'culture'. Culture in this sense is the sum total of one's norms of behaviour, one's values, attitudes to spiritual and religious development, to society, to family and to personal growth and development, to life in general. It is influenced by our heritage, traditions, legacies and our present circumstances. Culture is thus the vehicle and platform for maintaining historical linkages and for shaping one's environment. It guides and inspires a people, giving them a personality of their own. It influences the environment, provides historical continuity and opportunities and sets out a veritable road map for future development.

Over the years the various cultural streams in Trinidad have assimilated. These streams have included the cultures of the former European colonizers, of the various 'mother' countries as well as internal innovations within them. To them have been added both North and, to a lesser extent, South American ideas, values, behavioural patterns, traditions and aesthetics. Today, evidence reveals the existence of a unique, syncretic emerging culture in Trinidad and Tobago. Intertwined with this emergent culture are major identifiable elements of cultural persistence in the Indo-Trinidadian psyche, as is very apparent in their everyday lifestyles. There is a kind of 'ethnic dualism' as parallel cultural traits exist side by side. This condition is by no means unique to the descendants of East Indian immigrants. It is common to the descendants of all of those who 'came to', 'arrived in', 'were imported to' or 'invaded' Trinidad and Tobago. This has no doubt been facilitated by the concentrated pockets inhabited by the various ethnicities, especially on the island of Trinidad.

What is the genesis of the Indo-Trinidadian presence in Trinidad and Tobago and in other neighbouring Caribbean countries? History tells us that it was basically a response to issues of labour. In the nineteenth and early twentieth centuries – from 1845 to 1917 – significant numbers of East Indian immigrants arrived in British colonial Trinidad to work on its plantations. They came as contract workers under a system of indentureship to restore the plantation economy that had literally collapsed through lack of labour. They departed India from the ports of Madras and Calcutta on sailing ships – initially ships with masts (*paljahaj*), and later steamers – and were known as bonded coolies (Bong Coolies). Those immigrants who originated from South India and came through the port of Madras (now renamed Chennai) were referred to as Madrassis. Over the 72-year period of Indian indentureship in Trinidad, 'a total of 9,396 "Madrassis" came … representing … 6.3% of the total arrivals … The remaining 93% came through the Indian port of Calcutta'.[1] With the docking of the last ship, the *SS Ganges* in 1917, a total of 320 voyages had been made across the 'Kala Pani' (Black Water) and *pagal samundar* (crazy sea) ferrying 147,592 immigrants.[2] By the time the Indian indenture system had legally ended in 1917, over 1.3 million Indians had departed India, and 500,000 of them had travelled to the Caribbean.

JAHAJI BANDALS AND THEIR CONTENTS

Those disembarking carried their entire worldly possessions tied up in a bundle on their head or shoulders. This was their *jahaji bandal*, in reference to this baggage coming off the ship, or *jahaj*. The bundle was, however, not only physical. Inside their heads, their hearts and their minds were, figuratively speaking, bundles containing more intangible belongings: their spiritual, philosophical, religious, intellectual, linguistic, artistic and other cultural characteristics, their norms of behaviour, attitudes, values, traditions, heritage and rituals, feasts and festivals. Their belongings represented the cultural traits of the various regions from where they originated. These included the states of Bihar (Patna, Chapra and Jamshedpur [Jharkhand]), Uttar Pradesh (UP) (Lucknow, Benares, Ayodhya, Faizabad, Gorakhpur, Bareilly, Vrindavan and Mathura), Madhya Pradesh, Andhra Pradesh, Punjab, Bengal, Orissa, Tamil Nadu, Kerala, and Pondicherry. They spoke and thus introduced over 16 languages into the Trinidad landscape. These included Hindi, Urdu, Awadhi, Punjabi, Bengali, Bhojpuri, Maithili, Brij Bhasha, Chhattisgarhi, Bundeli, Tamil (still used in Mariyama or Kali *puja*s), Malayalam, French, Telugu, Rajasthani and Sanskrit. These invisible bundles really encompassed an entire ethos, representative of their respective 'cultures'. Each arriving individual was a microcosm of the macrocosm that was India and its existing culture during the nineteenth and early twentieth centuries.

The Indian immigrants were absorbed as labourers on plantations throughout Trinidad, mainly in the sugar belt, hence the large concentrations of people of Indian origin who still live in these areas. While the indentured workers were contracted on specific terms and conditions, these were observed more in principle than in practice. They lived in deplorable conditions, experiencing many social and economic problems. This, however, is the subject of other chapters. But in spite of the sometimes inhuman treatment, they kept coming. They were also fleeing many ills found in their home societies – political, social and economic.

In 1917, the system of indentureship formally ended with the enactment of legislation terminating this controversial practice. Many of the immigrants had already opted to remain in the country, having bought swamp and other substandard lands and successfully converted them to productive agricultural use. At the end of the period, a total of 80 per cent of the indentured immigrants had opted to remain in the colony and to make Trinidad their home. They were determined to become part of the social, economic, political and religious fabric of the communities in which they lived and the society as a whole.

Until the 1950s, Indo-Trinidadian settlements were still mainly concentrated in the rural areas where the immigrants had originally purchased lands and where other agricultural employment was available. In terms of integration and societal acceptance, Eurocentricity and social stratification were prevalent and in the 1950s, the East Indian segment of the population existed at the bottom of the social ladder. The handful of First Peoples or Amerindians of mixed blood who lived in Trinidad did not feature in this social hierarchy,[3] instead existing outside of it. In the year 2000, the second and third generation descendants of Indian immigrants, now Indo-Trinidadians, comprised a total of 40 per cent (504,946) of the population.[4] They also accounted for a significant percentage within the mixed population (20 per cent or 252,473 out of a total of 1,262,366) of Trinidad and Tobago.[5] Over 90 per cent of these people of Indian origin live in Trinidad, the larger of this twin-island republic.

100 YEARS AFTER THE END OF INDIAN INDENTURE

After the centennial anniversary of the end of the Indian indenture system, what does Trinidad and Tobago have to show, artistically, for the presence of successive generations of Indians in the country? Has it retained anything, and if so, what? Have the major performative traditions, the rituals and festivals brought from India by immigrants been transplanted into this landscape? And how have the pre-existing rituals and festivals of Trinidad been influenced by the presence of the Indo-Trinidadian? Thousands of flags, multicoloured pennons, fly atop flagpoles in Trinidad. These prayer flags fly throughout the island: in homes, along roads and in temples. What is the symbolism of these flags or *jhandi*s that dot our landscape? How do rituals, festivals and other visible signs of Indo-Trinidadian presence compare with counterparts in the appropriate areas of Indo-Trinidadian antecedents in India? Many of these traditions have been recorded but their nature and purposes have not been fully investigated with the intention of illuminating their multiple facets and establishing their links with the ancestral environment.

IDENTIFYING RITUALS AND FESTIVALS AND LOCATING RESEARCH AREAS IN TRINIDAD AND INDIA

I have located the rituals and festivals in terms of historicity, geographic sociology (gender, social stratification and mobility issues), economic and anthropological cultural approach in India and in Trinidad. The study also included the cosmological and phenomenological approach with regard to their antecedents and their reflections in Trinidad. The analysis used the following comparators for each event: form, format, faith, festivity, music, dance form, food, technology, gender issues and some economic issues. In this regard eight events have been identified: Ramleela in Felicity and Faizabad–Ayodhya; Diwali in Trinidad and Chitrakoot; Christmas in Trinidad and Chennai; Maha Shivaratri in Trinidad and Benares; Carnival in Trinidad (1783) and Goa (1510); Phagwa in Trinidad and Vrindavan; Hosay in Trinidad and Lucknow; and Jhandi or Prayer flags in Trinidad and UP, Bihar and Jharkhand.

RAMLEELA

One of the literary-cum-religious texts brought to Trinidad by indentured Indians was the Ramayana. It is the epic story of Ram – the story of the circumstances of his birth, youth, marriage and banishment, his life in exile, battles and his return to claim the kingdom of Ayodhya in northern India. The Ramayana tradition has been perpetuated in Trinidad and India over the years through literature and the creative and performing arts. These include *katha*(s), Ramayana *yagna*(s), artistic expressions on the theme and of course the Ramleela village theatrical tradition.

The Ramleelas of the First Felicity Ramleela and Cultural Group in Trinidad and the Ram Janaki Mandir of Sahabganj in Faizabad–Ayodhya in India can be compared and contrasted to illustrate the dynamic changes that are taking place in the respective events in both environments. Despite being so distant from each other, the events are similar even though there has been no physical contact between the two. Although the religious persuasions of Felicity are more diverse – including Hindus, Muslims and a series of Christian churches – within the Hindu fold, the narrative of the story remains the same. The folk performance itself, which is the telling of the epic story of Shri Ram (Rama), retains its open-air presentation (*maidan* Ramleela) with similar costuming and music. There is a non-linear narrative style in the composition of Tulsidas's *Ramcharitmanas*; the storytellers (*sutradhars*) of both Ramleelas follow a cyclical process that is so common to the Indian philosophy of life and hence contained in all of its artistic expressions, including music and dance. In Felicity, the performance takes 11 days while in Sahabganj it is 15 days, both returning to the main story for a satisfying conclusion.

The performances capture the heroic romance through a judicious mix of *rasa*s, or human emotions. These include the following sentiments: love; marvel or wonderment; the odious; the heroic, valour; grief, compassion or the pathetic; fury, anger; the terrible; the comic, the laughable; and peace. Three of the most popular moods, or *rasa*s, expressed in the folk drama are valour, grief and love in separation or longing for the return of the loved one. The use of both verbal and nonverbal language, of music, of facial and other body language and expressions is complex and rich in both Felicity and Faizabad–Ayodhya.

The Ramleela festival straddles two separate localities, each with distinct identities, characteristic features and motivations. The Ramleelas of both Felicity and Sahabganj seem to have maintained their religious, ritualistic and entertainment aspects. While they are dramatized from the same text, their respective directors lay emphasis sometimes on different aspects of the story. They have undergone significant changes due to the changing social, political and economic environment and the technical evolution taking place around us daily, in sound, light and information technology (IT).

In the Ramleela of the Ram Janaki Mandir, Sahabganj, there was an absence of female performers. Late performance timings interfered with the timings of the working population and reduced the funding of the production. The costuming was less colourful. The *maidan* Ramleelas of Faizabad and Ayodhya are rapidly declining, giving way to *manch* productions. The Durga Puja festivities taking place at the same time in those venues are now heavy competitors for the financial support of the business community and audiences, as I witnessed during the 2008 Ramleela season in Ayodhya. The massive audiences (thousands) at the Durga Puja festivities seemed to have been at least a quadruple of those at the Ramleela, leaving many Ramleela supporters concerned about the future of the *maidan* Ramleela in Faizabad–Ayodhya.

Figure 7.1 A soldier in Ravan's army metaphorically 'shooting fire' at his opponents in the Ram Janaki Ramleela in Faizabad–Ayodhya, UP, in 2008

Source: S. Balkaransingh.

While in Ayodhya the *maidan* Ramleela seems to be rapidly declining in appeal and financial patronage, in Trinidad it still maintains its overall appeal notwithstanding the problems of financing the event. Even though there are an increasing number of *manch* Ramleelas in recent times, the *maidan* Ramleela still triumphs. Kamal Ramsubeik, chairman of the National Ramleela Council of Trinidad and Tobago, noted, 'There are few *manch* [stage] Ramleelas when compared to the over thirty active *maidan* [savannah] Ramleelas in Trinidad' (Figure 7.2).⁶ The memory of the epic refreshes itself annually, bringing larger numbers of participants, both spectators and performers, especially from among the young. At least 30,000–40,000 people attend the 11-day performance of the First Felicity Ramleela Group. This is due to a number of factors: the inclusion of colourful and rich costuming, female participants in the Leela itself and the gradual reduction

Figure 7.2 Ramleela performance, Trinidad, 2009

Source: Edison Boodoosingh.

of Hindu 'caste' issues in the selection of character roles to be performed. There are generous helpings of local satire and humour. The Leela is thus constantly reinventing itself. There is also an open-air, festive environment created by the spectacle, where there are food and delicacy stalls, games, other entertainments, fashion conscious spectators, a meeting place for the community and the prospect of enjoying wholesome entertainment with added moral and religious instruction. The event is gradually adopting a more secular approach, generally, even as the rules and regulations of performances are adhered to.

In Trinidad, the Ramleela competes with another major festival, Carnival, in terms of audience, spectacle, wholesome entertainment, socio-economic activity and community development. It provides moral education, philosophical thoughts, political idealism and correctness, ethical behaviour and family entertainment. Yet it continues to be relegated to being only a 'religious event'. As such, there is still a need for the Trinbagonian population to discover itself through the Ramleela and exhibit that pride of ownership, for it is at once the source of our being, our living heritage and social and economic capital, waiting to be tapped for our development and for its tourism potential.

DIWALI

Diwali is another festival that can be compared between Trinidad and India. It is celebrated annually, just after Ramleela but within the same month of Kartik of the Hindu lunar calendar (September–October). This festival comprises a series of events, occurring over five successive days, each connected with different historical antecedents. Diwali has many aspects to its celebrations, both of a ritualistic and festive nature.

The geographical areas selected for observing the Diwali festival were the whole of Trinidad and Chitrakoot in India. The town of Chitrakoot, also spelled Chitrakut, is one of the celebrated pilgrimage spots in India, being the legendary place where Ram, the hero of the epic Ramayana of sage Valmiki and later god-hero Shri Ram of Goswami Tulsidas's *Ramcharitmanas*, spent a significant amount of time during his exile from his birthplace, Ayodhya. Chitrakoot was chosen because of its mixture of Bundeli and Bhojpuri culture. Half of Chitrakoot is in Bundelkhand, the other half in the Bhojpur region of UP. Like in Trinidad, Diwali in Chitrakoot is a purely vegetarian, non-alcoholic and non-gambling affair with some emphasis placed upon themes of environmental awareness.

CHRISTMAS AND CARNIVAL

Christmas and Carnival were introduced into Trinidad by Europeans. Christmas was brought to southern India by early Christian missionaries, while the Portuguese introduced Carnival in Goa after 1510 CE. Many East Indian immigrants to Trinidad came either directly from south India or through the southern port of Madras (Chennai). There is no documented evidence of Goans coming to Trinidad as immigrants. Less than 1 per cent of those who arrived in Trinidad were Christians, and there is also no documented history of their bringing these two festivals as part of their traditions. However, a statistically significant number of Indo-Trinidadians were converted to Christianity, especially from 1869,[7] long before the end of indentureship (1917–1920).

The Christmas and Carnival festivals in Trinidad were integral parts of the acculturalization process. The official religion of the then colonial state of Trinidad was Christianity; thus the Indo-Trinidadian population was greatly influenced by it and in turn influenced Christian rituals and festivals. Today,

Christmas and Carnival in their current local forms are eclectic events, significantly influenced by Indo-Trinidadians.

With respect to Christmas, there are similarities and differences in the observances and the role of the Indo-Trinidadian in the Trinidad Christmas compared to that of the Indian in a Chennai Christmas. In both Trinidad and Chennai, Christmas exists in syncretic forms, each influenced by aspects of 'Indian culture'. In both places it is domestic, home-based and celebrated with family, close friends and relatives with a degree of sobriety and restraint. Secularism has blended with religious observances. The symbols and festivity of the season – the Christmas tree, the giving of gifts and Santa Claus's role – are apparent in both religious and commercial areas. Even secular consumption patterns have blended with charity, goodwill and the perpetuation of family traditions of togetherness during the season.

While food, music and dance are common features in both environments, there are major differences. With regard to food, Trinidad's eclectic menu is somewhat different from that of Chennai, where tastes and expenditure diverge significantly (Figure 7.3).

In Christian society there is less vegetarianism, with meat and sea foods being readily consumed, provided that these are affordable to the family's

Figure 7.3 A typical eclectic Christmas meal in Trinidad (chef: Jassie Singh)

Source: Karla Ramoo.

purse strings. These non-vegetarian dishes are limited because of relatively high prices. In Hindu homes, traditional vegetarian meals are the standard fare. At the commercial level, all menus are available, both Indian and foreign. With respect to desserts, cakes, pastries and *methai* are readily available. Alcoholic beverages are also easily accessed, and it is not unusual to find vegetarians consuming vegetarian meals and pastries with a variety of alcoholic beverages in Trinidad.

Music and dance are integral aspects of the festival in both environments. In Chennai, the music, however, reflects marked differences. The Christians sing their carols and Christmas songs in various languages. The rest of Chennai participate in the annual Margazhi Utsav (music and dance and now also film and theatre festival) that extends all over Chennai with its over 300 performances.[8]

While for the Hindus of Chennai, the religious aspects of the celebration carry little significance, they are important for the Christians, who hold Christmas mass in all their churches in several languages, catering to the various linguistic realities of the area. In both environments, women are an integral part of the preparations for the season. They clean and decorate the home, prepare food and drink and entertainment. They are both performers and audiences in the offerings of music and dance. In Trinidad, women can be found in every sphere of the festivities – in the home, church, community service and in the fields of entertainment. They participate in the church choirs, in Parang music and in other public concerts as musicians and music conductors.

With respect to the carnival, the Trinidad Carnival represents a feeling, an attitude and a way of life. Similar to the Goa Carnival, it is full of theatre and pageantry, splendour, majesty and pomp. These carnivals display talent, creativity, innovation and craftsmanship. They dramatize social and political commentary, using satire, burlesque, mimicry and witticism, and evoke outright laughter. These carnivals are great 'polymorphs' encompassing the creative, performing, literary, plastic and culinary arts and influencing the very psyches of their followers.

While Hindus, Muslims and a sprinkling of other religious groups came from India (approximately 88 per cent of the migrants were Hindus; the remaining migrants comprised of mainly Muslims at 11 per cent and a few Sikhs, Christians and Buddhists[9]), 'the Indian society in Trinidad has been shaped more by Hindu philosophical values and Indian culture-norms, behavioural patterns, value systems and folk ethics, and its aesthetics, rather than solely by religious edict and ritual'.[10] Many researchers[11] have made passing references to the involvement of this sizeable group of Indo-Trinidadians in the Trinidad Carnival. They have contributed to the evolution of the festival through mythology, entrepreneurship and industry, artistry and patronage. Their influence is visible in the costume designs, street parades, music and management. As Nunley and Bettelheim recorded, with the 'introduction of the wheeled Kings and Queens, borrowed from the East Indian Hosay festival ... the [carnival] costumes grew in scale'.[12] Many carnival band leaders and designers have also used Indian themes, icons and music in their respective portrayals, thus influencing carnival aesthetics. These include Wendy and Ivan Kallicharan and Lionel Jagessar in San Fernando, and Raul Garib, Peter Minshall and Brian McFarlane in Port of Spain. For example, designer Peter Minshall's 'Mancrab', the king of his 1983 band River, came 'on stage, moving to the sound of East Indian tassa drums' and 'the borrowed foot movements of *Kathakali* ...' in the 1998 Port of Spain Carnival.[13] Even with the invention and development of the steel pan by pan pioneers, the Manette brothers in the 1940s, the method of 'note' reproduction (heating and 'tuning' with a hammer and rubber-tipped sticks) was influenced by the Indo-Trinidadian *tassa* drummers, who had used this technique since the 1850s to produce clear crisp sounds, or 'rolls', to lengthen the note.[14] The steel pan musicians also emulated their *tassa* counterparts by hanging the instruments around their necks with straps to facilitate processional mobility.[15] Indo-Trinidadians are part of every aspect of the Carnival.

Indo-Trinidadians have also introduced the rituals of Maha Shivaratri, the festival of Phagwa or Holi and the Islamic commemoration of Hosay or Muharram into the Trinidadian landscape. The mausoleums or tombs of the martyrs, Hassan and Hussein, are constructed annually, paraded on the streets until the Day of Ashura and then immersed in water with all the appropriate rituals. On one of the days of Muharram, short flags are brought by members of the community and placed on the *chowk*, honouring the memory of Abbas, the brother of Imam Hussein who sacrificed his life in the service of Islam (Figures 7.4–7.5). The flags are then paraded during the night's procession, similar to the annual ritual in Lucknow, UP. Today, thousands of prayer flags, or *jhandi*s, fly in every nook and cranny, in the compounds of homes, along roads leading to festive sites and on beach fronts during ritual baths in the Hindu holy month of Kartik. Indo-Trinidadians have coloured the landscape of Trinidad.

Figure 7.4 'Promise' flags on the *chowk* of Gulam Hussein Yard, St James, during Trinidad Hosay

Source: S. Balkaransingh.

Figure 7.5 Tazias of St James returning after prayers on Ashura, to be later immersed in the sea

Source: S. Balkaransingh (2009).

FINDINGS

GENERAL

In general, the research has revealed significant changes in the rituals and festivals of Trinidad and Tobago in terms of form, format, festivities and gender relations. These include changes in music, dance forms and food patterns in Trinidad. The general findings include:

1. There are recurring patterns of common symbols within the rituals and festivals. These relate to the symbols of light, of divinity, fertility, the seasons and the use of sound vibrations or music for conveying emotions.

2. There are recurring patterns of legends and myths, carried over time, in the rituals and festivals.

3. Lunar cycles and seasons have a common role in the determination of annual events. This includes the common use of calendars (Roman-Gregorian, which begins in December; the Samvat, beginning in Chaitra or March–April; and Islamic, beginning in the month of Muharram).

4. Each of the performative traditions examined contained aspects of the *transportive* (Hosay, Mass, Phagwa) and *transformative* (Mass, Ramleelas, *swarup*s versus *patra*s) introduced by the performers and sometimes by the audiences themselves.

5. There have been significant interplays between the *text* and *context* in the respective traditions. For instance, the Ramleela text is often translated into contemporary context and reinterpreted; there are also interplays between the 'greater' brahmanical, sanskritic tradition and the 'little' folk tradition. Sometimes the interplays are so inconspicuously interwoven that one is unable to identify the differences. These are common occurrences in the Ramleela, Diwali, Christmas, Carnival, Phagwa and Muharram where the audiences shift roles from being spectators to participants (pilgrims and devotees).

6. In the observances or performances of the rituals and festivals, the senses are utilized to effect transcendence, to shift awareness and to create separate realities, all with the aim of reconfirming faith.

7. Religion versus culture – while many of the rituals and festivals have their genesis in religion, over time there has been a blurring between the religious aspects and the cultural lines in these events in both countries. This is visible in the Carnival, Hosay, Ramleela, Phagwa and Diwali of both environments, but more so in Trinidad.

8. Gender Issues: There has been a significant change from the initial participation of mainly male members of society in many festivals. Today both sexes are involved in the performative traditions of Muharram or Hosay, Ramleela, Phagwa (Latmar) and Carnival.

9. Many of the ancient arts, motifs and designs that were visible in rituals and festivals in Trinidad are rapidly disappearing. These include the décor in Hosay and its performative aspects of *jharoo* (broom dance) and *banaithe* (fire dance), the fire-pass (walking the fire) and steel pan music on the road (including pan round the neck) during Carnival.

SPECIFIC

1. Science, technology and innovation have been used to significantly change the presentational dynamics of these celebrations. These are visible in the use of fabric, in costume designs, the use of lights (firecrackers in Ramleela, Diwali, Christmas, Hosay Carnival and Maha Shivaratri) and in sound reproduction (digital music and tape amplification).

2. There has been a loss of experiential memory in many of these performative traditions leading to indigenizing (the creolizing) of culture. The people who maintain the tradition of Hosay have lost the knowledge of its history, of its drumming rhythms, the names of prayer flags and even the use and pronunciation of proper Indian-derived names. There is also confusion between piety and festivity in Muharram or Hosay in Trinidad.

3. In Trinidad, the rituals and festivals hold religious, social, economic and entertainment value.

4. There is an interconnectedness of the themes that run through the festivals of Carnival, Maha Shivaratri and Holi or Phagwa.

CONCLUSION

While this chapter has centred primarily on the contributions of Indo-Trinidadians in the field of the performing arts, their contributions have spread to every facet of national life – in literature, agriculture and engineering; in science, technology, medicine and every aspect of education; in law, labour matters, finance and the service sector; in politics and national governance. The country has also had many Indian lawmakers including two prime ministers of Indian origin.

While the Indo-Trinidadian community has had a history of living in this environment for over 172 years, there exists a persistent feeling of cultural marginalization and alienation. The Indo-Trinidadians' experience of documented discrimination then and now in various fields of public service and the arts and their stereotyping as 'drunkards' has not fazed their resolve to be 'Trinis to the bone'. Despite many attractive options for foreign migrations (in the 1940s, 1962 and 1988), Trinidad continues to be 'home'; it has created a legacy (tangible and intangible) of cultural persistence. This can be attributed to the philosophical approach of Indians and their successors wherever they are domiciled or scattered. It is embodied in their unique worldview, *vasudhaiva kutumbakam* – the world is one family, similar to today's concept of the 'global village' – allowing for movement across borders.

NOTES

1. Tikasingh (2012, 23).
2. Deen (1994).
3. Braithwaite (1953, 1954).
4. Census of Trinidad and Tobago, 2000.
5. Census of Trinidad and Tobago, 2000.
6. Personal interview, July 2008.
7. Sookdeo (2008, 153–156).
8. *The Hindu* (2006). See also *New Indian Express*, 15 December 2006, and the *Deccan Chronicle*, 20 December 2006.
9. These figures were derived from the Annual Reports of the Protector of Immigrants, Calcutta 1874–1917. See Vertovec (1992, 33).
10. Balkaransingh (2016, 165).
11. Ahye (1978); Hill (1997 [1972], 1983); Constance (1991); Blake (1995); Crowley (1996); Sankerali (1998); Liverpool (2001).
12. Nunley and Bettelheim (1988, 84).
13. Schechner and Riggio (1998, 185).
14. Ellie Manette is credited with being the first person to use ball-shaped, rubber-tipped sticks to play the pan.

15. There is still a category called 'pan round the neck' in the Steel Band Festival. See Balkaransingh (2016, 167–168).

BIBLIOGRAPHY

Ahye, Molly. 1978. *Golden Heritage: The Dance in Trinidad and Tobago*. Trinidad: Heritage Cultures Limited.

Ali, Maulvi Mirza Gulam Abbas. n.d. *Life of Imam Husain (The Saviour)*. Mumbai: Haidery Kutub Khana.

Ali, S. V. Mir Ahmed. 1964. *Husain: The Saviour of Islam*. New York: Anjumane Aza Khana -Azhra.

Alladin, M. P. 1969. *The Monstrous Angel: Forty Poems*. Trinidad: N.P.

———. 1970. *Folk Dances of Trinidad and Tobago*. Trinidad: N.P.

Bakker, Hans. 1986. *Ayodhya Part 1: The History of Ayodhya from the 7th Century B.C. to the Middle of the 18th Century, Its Development into a Sacred Centre with Reference to the Ayodhyāmāhātmya and to the Worship of Rāma according to the Agastyasamhitā*. Groningen: Institute of Indian Studies, University of Grogenhein.

Balkaransingh, Satnarine. 1995. 'The Muharram Massacre of 1884'. *Natrang: Nrityanjali Theatre Journal* 1 (8): 7–9.

———. 1999. 'Chutney Crosses Over into Chutney Soca in Trinidad and Tobago Carnival'. In *Identity, Ethnicity and Culture in the Caribbean*, edited by Ralph R. Premdas, 47–53. St Augustine: School of Continuing Studies, University of the West Indies.

———. 2000. 'Multi-Culturalism and Representation: The Indo Trinidadian Folk Music on the Carnival Stage Changes Name to Chutney and Chutney Soca'. *Natrang: Nrityanjali Theatre Journal* 1 (12): 20–25.

———. 2016. *The Shaping of a Culture: Rituals and Festivals in Trinidad Compared with Selected Counterparts in India, 1990–2014*. Heartfordshire, UK: Hansib Publication.

Baumer, Bettina. 2006 [1997]. *Mysticism in Shaivism and Christianity*. New Delhi, India: D. K. Print World Ltd.

Beg, M. A. 2000. *The Guide to Lucknow*. Lucknow: Royal Printing Press.

Bezbaruah, M. P. (ed.). 2010. *Fairs and Festivals of India*, vols. 3–5. New Delhi: Gyan Publishing House.

Bhattacharya, B. 1993. *Saivism and the Phallic World*, vol. 1. New Delhi: Munshiram Manoharlal.

————. 1999. *Varanasi Rediscovered*. New Delhi: Munshiram Manoharlal.

Blake, F. I. R. 1995. *The Trinidad and Tobago Steel Pan: History and Evolution*. Port of Spain: Self-published.

Braithwaite, Lloyd. 1953. 'Social Stratification in Trinidad: A Preliminary Analysis'. *Social and Economic Studies* 2 (2/3): 5–175.

————. 1954. 'The Problem of Cultural Integration in Trinidad'. *Social and Economic Studies* 3 (1): 82–96.

Brereton, B. 1979. *Race Relations in Colonial Trinidad 1870–1900*. Cambridge: Cambridge University Press.

Chelkowski, Peter J. (ed.). 1979. *Ta'ziyeh: Ritual and Drama in Iran*. New York: New York University Publications and Soroush Press.

Constance, Zeno Obi. 1991. *Tassa, Chutney and Soca: The East Indian Contribution to the Calypso*. Trinidad: Jordan's Printing Service.

Crowley, Daniel. 1956. 'The Traditional Masks of Carnival'. In *Trinidad Carnival, a Republication of the Caribbean Quarterly, Trinidad Carnival Issue* 4 (3–4): 75–76.

Dabydeen, David, and Brinsley Samaroo (eds.). 1987. *India in the Caribbean*. London: Hansib Publishing Ltd.

Datta, Kali Kinkar. 1974. *The Comprehensive History of Bihar*, vol. 3, parts 1–2. Patna: Government of Bihar.

Deen, Shamshu. 1994. *Solving East Indian Roots in Trinidad*. Trinidad: H. E. M. Enterprises Trinidad Limited.

Gadgil, D. R. 1971. *The Industrial Evolution of India in Recent Times, 1860–1939*. Bombay: Oxford University Press.

Hill, Errol. 1997 (1972). *The Trinidad Carnival: Mandate for a National Theatre*. London: New Beacon Books.

————. 1983. 'The History of Carnival'. In 'The Social and Economic Impact of Carnival', Seminar held at the Institute of Social and Economic Research, University of West Indies, St Augustine, Trinidad, 24–26 November, 8–39.

Klass, Morton. 1988. *East Indians in Trinidad: A Study of Cultural Persistence*. Long Grove, IL: Waveland Press Inc.

Korom, Frank J. 2003. *Hosay Trinidad: Muharram Performances in an Indo-Caribbean Diaspora*. Philadelphia: University of Pennsylvania Press.

La Guerre, John. 1985 [1974]. *Calcutta to Caroni*. St Augustine: University of the West Indies.

Liverpool, Hollis Chalkdust. 2001. *Rituals of Power and Rebellion: The Carnival Tradition in Trinidad and Tobago, 1763–1962*. Chicago: Research Associate School Times Publication and Frontline Distribution International.

Look Lai, Walton. 1993. *Indentured Labor, Caribbean Sugar: Chinese and Indian Migrants to the British West Indies 1838–1918*. Baltimore: Johns Hopkins University Press.

Nunley, John, and Judith Bettelheim (eds.). 1988. *Caribbean Festival Arts: Each and Every Bit of Difference*. Seattle: University of Washington Press.

Premdas, Ralph R. (ed.). 1993. *Identity, Ethnicity and Culture in the Caribbean*. St Augustine: School of Continuing Studies, University of the West Indies.

Rodrigues, Maria de Lourdes Bravo da Costa. 2004. *Feasts, Festivals and Observances of Goa*. Goa: L&L Publications.

Sankeralli, Burton. 1998. 'Indian Presence in Carnival'. *TDR (1988–)* 42, no. 3, Trinidad and Tobago Carnival (Autumn): 203–212.

Schechner, Richard. 1983. *Performative Circumstances: From the Avant Garde to Ramlila*. Calcutta: Seagull Books.

Schechner, Richard, and Milla C. Riggio. 1998. 'Peter Minshall: A Voice to Add to the Song of the Universe—An Interview'. *TDR (1988–)* 42, no. 3, Trinidad and Tobago Carnival (Autumn): 170–193.

SookDeo, A. N. 2008. 'Involuntary Globalization: How Britain Revived Indenture and Made It Largely Brown and East Indian (Trinidad 1806–1921)'. *Man in India* 88 (1): 5–28.

Tikasing, Gerad. 2012. *Trinidad during the 19th Century: The Indian Experience*. San Fernando, Trinidad: R. P. L. Limited.

The Hindu. 2006. 'Music Season: The Chennai December Festival'. 8 December.

Vertovec, Steven. 1992. *Hindu Trinidad: Religion, Ethnicity and Socio-economic Change*. London: Macmillan Education Ltd.

8

EMIGRATION AGAINST CASTE AND THE GLOBALIZATION OF CASTELESSNESS*

Gajendran Ayyathurai

The understanding of caste or casteism and resistance against it beyond South Asia remains rudimentary. Popular subfields such as South Asian studies, postcolonial studies, Indian Ocean studies and Indian diaspora studies have been woefully deficient in engaging with caste as a foundational problem in the history of the Indian subcontinent. Likewise, such disciplines have not given much-needed focus to the caste-free (and anti-caste) culture, politics, economy and history of caste-oppressed communities in the precolonial, colonial and postcolonial periods. This has led to a lopsided understanding of, for instance, the re-establishment of caste through colonial apparatuses and how the privileged-caste groups, such as Brahmins, re-entrenched themselves to turn the British Raj into a British–Brahmin Raj.[1] Significantly, however, we have now begun to learn about the multiple movements and discursive and non-discursive practices of the marginalized communities who challenged the domination of self-privileging-caste groups in colonial and

* This chapter has been revised from its original publication in *Essays in Philosophy* 22, nos. 1–2 (2021): 45–65, reprinted by permission of the author and the publisher. It is a contribution to *Critical Caste Studies*, a new interdisciplinary subfield initiated by the author with scholars from India, Europe and North America, which views caste as a philosophical, social, cultural, political, economic, historical and international problem. The author is grateful to the Indo-Caribbean brothers and sisters who generously shared with him their home shrines, temples, archives, memories and histories. The author dedicates it to the caste-oppressed Indian women, men and children who, after their emigration from South Asia, have become casteless Indo-Caribbeans.

postcolonial India.[2] In this chapter, I examine how immigration, emigration and transmigration were part and parcel of the repertoire of resistance of caste-oppressed Indians, taking particular examples from the experiences of Indian migrants who settled in the Caribbean.

The institutionalized structures and violent practices of race, caste and gender have always been crucial push factors of migration in the modern period. Recent philosophical and interdisciplinary studies have engaged with how aspects of race, gender and nationality intersect with migration.[3] However, thus far, theories of migration and philosophies of immigration have inadequately engaged with the emigration of caste-oppressed communities during European colonialism in South Asia or with the postcolonial transmigration of such communities between the Global South and the Global North. The hitherto unexamined interrelationship between colonial policies and the emigration of Indians against caste, on the one hand, and the reconstruction of a caste-free life overseas by oppressed Indians, on the other, provide critical philosophical, cultural, political, economic and historical dimensions to migration.

Colonial racial capitalism depended upon comprador privileged-caste groups for its success (and stability). A large majority of Indians were, as a result, culturally *othered*, spatially segregated and economically underprivileged as lower castes and untouchables through the colonial state's legitimization of precolonial privileged-caste identities and practices. The Brahmins – who constituted not even 5 per cent of India's population, then and now – reaped maximum benefits through the propagation of their caste-power and by utilizing British colonial apparatuses.[4] Such caste groups not only viciously appropriated the labour and land of the oppressed communities but also normalized their dependency on colonialist, casteist structures.[5] Nonetheless, the emergence of the Slavery Abolition Act of 1833 in Europe, and the ensuing colonial Indian indenture policy introduced to circumvent it, unwittingly created an opportunity for subordinated Indians to resist religio-casteism, caste-imposing religious prescriptions or identities and labour exploitation by privileged-caste men, by migrating within and emigrating outside South Asia.[6]

Communities in diverse linguistic regions and their organic intellectuals welcomed indentured emigration to plantation and mining colonies from 1834 as a chance to seek emancipation from the casteism of Brahminical groups. This stance of the underprivileged was in rejection of the caste-nationalism of the privileged castes and their opposition to the colonial indenture policy.[7]

Unsurprisingly, the emigration of the marginalized not only led to their breaking free from the domination of casteist groups but also enabled them to re-member and re-establish caste-free cultural and religious identities overseas. It also guaranteed a better economic and social environment for the repatriated after their return.

The modern emigration of oppressed Indians, during colonialism or in the post-independence period, indicates that Indians abroad are not a homogeneous community, that is, 'Hindus'. In fact, categories and outfits such as 'Hindus', 'Hindu Associations', 'Hindustanis' and 'Sanatanis' in North America, the Caribbean and elsewhere have entrenched casteist divisions and discriminatory practices. They represent those emigrants from postcolonial India who were members of privileged-caste groups that disproportionately benefitted from state-subsidized medical and technical education.[8] The philosophy of multiculturalism, purportedly celebrating diversity and pluralism and advocating state and civil societal recognition of the categories and practices of privileged-caste Indians, is therefore problematic. Philosophers, historians, anthropologists and postcolonial specialists are yet to critically engage with the rise of local and global Brahminism. Evidently, lawsuits and reports in North America and Europe confirm the crises of casteism and racism between Indians inter se and in their interrelations with Africans, African Americans, Afro-Europeans and Afro-Caribbeans.[9] What are presented as entitlements of the 'Hindu Indian Americans' and 'American Hinduism' in 'multicultural' America, for instance, are based on a concerted effort to maintain 'that the caste system was never religiously sanctioned' by Hinduism and thus was not central to Hindu practice'.[10] Such manoeuvres have actually led to the exponential establishment of Brahminical temples by privileged-caste groups and the entrenchment of casteism or American Brahminism in the United States (US). In contrast, the assertion of castelessness made by diverse vernacular Indian communities after their emigration to the plantation colonies and further transmigration points to their divergence from and challenge of caste-reinforcing 'Hindu' homogeneity in multicultural societies.

In this chapter, I argue that the Indian diaspora is divided into privileged-caste and caste-free or anti-caste groups, and that caste-based social, cultural, political and economic exclusion, which is historically associated with the invention and oppression of self-privileging-caste groups, is present within the Indian diaspora. This study particularly points to the contexts of emigration where Indian communities were oppressed under caste in colonial India but considered themselves caste-free and chose to emigrate across the Indian, Atlantic and Pacific Oceans. More importantly, it also examines how the Indians who emigrated against caste or casteism both found agentic religio-cultural self-emancipation and established the collective transformation of their social life in the faraway lands of the Caribbean.

To counter the Slavery Abolition Act of 1833, the British introduced a policy of Indian indenture in 1834 to recruit Indian labourers for the plantation colonies. Regarding the indentured Indians in the Caribbean, Lomarsh Roopnarine writes:

> For over three-quarters of a century (1838–1920), British, Danish, Dutch, and French governments transported an estimated 500,000 indentured Indian laborers from the Indian subcontinent to the Caribbean. The laborers were distributed over British Guiana (238,960), Trinidad (143,939), Suriname (43,404), Guadeloupe (42,236), Jamaica (37,027), Martinique (25,404), French Guiana (8,500), Grenada (3,200), Belize (3,000), St. Vincent (2,472), St. Lucia (2,300), St. Kitts (361), Nevis (342), and St. Croix (325).[11]

Many indentured labourers had little idea where they were going. The plantation colonies were not hospitable, but some envisioned that such distant lands would offer them a personal and collective transformation. Given the hard labour requirements of plantation economies, caste-oppressed agrarian Indians constituted the majority of the emigrated.[12] And yet, paradoxically, caste or casteism remains very much present outside India. Some Indo-Caribbeans even re-invented their identities as Brahmins and Kshatriyas by purportedly relying on colonial documents and tracing their ancestral connections.[13]

Despite these reactionary episodes, for most migrants, emigration was the means by which oppressed Indians succeeded in re-embedding castelessness, both during and after their indenture in the European plantation colonies. That is, although the virulence of colonialism and casteism disembedded marginalized Indians from their local life-worlds in India, through the indenture contracts they re-embedded themselves in casteless time and space overseas.[14] And this – I will show – is evidenced in the caste-free consciousness, identity and practices of some Indian communities in the

Caribbean. The indentured Indians and their descendants believe that their individual and collective life is not putatively determined by or dependent on their birth into a caste, particularly as a lower caste or untouchable. Instead, they retain diverse positive vernacular identities and reject such caste categories, which were originally invented by and imposed through Brahmin-male power. Nonetheless, I point toward a struggle within the religious practices of the Indo-Caribbean diaspora between those who are cultivating and strengthening a caste-free identity (characterized by inclusive practices) and those who re-invent and re-impose a caste-based identity (characterized by Brahmin-male dominated exclusionary ideologies, institutions and practices).

BRAHMIN-MALE POWER, INDIAN INDENTURE AND CASTE-FREE INDIANS

It is true that the colonial indentured labour policy was designed to maintain European empires across the world; it was, as some have described it, 'A New System of Slavery'.[15] However, for oppressed Indian women, men and children, the European indenture contract was an opportunity to escape internal religio-casteism. The prosperity of male privileged-caste members meant that the segregated majority of Indians were denied educational, economic and other opportunities of colonial modernity. Privileged-caste women themselves were also at the receiving end of Brahmin-male power and its violence.[16] Although only a small percentage of emigrants were women, they did not hesitate to grasp the opportunities of indenture. Gaiutra Bahadur shows how Brahmin women left India and vowed never to return because of the sexual and other forms of oppression they were subjected to by privileged-caste men.[17] Indian diaspora studies confirm that such women found more sexual and labour autonomy overseas than in their 'homeland', retaining ownership of their own houses, land and cattle.[18]

Caste or casteism was an unambiguous push factor in the emigration of Indians subjugated as lower castes and untouchables since the precolonial period, although there were some pull factors, such as contractual wage employment. In fact, casteism and colonialism became a double-edged sword which ruptured multiple native vernacular Indian communities. This is amply evident in the words of anti-caste organic intellectuals such as Iyothee Thass (1845–1914). Thass openly wrote against the caste-based exploitation and marginalization of, and cultural violence against, a large majority of Indians by minority groups of Brahmins who flourished under European colonialism. He urged the reading public to call the Indian National Congress, which led the Indian national movement, a 'Brahmin Congress'.[19] More directly, Thass was against the stand of the Brahmin-male controlled Congress against the British indenture policy as a way to preserve the caste-oppressed Indians under Brahmin exploitation in India. In contrast, Thass and his fellow anti-caste Indians showed how repatriated Indians from Mauritius, Trinidad and Tobago, Guyana, Fiji and South Africa brought back prosperity, which was not otherwise possible due to Brahminical oppression in India.

The significance of emigration against caste was evident in the case of 'An Australian' who had migrated from south India to Australia in the 1870s. The Australian, who identified himself as a Tamil Buddhist but never revealed his name due to fear of reprisal from privileged-caste groups as well as colonial authorities, joined hands with Thass to establish a caste-free vocational training school for oppressed Indians called the 'Non-Caste Dravidian Industrials Limited' in Madras (south India) in 1909. Likewise, other indentured-turned-freemen from the Tamil-speaking regions who stayed in their destination countries demonstrated their self-emancipation abroad. For instance, they began to represent themselves as casteless persons through establishing Buddhist associations in Ovenport, Durban and Natal in South Africa and publishing and circulating Tamil magazines, such as *The Tamilian* (1907–1914). These intellectuals, organizations and publications critiqued Brahminical capitalism and casteism and contrasted it with the caste-free memory, knowledge traditions, Buddhist culture and historical sense of castelessness of the marginalized Tamils and other Indians in the early twentieth century.[20]

In the Caribbean, after the independence of the plantation colonies, many Indo-Caribbeans moved to the United Kingdom (UK) and the Netherlands, and then to the US and Canada. Clearly, their breaking free from privileged-caste groups in India enabled the possibility to establish new ways of life to transform themselves and reconstruct and re-embed new societies sans caste. It is only right that we examine some instances from the Caribbean to learn about how the Indians who decided not to return to their homeland after their indenture dealt with caste.

INDENTURED INDIANS AND THE PROBLEM
OF CASTE IN THE CARIBBEAN

The rise of caste or casteism among some Indians in the Caribbean is indeed paradoxical to see. Caste was not a factor or a condition in the recruitment of indentured labourers. The main requirement was their capacity to do hard plantation and mining work in hostile environs across the world. Nevertheless, some indentured Indians and their descendants re-invented themselves as privileged-caste members, making sure that some of their fellow migrants from the same linguistic backgrounds were also recruited into such exclusionary social formations. A direct consequence of this re-institutionalization of caste in the Caribbean was the scrambling to identify oneself as privileged by birth. This was to gain more favourable work and monetary, sexual and other benefits. More perniciously, it led to the subordination of fellow Indians according to their language, food habits and colour as lower castes in the plantation colonies. Peter van der Veer and Steven Vertovec have shown through their pivotal study that 'Caribbean Hinduism' is nothing but the privileged-caste-dominated religious institutionalization of 'Brahmanism'. As is the case in India, those who self-identified and promoted themselves as Brahmins re-planted caste in the Caribbean.[21] This meant that Brahmin-male power re-emerged among Indians overseas to whom caste identity had not mattered in the first place or whose privileged-caste identity and ensuant lack of agrarian knowledge would have made them poor recruits for indentured labour. It also meant that the bonds formed 'across caste and religion' on the perilous and long voyage, the 'close social ties of *dipwa-bhai* and *dipwa-bahan* (depot brothers and sisters) and *jahaji bhai* and *jahaji bahan* (ship brothers and sisters)' were betrayed after the arrival of the migrants at their distant destination.[22] As a result of the rise of re-crafted Brahmin identity and power (often through unverifiable personal claims), a birth-based and hierarchical Hindu religious social structure was perpetuated in the Caribbean. Migration and transmigration during colonialism and after independence (to Europe and North America) have exacerbated and reinforced the casteist tendencies of self-privileging Indian migrants.[23]

In Guyana, there is evidence of a Shaivite temple in Berbice which is said to have existed since 1846. Nonetheless, five Brahminical *murti*s – that is, Brahma, Vishnu, Shiva, Shakti and Hanuman (Shakti is the only goddess in this ensemble of gods) – and their other derivative avatars as well as Ganesha, began to take root in the Caribbean only in the 1920s, after the indenture policy came to an end. Indians who were influenced by north Indian religious movements, such as the Arya Samaj, sought to recruit Indo-Guyanese into their fold by promoting reformist ideas, such as priesthood for non-Brahmins.[24] Crucially, Indian Muslims and worshippers of regional deities (such as the goddess Kali) were some of the first to assert their inclusive religio-cultural practices (inter-ethnic) through festivals such as Muharram and Kali Puja with animal sacrifice and communal feasts. However, those who promoted themselves as Brahmins were in favour of a Caribbean Brahminism, the caste-based re-establishment of exclusionary cultural, economic and social institutions and practices in which Brahmins remained the most superior group in the Indian diaspora. This was in contrast to the Kali, Arya Samaj, Muslim, Christian, Indo-African and other more egalitarian and inclusive Indo-Caribbean traditions.

Self-privileging-caste men thus shaped the emergence and institutionalization of what is called the 'Sanatani Dharma', the Brahminical myth that there is an eternal order or duty or righteousness which a Hindu ought to follow at all times and in all spaces. Such claims were first propagated with the establishment of the Sanatan Dharma Maha Sabha (SDMS) in Trinidad in 1951, through the efforts of Bhadase Sagan Maraj, who aimed to reach out to the Indian diaspora in the Caribbean. The SDMS unambiguously stood for Brahminical values and identity.[25]

Not surprisingly, the Indo-Guyanese took a cue from the SDMS of Trinidad and established their own Guyana Hindu Dharmic Sabha (GHDS) in 1974. Reepu Daman Persaud founded the GHDS and remained its president until he passed away in 2013. His name carries the prefix Pandit, referring to his Brahmin identity (although some non-Brahmin privileged-caste priests also refer to themselves as Pandits in the Caribbean). The arrival of Reepu Persaud's father, Durga Persaud, in Guyana in 1914, purportedly with a caste-bearing colonial document, authenticated his descendant as a Brahmin, allowing him to bear the mantle of the institutionalization of the GHDS. The organization presently oversees over 125 temples in Guyana, including some caste-free examples such as the Kali temples. After Reepu Daman Persaud's demise, his daughter Vidhya Persaud was elected to be the next president of the GHDS in 2013. Interestingly, she says that 'even though she is a vegetarian, teetotaller and a Hindu, the pandits, that is, the brahmin priests of GHDS, are not happy about her being the president, since she is a woman'.[26] Such gender disparities have led to the formation of the Mahila Mandali (the women's association) within the GHDS. Nonetheless, it is clear that the GHDS, its priest-training programmes and other festivities stand neither for gender equality nor for the anti-caste integration of the Indo-Guyanese but instead for caste-based unequal integration.

Suriname received its first indentured labourers in 1873. They were mostly from the United Provinces and Bengal Presidency of British north India (Uttar Pradesh [UP] and Bihar in present-day India). As in other parts of the Caribbean, the Indo-Surinamese were mostly lower-caste Indians and Muslims, but the Brahminical gods, goddesses and temples took shape in Suriname along with the dominance of those Indians who self-identified as Brahmins. They found success with the establishment of certain Surinamese laws in their favour. For instance, only Brahmin males were deemed qualified priests and allowed to officiate at marriages of Indo-Surinamese who identified themselves as 'Hindus'.[27] In fact, like Trinidad and Guyana, Suriname also has its own Sanatan Dharm Maha Sabha (SDMS-Suriname) which, as a Brahmin-dominated association, institutionalizes Brahminical religio-cultural practices.

Indo-Surinamese Brahmin priests are clear when they say that 'caste is permanent because it is Sanatani dharma, and vice versa. And as per Sanatani dharma even Sanatani brahmin women cannot become *pandita* [priestess] but only *pracharika* [propagator]'.[28] Such caste-inflected standpoints in the Indian diaspora mirror the rise of Brahminical or Hindu fundamentalism in colonial and postcolonial India[29] and the advent of global Brahminism. The latter entails the international ascendance of local racism and casteism among a minority of the Indian community who consider themselves Brahmins. By mythically imposing a birth-based *varna* (colour) and *jati* (caste), they culturally and economically benefit while violently perpetuating casteism overseas. Such tendencies can also be mimicked by some non-Brahmin privileged groups.

The inauguration of the SDMSs of Trinidad, Guyana and Suriname in the twentieth century points to the social and self-transformation of indentured Indians and their descendants in the Caribbean. Their rise now as 'Sanatanis', Indians who identify themselves as 'orthodox Hindus', is a euphemism for a caste-based identification of oneself as a Brahmin or non-Brahmin privileged-caste member. The institutionalization of such caste-based identities is evident in places of worship (temples), marriage rituals and practices, food restrictions (vegetarianism), educational institutions and birth-based Brahminical occupations (priesthood). Paradoxically, some of the descendants of Indian indentured labourers, who were mostly from caste-oppressed communities, are now increasingly self-proclaiming their supposed Brahminical identities. Problematically, such orthodoxies begin to be valorised by some Indians as the *only* Indo-Caribbean identity.

The Indians who dared to break free from the shackles of caste or casteism and became indentured labourers have, however, documented their perspective. One poem reads, 'Brahmans and Kshatriyas ... Who attach untouchability ... While keeping the company of prostitutes ... The subjects escaped and came to the islands ... India turned on her side'.[30] Their caste-free religio-cultural institutions and practices have also continued to thrive in the Caribbean – in opposition to and differing from the Sanatani Brahminical claims. This anti-caste spirit and historical sense of castelessness can be seen among the Indo-Guyanese, for instance, who have retained vernacular Kali and Amman religious practices – identified as 'the Madras Tradition'.[31] Understanding these casteless modes of worship and practices reveals how the Indo-Guyanese have held on to their ancestral caste-free values in order to establish a casteless society in the Caribbean.

THE POLITICS OF THE BRAHMINICAL CO-OPTING OF KALI AND AMMAN

Caste-free temples, deities, priests, priestesses and worshippers are diverse in Guyana. They have a long and intricate history of connection to the Indo-Guyanese communities since their arrival in 1838. In fact, some anti-caste Indo-Guyanese point out that their own ancestors played a crucial role in establishing the very first temples of Guyana. Keith McNeal poignantly writes in the context of Kali worship in Trinidad, 'Parameshwarie and Katerie, although derived from different Indian geographic zones, meet at the kali temple for those seeking the divine intervention of *Shakti*'. Furthermore, he records that such non-Brahminical traditions have been 'gaining ground among increasingly wide segments of the Guyanese Hindu community and among Afro-Creoles as well'.[32] Historically, it is as part of the lore of indentured Indians and their descendants that many of these non-Brahminical deities, such as Parameshwarie, Kali, Katerie, Siparee Mai, Sangili Karuppan, Muni, Madurai Veeran, Maari Amman, and so on, were brought from across the Indian subcontinent to Guyana. Thereafter, due to colonial, racism-inflected Christianity, on the one hand, and the gradual ascendance of Brahminical deities and rituals, on the other, these non-Brahminical traditions have assumed distinct identities in diverse localities of the Caribbean.

McNeal, however, misreads changes in the non-Brahminical Caribbean traditions when he says that behind the animal-sacrifice-oriented deities in the Caribbean is the 'Hindu conceptualization of cosmic power or energy that emanates from the devis, or female goddesses, that generates and continues to activate the universe'.[33] This is a condescending co-option of the non-Brahminical deities and worship of the Indo-Caribbeans into Brahminical categories and practices. The category 'Hindu' was not popular even in colonial India of the early twentieth century when indentured emigration came to an end. The indentured Indians were mostly unconnected to Brahminical religio-cultural notions. In fact, they were victims of the caste-based violence of privileged-caste groups who claimed a 'Hindu' identity after the British promotion of this category.[34]

Some scholars who study the Caribbean, North American and European Indian diaspora carelessly foist the category Hindu on communities which are unconnected with or would not like to be identified *solely* as Sanatanis (orthodox privileged-caste groups). Such misrepresentations are based on seeing the Indian diaspora as *only* Hindus. They not only overlook the modalities of Brahminical impositions but also legitimize the co-option of linguistically diverse and polytheistic non-Brahminical deities of India into a monolithic Brahminical or Hindu Shakti and *devi* form. For that matter, what is also usually identified in the Caribbean as the 'Madras Tradition' does not shed enough light on the critical caste aspects of non-Brahminical deities, temples, priests and publics.

TRACES OF CASTE-FREE IDENTITY AND TRANSFORMATIONAL MODES OF WORSHIP

The caste-free temples in Guyana focused upon here are of two kinds: (*a*) Kali temples and (*b*) Mariamman temples. Such temples, however, house multiple other non-Brahmin deities (as well as some Brahminical deities) from diverse regions of India. These temples mostly have priests, although priestesses serve in various non-Brahmin temples from time to time across Guyana.

Kali and Mariamman temple architecture mostly does not feature the imposing grandeur of Brahminical temples. The deity is supposed to be accessible to all devotees. As soon as they enter these temples, worshippers are instantly surrounded by and connected to the deities that are there. This clearly contrasts with the hierarchical spatial divisions of Brahminical temples, which mimic caste and gender structures in their arrangement; the descending order of gods, goddesses, priests and worshippers can be seen in the design, and separate entrances and seating arrangements exist for men and women. In addition, patriarchal concerns prevent menstruating women from entering such temples. In the non-Brahmin temple complexes in Guyana, a female deity can be found at the very entrance. It is usually either a Kali amma(n) (mother Kali) or Kateri amma(n) (mother Kateri) and not Ganesha as is the case in Brahmin temples. Women also retain a lot more autonomy in their access and worship in comparison to their experience in Brahmin temples. However, gender-based violence and suicide rates of women are very high in the Caribbean, irrespective of their religious affiliations.[35]

Although a shrine might be identified as a Kali temple, it invariably hosts a pantheon of deities, some of which are even absent in Brahminical temples in Guyana or India. Christ, Mary and Islamic images may also be present among the diverse non-Brahminical deities (in-between them and not at the periphery). The priest of a Kali temple says:

> Muslims and Christians regularly visit the Kali shrine for healing their psycho-somatic challenges in life. While the Muslim and Christian worshippers retain their own distinct religious identity, they liberally accept Kali as well to ward off their travails and to seek well-being through her blessings.[36]

In addition, the Kali shrine priest explains that he wanted to express Kali's and his own 'we feeling' to these Muslim and Christian worshippers by keeping Mary, Christ and images of Islam in the shrine on par with Kali and other vernacular caste-free deities.[37]

Clearly, the heterodox aspects in this Kali worship and the inclusive casteless religiosity of the worshippers can be seen in three ways: (*a*) despite the non-Brahminical identity and religious space of Kali, Brahminical deities are also incorporated into the shrine; (*b*) besides non-Brahmin and Brahmin deities, other religious deities and images of Muslim and Christian traditions are also vital to the Kali shrine and worship; and (*c*) animal sacrifice, alcohol and smoking are indispensable features of Kali rituals. These practices not only reject the Brahminical stigmatization of such rituals but also empower the meat-eating, alcohol-drinking and smoking habits of the devotees of Kali, who are invariably disparaged by the Brahmin-male gurus in the Caribbean as is the case elsewhere. Evidently, there is a rejection of the Brahminical exclusionary practices that manifest in the worship of Brahminical deities, thereby embedding casteless and raceless spatial and temporal values. In the Kali temples of Guyana, the caste-free consciousness and identity of the devotee as well as the priest is apparent.

The Mariamman temples of Guyana are remarkable for their distinctness as not only the place of a non-Brahmin deity but also a space where casteless subjectivity is reinforced. Architecturally, the Mariamman shrines are almost extensions of the houses of their multilingual and modern priests. The main deity in one temple is, of course, Mariamman. It features a replica of the Mariamman temple of Samayapuram in Tamil Nadu, south India, as a marker of caste-free memory and a casteless Tamil influence 9,000 miles away. In fact, this Mariamman temple entrance welcomes a worshipper with a Tamil god, the dark-skinned Sangili Karuppan, who wears a chain around his body and is a protecting deity of the worshipper. Then one moves to see Muniandavan, another Tamil god who is also known as Muniandi or Munieaswaran in Tamil Nadu today and is a popular deity of the casteless Tamils. Muniandi is also a reference to Buddha, who was also known as Muni or Sakyamuni among the Tamil Buddhists and others across the world due to his attainment of nirvana through his meditating prowess.[38] Next, one passes on to pray to Madurai Veeran, another Tamil god whose origin is traced to Madurai in Tamil Nadu. This deity is also known for his valour, as the Tamil word *veeran* signifies. He is also a popular deity among the casteless Tamils due to a legend about his struggle against caste or casteism in the Tamil speaking regions of South India. Finally, one reaches the goddess Mariamman, the main deity. She is adorned with *kumkumum* (vermilion) on the forehead and a red sari wrapped around her body. Ritual items such as neem and mango leaves in bowls of water, a semi-husked coconut and a sickle to cut it, camphor on a plate to be lit and *sambirani* (incense powder) to be put in a simmering charcoal pan are kept ready for the priest's ritual performances. Interestingly, the priest encourages the participation of worshippers in these rituals while he chants the Tamil words in praise of Mariamman, which are mostly intelligible to the worshippers. Adjacent to the Mariamman deity is a pit where a fowl or a goat or a pig is sacrificed on important occasions. The meat of these sacrificed animals is then cooked for communal feasts in the temple complex, which is meant to emphasize caste-free commensality. These practices markedly diverge from those found in Brahmin temples, where caste-based asymmetrical social gatherings, followed by handouts of small plastic packets of vegetarian devotional-foods (*prasad*) predominate.

In the Mariamman temples, the priests, priestesses and devotees occupy a caste-free horizontal space and experience a direct communion with the goddesses and gods through their own ritual performances aided by the priest. Considering the caste-valorising and 'north Indian' predominance of the Sanatani associations in Guyana and their interlinkages with other such organizations in Trinidad and Suriname, a Mariamman priest said:

> There is marginalization of non-Sanatani Indo-Guyanese with alternative beliefs, practices and associations which are interreligious and interracial. Kali and Mariamman temples have always been known for their inclusivity of Muslims and Christians as well as Africans, Chinese and native Amerindians. Disparagingly, such humanistic Indo-Guyanese religio-cultural practices and traditions have been dubbed as *obeah* (African religious cult).[39]

Nonetheless, Kali and Amman priests say that integrating such Indo-Guyanese traditions is becoming more popular among the Guyanese in general. This is because they are embedded in a working-class-oriented, interracial and casteless society.

CASTE-FREE PRIESTS AND RITUALS OF HEALING

Unlike the Brahmin priests of Sanatani temples, the priests of Kali and Amman temples do not identify themselves by caste. A Kali temple priest said that 'caste-claims of priests are not only shameful but also anti-God'.[40] In fact, such temple priests explain that the caste-based hierarchy perpetuated via the Brahminical deities is also a senseless degradation and alienation of the worshippers even as their financial support is sought for the prosperity of the Brahminical temple complex. In contrast, the Kali and Amman priests promote caste-free accessibility for any common worshipper, woman or man. Their ritual chanting is mostly in simple English and/or Tamil, unlike the Brahmin priests' English sermon interspersed with Sanskrit (and Hindi) that is mostly unintelligible to worshippers.

The Kali and Amman priests often directly involve the worshippers in their rituals. The close proximity of the priest and their bodily touch enhances the healing experience of the worshippers. Such oneness between the priest and the devotee encourages a reassuring self-empowerment as well as a collective casteless belongingness. This sits in opposition to the spatial segregation and non-touching interaction between Brahmin-male priests and their followers. There is no glaring relationship of dominance and subordination between the Kali and Amman priests and their devotees. In fact, these priests deliberately practice closeness. For instance, one Kali temple priest has seating arrangements in the shrine in such a way as to facilitate an equal communion with his worshippers, even though only the priest knows the rituals of healing. In this arrangement, the devotee benefits from the immediate support engendered by the plain-speaking nature of the priest and the proximity of the surrounding goddesses, gods and fellow worshippers. Animal sacrifice and community feasts thereafter foster togetherness on a shared sacred ground, aiding those present in overcoming their life challenges.

True to the interracial and interreligious nature of the devotees, the Kali and Amman priests show an ethical understanding of humanity by rejecting caste and race differences. Some have interracial partners. Particularly, they understand caste as casteism. In this sense, a Mariamman temple priest said, 'Claiming one's identity as a brahmin priest is bogus and it is meant to gain material prosperity by putting down the devotees of the deities they officiate as priests'.[41] Instead, such priests say that all humans face unsettling moments in their lives irrespective of their births. Healing devotees by invoking the sacred blessing of the deities is seen as incumbent on the priests or priestesses if one identifies as such. In this sense, the caste-free non-Brahmin deities, their priests and their ritual performances offer an explicit healing function through what could be called 'casteless inclusive integration'. It is through such non-discriminatory, religio-cultural interpretations and healing practices that caste-free identity in general, and casteless Tamil identity in particular, is forged, the Mariamman priest said.

EMIGRATION, TRANSMIGRATION AND THE GLOBALIZATION OF CASTELESSNESS

Among all the push factors behind Indian indentured emigration, the most virulent was the problem of caste or casteism under the colonial regime. The ascendance of privileged-caste groups and their collusion with the British colonialists branded certain Indians as lower castes and untouchables, leading to increasing losses of labour, water, land, education, jobs and dignity in nineteenth- and twentieth-century colonial India. Not surprisingly, these groups welcomed the indentured labour policy and sailed away, emigrated and transmigrated, to shed their subordination under caste. Multiple Indian diaspora sources confirm that nearly 80 per cent of them vowed never to return to India. This is because they feared their re-casteing as subordinates by privileged-caste groups, such as Brahmins.

Disconcertingly, some indentured Indians, true to their birth-oriented, caste-based beliefs and identities, not only reinvented their homeland deities and temples but also *othered* fellow Indo-Caribbeans and Afro-Caribbeans for their caste-free ways of life. The Sanatan Dharma *sabha*s in the Caribbean served to reinforce Brahminical orthodoxy, elevating the privileged and their prosperity, while relegating Indian Muslims, Indian Christians and casteless Indians as inauthentic Indo-Caribbeans. It is through them that the Brahmin and Kshatriya identities of the priests, patrons and devotees were established. In addition, they continue to adhere to caste-valorising endogamous marriage and business interests. The prefix 'Pandit' before an Indo-Guyanese name, as is the case elsewhere in the Caribbean, helps a person of Indian origin to elevate himself as a privileged-caste man over other Indians who are denied or do not embrace such titles (although some casteless and anti-caste Indo-Guyanese priests of Kali and Amman temples also identify themselves as Pandits). Personal claims and recognition by one's group only matter in such caste-based elevation of one's status and prosperity as middle- or upper-class priests. Unsurprisingly, some Brahmin-Pandits drive luxury cars, live in palatial homes and often fly across the Caribbean and North America as the most sought-after priests, while other Brahmin-Pandits, in-addition to and perhaps because of their priesthood, have become successful entrepreneurs or work for corporate enterprises. Considering the guarantee of immense prosperity, some who self-identify as Brahmins, even though they are not fully sure about the caste of their own parents and grandparents, have chosen the career of priesthood by quitting their higher-education-based jobs. There are instances of claims of Brahmin identity by Indo-Caribbeans turning out to be false when their ancestry is traced back to villages of north India where Indians oppressed by caste, those categorized as lower castes and untouchables, live.[42]

Sanantani *sabha*s are wealthier and control predominantly Brahmin-oriented temple and educational enterprises. But some of them have co-opted non-Brahmin traditions such as Kali and Amman temples. The Sanatani *sabha*s have the support of privileged-caste-based 'Hindu' associations in India and North America and vice versa. Predictably, the Sanatani *sabha*s disparage the interracial and interreligious influence of Christianity and Islam on the Indo-Guyanese, even as they promote caste-reinforcing social relations within and through them. For these reasons they seem to have belied the hopes of their own indentured ancestors for caste-free social and self-transformation.

In contrast, the non-Sanatani women and men continue to hold the ethical values of their ancestors. Clearly the Indo-Caribbeans who do not identify themselves by any caste have re-embedded their castelessness. Indo-Guyanese individuals relate how their ancestors arrived in the Caribbean from diverse linguistic zones of India, but they are also proud of their ancestors' forging of interracial and interreligious casteless identities in Guyana. Re-embedding diverse caste-free deities, such as Kali and Amman, and building temples of interreligious inclusion stand apart from the Brahminical deities and temples of the Caribbean (and North America and Europe), where the Brahmin and Kshatriya identities of the priests, patrons and devotees are reinforced.

Have the Indians who emigrated to escape caste oppression in colonial India succeeded, close to 200 years after their voyage? When we examine the lives of the Indo-Guyanese descendants of indentured Indians, it is evident that some have. These communities follow vernacular Kali and Amman traditions in the Caribbean, shunning caste, as their ancestors did. In fact, such Caribbean Indians are the harbingers of the globalization of castelessness. That is, they find Brahminical identity, priesthood and temples abominations against fellow Indians, the Indian diaspora and their caste-free humanity. Among such Indo-Caribbeans there is thus a sense of self-transformation and belonging in a casteless society. Nonetheless, the lack of critique against caste, like race, in (South Asian) academic theory and practice has constrained a rigorous understanding of the deep history of castelessness in the diverse linguistic regions and communities in India and the Indian diaspora.

NOTES

1. See Fuller and Narasimhan (2014).
2. See Aloysius (1997).

3. See De Genova (2006); Song (2018); Cole (2000).

4. Fuller and Narasimhan (2014).

5. Aloysius (1997).

6. See Ayyathurai (2020).

7. See Ayyathurai (2011).

8. See Subramanian (2019).

9. See Diwakar (2020); Dhanda et al. (2014). Regarding the Indian government's effort 'to avoid international scrutiny of caste discrimination', see Berg (2018).

10. Kurien (2006).

11. Roopnarine (2009).

12. Roopnarine (2018).

13. See van der Veer and Vertovec (1991); Rocklin (2019).

14. For disembedding and globalization, see Eriksen (2007).

15. Tinker (1974).

16. See Sinha (1995).

17. See Bahadur (2013).

18. See Mishra (2016); Fokken (2015).

19. Ayyathurai (2011).

20. Ayyathurai (2011).

21. van der Veer and Vertovec (1991).

22. Roopnarine (2018).

23. See Vertovec (1992).

24. Personal interview with Yog Mahadeo, 5 September 2019, Georgetown, Guyana.

25. See Jayaram (2006).

26. Personal interview with Vidhya Persaud, 14 September 2019, Georgetown, Guyana.

27. See Hoefte (2014).

28. Personal interview with Pandit Nitin Jagbandhan, 23 September 2019, Paramaribo, Suriname.

29. See Ludden (1996).

30. Carter (1996, 80).

31. See Kloss (2017).

32. McNeal (2003, 236–237).

33. McNeal (2003, 242).

34. See Marshall (1970).

35. See Lal (1985).

36. Personal interview with Pandit Parasaram Samaroo, 18 September 2019, Timehri, Guyana.
37. Personal interview with Pandit Parasaram Samaroo, 18 September 2019, Timehri, Guyana.
38. Ayyathurai (2011).
39. Personal interview with Pandit Deodat Muridall Tillack, 11 September 2019, Georgetown, Guyana.
40. Personal interview with Pandit Parasaram Samaroo, 18 September 2019, Timehri, Guyana.
41. Personal interview with Pandit Deodat Muridall Tillack, 20 September 2019, Georgetown, Guyana.
42. Personal interview with Swami Aksharananda, 19 September 2019, Cornelia Ida, West Coast Demerara, Guyana.

BIBLIOGRAPHY

Aloysius, G. 1997. *Nationalism without a Nation in India*. Oxford: Oxford University Press.

Ayyathurai, Gajendran. 2011. 'The Foundations of Anti-Caste Consciousness: Pandit Iyothee Thass, Tamil Buddhism, and the Marginalized in South India'. PhD dissertation, Columbia University, New York. https://anthropology .columbia.edu/content/anti-caste-consciousness-tamil-buddhism. Accessed 26 May 2022.

———. 2020. 'Living Buddhism: Migration, Memory, and Castelessness in South India'. *History and Anthropology* 31 (5): 1–19. DOI: 10.1080/02757206. 2020.1854751.

Bahadur, Gaiutra. 2013. *Coolie Woman: The Odyssey of Indenture*. Chicago: University of Chicago Press.

Berg, Dag Erik. 2018. 'Race as a Political Frontier against Caste: WCAR, Dalits, and India's Foreign Policy'. *Journal of International Relations and Development* 21 (4): 990–1013.

Carter, Marina. 1996. *Voices from Indenture: Experiences of Indian Migrants in the British Empire*. Leicester: Leicester University Press.

Cole, Philip. 2000. *Philosophies of Exclusion: Liberal Political Theory and Immigration*. Edinburgh: Edinburgh University Press.

De Genova, Nicholas. 2006. *Racial Transformations: Latinos and Asians Remaking the United States*. Durham: Duke University Press.

Dhanda, Meena, Annapurna Waughray, David Keane, David Mosse, Roger Green and Stephen Whittle. 2014. *Caste in Britain: Socio-Legal Review*. Manchester: Equality and Human Rights Commission.

Diwakar, Amar. 2020. 'A Silicon Valley Lawsuit Reveals Caste Discrimination Is Rife in the US'. *TRT World*, 15 September. https://www.trtworld.com/magazine/a-silicon-valley-lawsuit-reveals-caste-discrimination-is-rife-in-the-us-39773. Accessed 26 May 2022.

Eriksen, Thomas Hylland. 2007. *Globalization*. London and New York: Bloomsbury.

Fokken, Margriet. 2015. 'Beyond Stereotypes: Understanding the Identities of Hindustani Women and Girls in Suriname Between 1873 and 1921'. *Tijdshrift Voor Genderstudies* 18 (3): 273–289.

Fuller, C. J., and Haripriya Narasimhan. 2014. *Tamil Brahmins: The Making of a Middle-Class Caste*. Chicago: University of Chicago Press.

Hoefte, R. 2014. *Suriname in the Long Twentieth Century: Domination, Contestation, Globalization*. New York: Palgrave Macmillan.

Jayaram, N. 2006. 'The Metamorphosis of Caste among Trinidad Hindus'. *Contributions to Indian Sociology* 40 (2): 143–173.

Kloss, Sinah. 2017. 'Manifesting Kali's Power: Guyanese Hinduism and the Revitalization of the Madras Tradition'. *Journal of Eastern Caribbean Studies* 43 (1): 83–110.

Kurien, Prema A. 2006. 'Multiculturalism and "American" Religion: The Case of Hindu Indian Americans'. *Social Forces* 85 (2): 723–741.

Lal, Brij. 1985. 'Veil of Dishonour: Sexual Jealousy on Fiji Plantations'. *Journal of Pacific History* 20 (3): 135–155.

Ludden, David (ed.). 1995. *Making India Hindu: Religion, Community and the Politics of Democracy in India*. Delhi: Oxford University Press.

Marshall, P. J. 1970. *The British Discovery of Hinduism in the Eighteenth Century*. Cambridge: Cambridge University Press.

McNeal, Keith. 2003. 'Doing the Mother's Caribbean Work: On Shakti and Society in Contemporary Trinidad'. In *Encountering Kali: In the Margins, at the Center, in the West*, edited by Rachel Fell McDermott and Jeffrey J. Kripal, 223–248. Berkeley and London: University of California Press.

Mishra, Margaret. 2016. '"Your Woman Is a Very Bad Woman": Revisiting Female Deviance in Colonial Fiji'. *Journal of Women's Studies* 17 (4): 67–78.

Rocklin, Alexander. 2019. *The Regulation of Religion and the Making of Hinduism in Colonial Trinidad*. Chapel Hill: University of North Carolina Press.

Roopnarine, Lomarsh. 2009. 'The Repatriation, Readjustment, and Second-Term Migration of Ex-Indentured Indian Laborers from British Guiana and Trinidad to India, 1838–1955'. *New West Indian Guide* 83 (1–2): 71–97.

———. 2018. *The Caribbean Indian: Migration and Identity in the Diaspora.* Jackson: University Press of Mississippi.

Sinha, Mrinalini. 1995. *Colonial Masculinity: The 'Manly Englishman' and the 'Effeminate Bengali' in the Late Nineteenth Century.* Manchester: Manchester University Press.

Song, Sarah. 2018. 'Political Theories of Migration'. *Annual Review of Political Science* 21 (1): 385–402.

Subramanian, Ajantha. 2019. *The Caste of Merit: Engineering Education in India.* Cambridge, MA: Harvard University Press.

Tinker, Hugh. 1974. *A New System of Slavery: The Export of Indian Labour Overseas, 1830–1920.* Oxford: Oxford University Press.

van der Veer, Peter, and Steven Vertovec. 1991. 'Brahmanism Abroad: On Caribbean Hinduism as an Ethnic Religion'. *Ethnology* 30 (2): 149–166.

Vertovec, Steven. 1992. *Hindu Trinidad: Religion, Ethnicity, and Socio-Economic Change.* London: Macmillan.

9

MEMORY, NOSTALGIA AND REALITY

A SOCIO-HISTORICAL PERSPECTIVE OF CULTURE AND EDUCATION IN THE GREY STREET COMPLEX

Tashmica Sharma

As the globe has experienced increasing population shifts from rural peripheries to towns and cities, urban expansion has become one of the most complex challenges.[1] The fabric and form of every city is continually restructured to cater to the arrival of new entrants and aspirants. Whether urban communities have been favoured or disadvantaged by such modifications, they remain inherently associated with their unique urban identity and its place-relationship.[2] This is because the identity of a city (with its urban morphology) becomes history once it is altered, and the place-relationship remains perpetual and preserved in the emotional memories of its urbanites.[3] The mnemonic and emotional elements of a particular location have long played essential roles in understanding the history of socio-demographic dimensions of urban environments.[4] The South African experience has been no different.

The socio-spatial systems of South African cities reflect the history of apartheid and its plethora of consequences for various disadvantaged groups.[5] Thus South African urban history has been a vital aspect for understanding the contemporary shapes and forms of its cities. The changing form of the central business district (CBD) of Durban, one of South Africa's major urban nodes, for example, has captured the attention of scholars from various disciplines. It has become a focus for researchers due to its remarkably rich history and diverse culture.

The historic distinctive trait of the Durban city centre was that it contained two CBDs: a white one at the core and an adjacent Indian business sector.[6] From the late nineteenth century, it was in this precinct (currently renamed after Yusuf Dadoo, an anti-apartheid activist) that many indentured and passenger Indians in Natal inexorably planted their footprints.[7] Previously a legislated Indian Group Area,[8] this precinct formed a fundamental economic and commercial component of the Indian CBD and served as an important contributor to the urban economy during the apartheid era.[9] It also served as an incubator for numerous Indian entrepreneurs and business houses, many of which have still retained their operations there to this day. The presence of multifarious Indian businesses not only brought about a sense of belonging but also gave this complex a cultural vibrancy. Often called a 'home away from home' for the South African urban Indian population, the complex encapsulated a rich cultural ambience with great recreational and institutional significance.[10]

The post-apartheid era has seen a changing townscape across the Durban CBD and transformation within all its precincts. However, the Grey Street Complex area still 'survives as the old business and residential centre for the Indian community in Durban, and indisputably as its cultural heart'.[11] Even after the demise of apartheid, Grey Street residents still reminisce about the trials and triumphs of their making of the 'mini-India' and their unique socio-spatial identity.[12] Their mnemonic attachment to this complex reminds the community of a romanticized and sentimental microcosm of South African Indian traditionalism, collectively lived and experienced.[13] Although undergoing rapid demographic and cultural transformations, the precinct is still associated with nostalgia for its historical spatial reference as the Grey Street Complex.

HISTORICAL CONTEXT

In order to understand the location of the Grey Street Complex, it is necessary to have an understanding of urban structures in the context of South African history. Cities of apartheid South Africa are considered to be distinctive beyond comparison.[14] This emanates from a colonial history of European and British imperialism – both of which provided a prototype model of urban segregation which was later inherited and schematized by Afrikaner nationalists for their apartheid doctrine.[15] The apartheid city model was also circumscribed by a series of restrictive legislation that garnered white domination in urban areas:

1. Natives (Urban Areas) Consolidation Act, 1923
2. Asiatic Land Tenure Act (Ghetto Act), 1946
3. Population Registration Act, 1950
4. Group Areas Act, 1950, 1966
5. Prevention of Illegal Squatting Act, 1952

It was against this backdrop that every South African city developed economically, socially and spatially. Black, coloured and Indian communities were forcibly removed from cities under the Group Areas Act and relocated to distant group area zones or rural townships.[16] Focusing particularly on the city of Durban, the concept of a dual CBD was evident from a very early stage when a minor Indian trading zone became an Indian CBD, leaving the rest of the city designated as a white CBD.[17] Despite this Indian zone, the entire city was still controlled by white domination, making the development of the Indian CBD both dependant on and subjected to the compromises of apartheid legislation.[18] Although the Indian CBD structure contained both the Grey Street Complex and part of the Warwick Junction Precinct – an extension of the Grey Street Complex – this chapter will focus on the former as the main Indian commercial and cultural hub.

SPATIAL PROFILE

The Grey Street Complex is a spatially modest precinct. Although it was geo-strategically positioned as a neighbouring secondary node to the white CBD, the Grey Street Complex remains spatially unchanged in its contemporary environment. The land coverage of this precinct (eliminating roads) is approximately 20 hectares in total.[19] From the north to south boundaries, the entire precinct is approximately 1 kilometre long, and from its east to west boundaries, it extends to approximately 700 metres at its greatest width. The locality map (Figure 9.1) represents the spatial delineation of the Grey Street Complex. The main street, from north to south, is Grey Street. It is enclosed by Derby Street and Dartnell Crescent as northern boundaries as well as Commercial Road as a southern boundary. The eastern boundary is formed by Albert Street. The western boundary consists of two parts: Cross Street (which is intercepted by Short, Brook and Bond streets) and Fishmarket Street (which includes the Cathedral-road interception). Nine

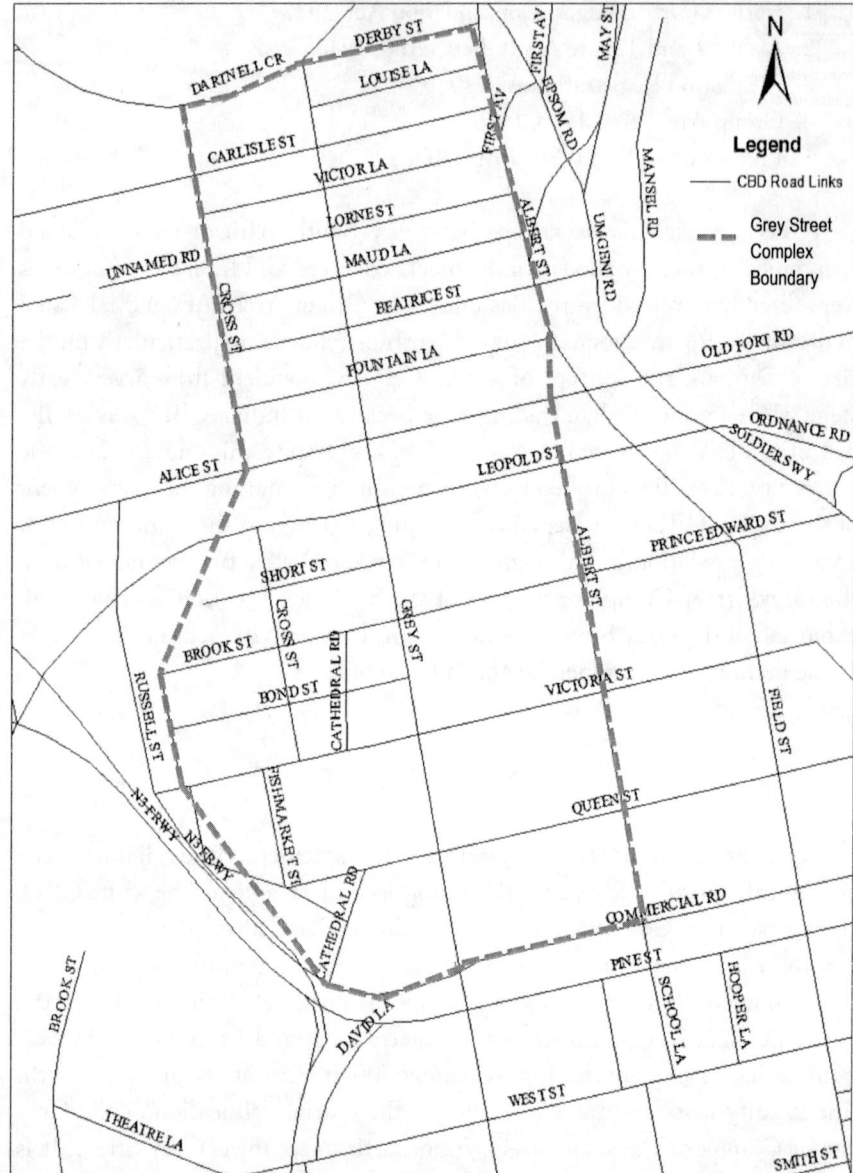

Figure 9.1 Grey Street Complex with spatial boundaries

Source: Map produced using ArcGIS software; shapefiles obtained from the Geographical Information Systems Department, University of KwaZulu-Natal.

Table 9.1 Apartheid and post-apartheid street names in the Grey Street Complex

Street names during apartheid	Post-apartheid street names
Alice	Johannes Nkosi
Beatrice	Charlotte Maxeke
Carlisle	Carlisle
Commercial	Dr A. B. Xuma
Leopold	David Webster
Lorne	Ismail C. Meer
Prince Edward	Dr Goonam
Queen	Denis Hurley
Victoria	Bertha Mkhize

Source: 'Durban, KwaZulu-Natal: Road Map and Street View', https://www.maps-streetview.com/South-Africa/Durban/roadmap.php (accessed 14 May 2016).

main intersecting streets parallel across Grey Street and form the inner matrix of this complex. The names of the parallel streets have changed in the post-apartheid era (Table 9.1).

Currently, the Durban CBD has new street names; thus, the aforementioned apartheid street names are no longer applicable to this precinct. However, the nature of this study is socio-historical, and it has utilized the previous street names as this precinct has been examined during the apartheid era. Additionally, the study has drawn on the memory and nostalgia of its previous residents who knew the previous names of all the streets and have particular emotional attachments and sentimental connotations associated with the former names of this complex and all the streets within it.

METHODOLOGY

For this study we have made extensive use of historical records. Documents such as Group Areas' memoranda, historical school paperwork, and the brochures, pamphlets and letters of several cultural organizations have provided archival data which are important sources for this study. In addition, these documents provide information about the circumstances under which the Indian community previously lived and their systems and principles at that time. Such records encapsulate a rich historical background of the study area – politically, socioculturally and economically.

A second source for this study has been a series of interviews with residents and former residents of the Grey Street Complex. The strength in receiving information from a qualitative interview is that it is reliable and valid because it is answered personally; it thus brings in elements from the actuality of the situation under examination.[20] However, it is important to note that the information received may be biased as a result of the personal experience and perception of the interviewee.[21] Thus, as a researcher, it is important to have a thorough understanding of the context and situation before accepting any information as authoritative. Triangulation has been used between interviews and documentary sources to as far as possible eliminate bias in our conclusions.

Communication during an interview is guided by a particular thematic framework or narrative approach with an interactive structure. For this chapter, the focus of the interviews was on memory and nostalgia. Semi-structured interviews have been conducted with informed consent of the interviewee, the data being obtained through open-ended questions. This approach has been selected as the study is based on the memory and nostalgia of the interviewee sample and is therefore more reliant on their mnemonic phenomenology rather than the specificity of the question.[22]

For this chapter, several interviewees were selected according to their profile and knowledge of as well as experiences in the area during apartheid. Most of them are at an advanced age and were interviewed individually. The interviewees are mainly residents of the Grey Street Complex and include businessmen and business women, newspaper reporters and senior community leaders of sociocultural and religious organizations that existed during the apartheid era. A brief description of the profiles of the interviewees is presented in Table 9.2.

The selection of the sample is a crucial element in the nature of the outcome of the study, and researchers need to exercise caution in the context of bias so as to prevent skewed results. There are several sub-categories of purposive sampling, each of which applies to a certain type of investigation based on the researcher's interest. The two variants of purposive sampling that have been employed for this study are expert and snowball. Expert sampling allows for the selection of the most knowledgeable authorities, specialists and practitioners in a specific field.[23] This type of sampling is pertinent to the study as experts have been selected to provide precise details on certain institutions. In addition to this, snowball sampling allows for the selection of individuals who display qualities that are most suitable to the investigation.[24] It is also a

Table 9.2 Profile of interviewees selected for the study

Interviewee	Profile	Date of interview
Mr Karsandas T. Manjee	• Former committee member of the Grey Street Indian Local Affairs Committee • Property development specialist – fixed property owner in the Grey Street Complex during apartheid	5 March 2016
Growfin Property Group	• Property experts and owners of several properties throughout the Durban CBD including in the Grey Street Complex	22 April 2016
Mr Ashwin Trikamjee	• President of the South African Hindu Maha Sabha • Former president of the Kathiawad Hindu Seva Samaj • Former president of the South African Soccer Federation	4 May 2016
Mr Ahmed Mahomad	• Chairman of the Juma Masjid (Grey Street Mosque) Trust • Committee member of the KwaZulu-Natal Interfaith Committee	19 May 2016
Mr Buddy Govender	• Senior manager of the Development and Environmental Planning Unit of the eThekwini Municipality • Co-founder and coordinator of 'The Casbah and Surrounds' webpage and 'Casbah edition'	30 November 2016

Source: Table compiled by the author based on information received during interviews.

way of selecting individuals who may possess expert knowledge for the study and is employed when a researcher is sampling with a defined intention.[25]

The final data analysis was structured using an inductive content analysis approach. Once the data was critically examined, structural categories were identified according to common themes emerging from the various data sources. The structural categories were then grouped and placed under higher order headings, which are based on the content of the objectives of the study. Classifying and integrating the information, with the guidance of a conceptual system, has provided an all-encompassing data analysis to explain how various socio-historical aspects of the Grey Street Complex have played a role in influencing memory and nostalgia within the community.

THE RISE OF A CULTURE IN GREY STREET

The year 1833 marked the end of slavery, but not the end of imported labour to colonial plantations. Up until 1917 more than 1 million Indians were transported to various colonial territories to work on plantations. British imperialism and feudalism translocated Indians to many enclaves around the globe. Durban in South Africa was one such region, where Indians arrived as indentured labourers between 1860 and 1911.[26]

The year 2017 marked the centenary of the abolition of the indenture system. What can be reflected upon, a century after its termination, is that it was not only significant due to its contribution to the historic urban and agricultural economies of South Africa, but also in its enrichment of the social and cultural pluralism of this country.[27] In addition to these pioneers, the advent of passenger Indians (traders who paid for their passage in 1874 and thereafter) also contributed to the commercial and urban form of cities in the country, especially Durban. Both these migrations gave rise to a new dimension for the Indian diaspora.[28] The history of the arrival of both indentured and passenger Indians in South Africa is so well known to society and in literature that it requires only a brief recitation in this section of the chapter. Nevertheless, it is important to understand that the history of Indian arrival in Durban is directly linked to the foundation, evolution and functionality of the Grey Street Complex.

THE EVOLUTION OF THE GREY STREET COMPLEX

The period between 1860 and 1911 recorded more than 150,000 Indians indentured as labourers in the sugar estates of colonial South Africa.[29] While the Government of Natal regarded the presence of indentured Indians as a temporary migration, the Indian colonial authorities viewed this as a permanent move.[30] D. S. Rajah argues that the profile of the first set of Indians who arrived in South Africa reflected a range of skills in various avenues of employment – priests, horticulturists, carpenters, weavers, domestic cleaners, tradesmen and atypically enough, a very small group of labourers.[31] Thus, the quest to obtain post-indenture employment was not a very challenging one for ex-indentured Indians because, soon enough, they were incorporated into the South African economy as craft workers, fishermen, tailors, laundrymen and household servants. Some ex-indentured Indians also found employment at the railway station, in shipyards as well as in coal mines. In addition to this, those who had a commercial background purchased land plots and became market gardeners while others enjoyed success in business.[32] The second set of indentured Indians arrived on 26 November 1860 in South Africa with even more diversification in their employment profiles. Table 9.3 exhibits the diverse skills of part of this second group of Indians.

Many of the commercial activities of ex-indentured Indians became increasingly concentrated in the Durban CBD because of its urban economic prospects and employment opportunities.[33] The need for renewed indenture contracts disappeared as Indians had the background skills to obtain the various types of employment available in Durban. This was also influential in facilitating their access to higher tiers of employment. Many ex-indentured Indians rapidly transformed their occupational profiles. Brookes and Webb point out that such variation in post-indenture employment was initially encouraged by the white community who supported this broadening of professions.[34] This diversification was further intensified by the arrival of passenger Indians.

THE ARRIVAL OF PASSENGER INDIANS

The first passenger Indians arrived in South Africa in 1874. Most passenger Indians came to Natal as businessmen. They immediately became aware of the commercial opportunities in Durban, initially serving the indentured community, and subsequently the African and white groups as well.[35] They soon began to transform the consumer market by supplying both products and services that were not only appealing to Indian consumers but also to the black and white communities.[36] In addition to their influence on the urban consumer market, passenger Indians were equally successful in the urban property market. They acquired several properties in the Durban CBD at a very early stage after their passage to South Africa.[37] While their acquisition of property may have been more evident in Durban, it also extended across various other urban nodes in the Natal province.[38]

This settlement eventually led to competition and conflict between Indian and white businessmen. The latter viewed the former as a threat, and subsequently influenced the local, provincial and national governments to introduce legislation to restrict Indian ownership and occupation of property to certain zones. While passenger Indians were contributing markedly to the development and growth of the city, their presence concerned the apartheid

Table 9.3 Occupational profiles of Indians on the *SS Belvedere*

Second group of indentured Indians (26 November 1860): *SS Belvedere*	
Initial occupational profile	Number
Gardeners	69
Priests	61
Soldiers	25
Dairymen	18
Pig rearers	16
Fruit producers	14
Salt dealers	11
Porters	11
Clerks	9
Herdsmen	8
Boatmen	7
Leather workers	6
Policemen	5
Messengers	5
Laundrymen	5
Oil pressers	4
Ironmongers	4
Traders	4
Undertakers	3
Barbers	2
Hunters	2
Jewellers	2
Confectioners	1
Weavers	1
Enamelware dealers	1
Total	**294**

Source: Singh (1960, 23).

government far more than they anticipated it would. Yet, the apartheid government continued to remain tolerant of indentured Indians entering the country due to their labour being a fundamental component of the South African economy.

THE DEVELOPMENT OF THE 'INDIAN CBD'

It is important to note that the development of the Grey Street Complex has to be considered in the context of the entire CBD of Durban. This is because the race–space delineation of this precinct was only legally determined at a very late stage in the apartheid era. The birth of the Grey Street Complex can be traced to the 1870s, when the Durban CBD already had a large concentration of Indians who had started businesses and acquired residency in a northwestern region of the city.[39] By the early 1880s, Durban had more than 60 Indian shops and approximately 118 fixed properties that were owned by Indians.[40] Thus an 'Indian hub' began to emerge and geo-strategically position itself in the city centre. Due to the profile of the urban consumer market in this centralized area, services and products for this community expanded very rapidly and it subsequently became known as the Indian CBD.

The continuous success of Indian traders antagonized white merchants.[41] Rajah asserts that the true potential of Indian traders was fully realized during the economic recession between 1882 and 1886, when employment was limited, and trading volumes were restricted. It was during this specific period that most black and Indian consumers became avid customers of Indian traders. Thus, the so-called Indian CBD acquired increased consumer popularity and this influence over the urban market attracted attention from the government.[42] It was at this point in South African history that the first expression of anti-Indian tendencies surfaced. Such anti-Indianism led to the establishment of the Wragg Commission in 1885, a document of the prevailing legislation governing Indian immigrants.[43] Although the commission stated that the dynamic role of Indian traders was significant for the urban economy, it also suggested that Indians should continue to remain in the colony only as indentured labourers. Subsequently, various laws were implemented in a concerted effort to destabilize and impede the growth of Indian capital as well as to impose limitations on Indians' acquisition of property (Table 9.4).

Towards the end of the nineteenth century, a large part of the Indian population was displaced from the Durban CBD and relocated to areas that came to be known as the Railway and Magazine Barracks.[44] By 1911, the population of the Durban CBD was in excess of 1,15,000.[45] Table 9.5 reflects that almost half of the population was made up of the Indian community at this time.

Table 9.4 Restrictive legislation imposed on Indians in the Durban CBD

Legislation	Description
Dealers Licenses Act (Natal) No. 18 of 1897	Required Indians to obtain trading licences in order to prevent them from competing with white merchants
Trading and Occupation of Land Restriction Act No. 35 (Pegging Act) of 1943	Prohibited Indians from occupying or purchasing properties which were previously occupied or acquired by the white community
Asiatic Land Tenure Act (Ghetto Act) of 1946	Restricted Asians from owning or occupying land in specific locations. Asians required a permit if the land was not occupied or purchased by Asians previously
Group Areas Act No. 41 of 1950	Determined the spatial location of different race groups
Industrial Conciliation Act No. 28 of 1956	Racially separated trade union movements and prohibited mixed trade unions

Source: Adapted from Chetty and Omar (1983) and Jithoo (1985).

With the presence of a very large Indian population in the CBD, it was logical for this community to settle at this particular location. The implementation of the Group Areas Act of 1950 dislocated approximately 140,000 Indians from the CBD. The Indian population in this precinct remained fairly similar from 1960 to 1970 but a very significant decrease, by more than 30 per cent, was evident by 1980 (Figure 9.2). This decrease was attributed to the political dynamics of uncertainty in relation to the racial zoning of the area according to the Group Areas Act.

MEMORIES AND NOSTALGIA OF A CULTURAL CHRONOTOPE

The Grey Street Complex is a cultural chronotope on the socio-spatial timeline of South African history. The residents of this precinct still have a place connection to the cohesive ensemble of cultures that existed in this part of the city during apartheid. The cultural connectivity of the community in this locality became integrated into their identities. Mr Buddy Govender, senior manager of Development and Environmental Planning of the eThekwini Municipality, nostalgically recalls his cultural experiences within the precinct:

Table 9.5 Reflection of the population percentage in the Durban CBD for 1911

Population composition of Durban (1911)	
Race group	Percentage (%)
African	19
European	34
Indian	47
Total	100

Source: Adapted from Croft et al. (1971) and Chetty and Omar (1983).

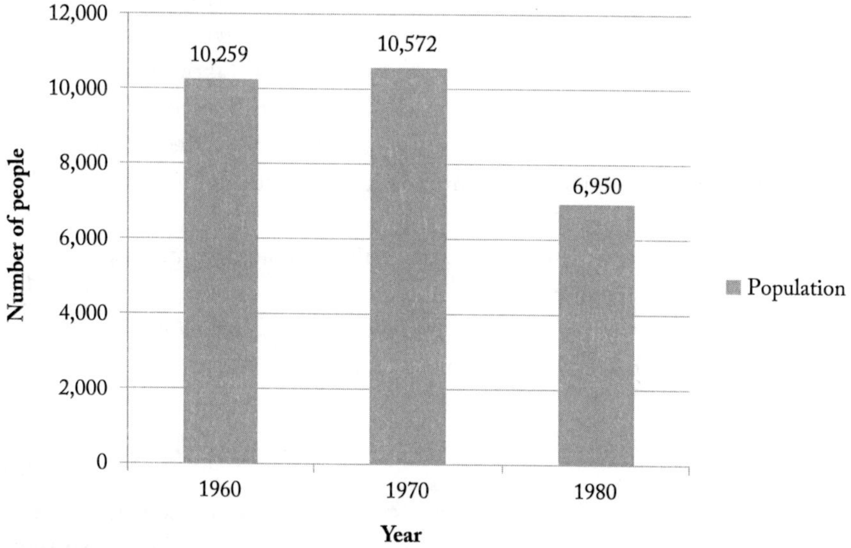

Figure 9.2 Population of the Grey Street Complex from 1960 to 1980

Source: Adapted from the Memorandum of the Central Durban Indian Area Protection Committee, 1982.

This was the most brilliant place to grow up in. It was a cosmopolitan area and a cultural time warp where we lived with broad vision. I remember how our vernacular was thriving and how pigeons would be flying over us while the Cathedral bell was ringing. I remember visiting the mosque and temple; we were all there no matter what our religion was and everyone came together to form a perfect blend.

We always celebrated together, if someone was happy, we were all happy and if anyone of us was sad, we were all sad. We had very little but we always turned it into something beautiful. The Grey Street Complex was a melting pot of cultures and the lifeblood of the community.[46]

Mr Ahmed Mahomad, chairman of the Juma Masjid Trust, reminisces about his cultural connection to the area, especially in terms of trust and religious tolerance:

Early traders interacted, trusted and lived a communal life. We had respect for everyone and a mutual respect for each other's religion and prayers. I remember how I used to light fireworks with my friends during Diwali. My family also enjoyed celebrating Raksha Bandhan. The mosque had a great relationship with the church, even today.

We saw everyone in our community as family. There was an intertwining of religion and culture and it was beautiful.[47]

The precinct became a microcosm of cultural cohesion and integration, one where the heritage of each of its residents existed in harmony. Evidently, the community of the Grey Street Complex never failed to educate future generations about their rich religious and cultural heritage.

CULTURAL VALUES AND CULTURAL ORGANIZATIONS

Religion, culture and education were essential in creating the value system within which the Indians lived as a community. Being the pioneers that they were, they took it upon themselves to create associations, societies, *samaj*s, *sangam*s, *sabha*s and *madrassa*s, not only to cater for the present but for the generations to come.

It must be emphasized that Indians held education and religion as paramount. Many adjustments were made at the dinner table in order to ensure that funding would be available to purchase the necessary stationery for the children's education, both Western and Eastern. The community built *patshala*s (traditional Hindu schools, taught by Brahmins) and *madrassa*s (schools for the study of Islamic theology and law) and attended these after English classes. To this day, it is observed that the Indian community still considers education a fundamental component to their living. Historically, small vernacular units served as the catalyst for the creation of religious institutions and organizations.[48]

The people who arrived from India tried as hard as possible to remain together in their own distinct groups in which they had lived in their motherland, especially the traders.[49] Consequently, the traders who were confined to the then Indian CBD were mainly Gujarati Hindu and Muslim groups, predominantly from Surat in Gujarat. One remarkable trait of these trader groups was that they could live in very confined spaces. So the trader would either be living behind or in a small flat above their retail shop. Their commitment to religion and education motivated them to quickly develop cultural institutions by which they could promote their own value systems.

Within the Indian community, culture and religion are inextricably intertwined regardless of faith. This can be seen when Christian Indian women wear sarees to church or in the way that mosques, in addition to their religious roles, also perform an important function in transmitting other artefacts of Islamic lifestyle or in how classical music and dance are integral to the Hindu faith. The three major religious groups that were present in the Grey Street Complex were Muslims, Hindus and Christians. These religious groups worked in harmony to establish various organizations and institutions to preserve culture and religion and provide the community of this precinct with an opportunity to receive an education. Various distinctive factors influenced the presence of each of these groups in this precinct as well as the formation of their associated cultural and educational bodies.

Christianity

The Christian community experienced very few difficulties in the formation of cultural organizations and institutions as these were established and developed by British and European missionaries, who also provided financial support for the maintenance and operation of their schools in the Grey Street Complex.[50] In particular, Anglicans, Methodists, Roman Catholics and Wesleyan missions were actively involved in Christian schooling.[51] Many of the missionaries who established schools could speak the vernaculars of the Indian community. Hence, they garnered support from Indians who were seeking education and cultural grounding in a foreign country. Table 9.6 provides a summary of the contributions made by early Christian leaders in this precinct.

Table 9.6 Contributions made by Christian religious leaders

Religious leaders	Contributions
Bishop Jean François Allard	Founder of Saint Joseph's Church in 1852 (one of the first churches in South Africa), later established as Emmanuel Cathedral
Reverend Ralph Stott	Established Methodist Chapel in Durban in 1876
Father John Baptist Sabon	Established Emmanuel Cathedral in 1902 and Saint Anthony's School in 1885
Dr Lancelot Booth	Established several mission educational facilities in 1887 which came to be known as 'booth schools' and built Saint Aidan's Church in 1887
Pastor J. F. Rowlands	Founder of Bethesda Temple in 1931

Source: Adapted from St Aidan's Mission Centenary Brochure (1983); Henning (1993); Govender and Naidoo (2010); Vahed (2013); Vahed and Waetjen (2015); Emmanuel Cathedral Historical Guide (2016).

Islam

The origins of Islam in South Africa can be traced back to 1667 with the arrival of the Cape Malays, far earlier than the period of indenture; however, they prayed in Jama'at Khanas (gatherings in an unsanctified house or place) and not in mosques.[52] Islam in the Natal province dates back to the arrival of indentured Indians, and of traders who were predominantly Muslim.[53] In particular, Muslim traders offered benefactions to those Muslims who were less fortunate and their symbiotic relationship allowed institutions such as the May Street Mosque in Greyville, to develop.[54]

The Islamic faith and traditions to be found in the Grey Street Complex are associated with one of the most well-known cultural and architectural hallmarks within the precinct, the Juma Masjid (Grey Street Mosque), which was the first mosque to be constructed in South Africa in 1884, and is also the largest in the southern hemisphere.[55] There were many prominent Islamic leaders in the Grey Street Complex who made contributions to culture in this precinct, as presented in Table 9.7.

Hinduism

Hinduism in the Natal province, like Islam, can be traced to the period of indenture. Hindus initially established places of worship on the plantations.

Table 9.7 Contributions made by Islamic leaders

Religious leaders	Contributions
Abubakr Amod Jhaveri	Arrived in 1874 and was considered to be the first trader in Natal; one of the first trustees of the Juma Masjid
Dada Abdoola	Local leader, political representative and responsible for the arrival of Mohandas K. Gandhi in South Africa
Ahmed Mohammed Tilly and Hoosen Meeran	Trustees and financial contributors to the West Street Masjid
Hajee Ahmed Mohammed Lockhat Trust	Established the Hajee Ahmed Mohammed Lockhat Wakuff Trust and founder of *madrassa*s in various areas of Durban in 1922
Abdulla Ismail Kajee	Spokesman for the Orient Islamic Institute and member of the South African Indian Congress (SAIC)

Source: Adapted from Sema (1985); Vahed (2013); Vahed and Waetjen (2015).

Table 9.8 Contributions made by Hindu missionaries in the precinct

Religious leaders	Contributions
Professor Bhai Parmanand	First Hindu missionary who visited South Africa in 1905 to provide central leadership to Hindus; established various Vedic institutions in the country
Swami Shankaranandji	Arrived in 1908; inspired the community to establish more cultural organizations and schools in the province; provided guidance and understanding of the significance of Hindu rituals and philosophy; established the South African Hindu Maha Sabha in 1912
Sir Srinivasa Sastri	Established the Hindu Tamil Institute as well as Sastri College in 1929
Bramha Sri Siva Guruswamigal	Established the Saiva Sithantha Sungum in 1937 and encouraged the community to form more South Indian organizations

Source: Adapted from Kathiawad Hindu Seva Samaj Souvenir Brochure, 1956; Surat Hindu Association Diamond Jubilee Brochure, 1975; South African Hindu Maha Sabha Centenary Brochure, 2012.

They preserved their religion and culture with very few amenities.[56] Many Hindu families practiced daily rituals at home as this was a tradition that was inherited from their Indian forebears. Community leaders noticed that there was a lack of central leadership and sent requests for Hindu missionaries to come from India to provide guidance and organizational foundation for Hindus in South Africa.[57] Some of the Hindu missionaries who made contributions to the country, and more specifically to the Grey Street Complex are presented in Table 9.8.

THE SUCCESS OF CULTURE IN GREY STREET

CULTURAL ORGANIZATIONS AND EDUCATIONAL INSTITUTIONS

The entire Indian community valued religion and cultural teachings to such an extent that they created the organizations displayed in Table 9.9. These organizations had subcommittees that engaged in various welfare, recreational and socio-religious projects which brought all elements of community life to the precinct. There was also a harmonization among all cultural bodies or groups despite their distinctive ideologies. These bodies did not only fulfil the religious and cultural needs of the Indian community, but helped to supply formal education which was a dire need during this time. Mr Ashwin Trikamjee, President of the South African Hindu Maha Sabha, recalls his experiences:

> The community ensured that cultural practices were sustained with great intensity. I remember when I started off in the South African Hindu Maha Sabha, we didn't even have decent offices or proper premises but we still continued.
> The community worked in harmony because we knew culture was important. If the Gujarati community built an institution, it was for everyone regardless of religion or linguistic group.[58]

The most significant role of most organizations was the raising of funds and providing personal donations to acquire fixed properties in the Grey Street Complex so that they could meet the demands of the growing population, especially for formal and vernacular education.[59]

Table 9.9 Cultural organizations in the Grey Street Complex

Religion	Organization	Year of establishment	Location
Islam	Juma Masjid Trust	1881	Corner of Grey and Queen streets
	West Street Mosque Trust	1885	478 West Street
	Madressa Anjuman Islam Trust	1889	101 Field Street
Christianity	Saint Aidan's Anglican Mission	1883	49 Cross Street
	Saint Anthony's Catholic Mission	1890	Corner of Centenary and Carlisle streets
	Emmanuel Cathedral	1902	48 Cathedral Street
	Bethesda Temple Society	1931	29 Carlisle Street
Hinduism	Surat Hindu Association	1907	127 Victoria Street
	South African Hindu Maha Sabha	1912	280 Grey Street
	Arya Prathindhi Sabha	1925	21 Carlisle Street
	Andhra Maha Sabha	1931	43 Leopold Street
	Saiva Sithantha Sungum	1937	37 Derby Street
	Shree Sanathan Dharma Sabha	1941	9a Crabbe Street
	Kathiawad Hindu Seva Samaj	1943	52 Lorne Street
	Natal Tamil Vedic Society	1951	Corner of Cross and Carlisle streets
	Gujarati Hindu Sanskruti Kendra	1992	5 Sydenham Road

Source: Adapted from Kathiawad Hindu Seva Samaj Souvenir Brochure, 1956; Surat Hindu Association Diamond Jubilee Brochure, 1975; Residential Development Memorandum of the Grey Street Area Indian Local Affairs Committee, 1979; Schedule of Community Facilities of the Central Durban Ratepayers Association, 1982; Gopalan (2012); Rosenberg (2012); Vahed (2010); Vahed (2013); Vahed and Waetjen (2015).

Vernacular language was one of the most important markers of cultural identity. Learning and speaking in the 'mother-tongue' was the closest link to their ancestral lineage, and therefore to their motherland, India. Integrated schooling not only gave a sense of identity to children but also inculcated a cultural grounding and traditional value system.

Ahmed Mahomad reminisces about the importance of education and religion:

> Our community progressed under very harsh conditions during the apartheid era. We had to build our institutions entirely on our own. In spite of this, we knew that we had to educate our children and preserve our traditions so that the legacy of our ancestors would live across generations. This was because our forefathers always taught us two things: that a place of worship was important to preserve our culture and that education was a very valuable component in our lives.[60]

Many of the schools established by the community were state-aided Indian (SAI) schools and predominantly vernacular.[61] It is important to be cognizant of the fact that in order to receive any financial aid from the government, the community had to adhere to certain criteria. More specifically, as pointed out by Govender and Naidoo, the community had to provide the following:[62]

1. School site (fully purchased and developed)
2. Classroom facilities and teachers
3. Principal's accommodation
4. Regular attendance with a viable student roll

Only when the government determined that these requirements were met, was financial aid provided. It is worth recording that the SAI schools listed in Table 9.10 supplied education to the entire community in the Grey Street Complex during the apartheid era as the government neglected them due to prejudice and discrimination.[63] Table 9.10 also indicates that the formal schools were state-owned and their administration managed by provincial authorities.[64] The platoon schooling system was implemented to accommodate large numbers of students and without it many generations of Indians would not have received an education.[65]

There were not many tertiary educational institutions in this precinct, as exhibited in Table 9.11. The Saint Aidan's Provincial Training College, established by Saint Aidan's Mission in 1904, provided an opportunity for students to obtain a teaching qualification.[66] Although the success of the college was short-lived with its closure in 1920, it did produce many qualified educators which alleviated the shortage of teachers in schools at the time, particularly in those for the descendants of indentured Indians.[67]

Table 9.10 Primary and secondary educational institutions (formal and vernacular) present in the Grey Street Complex during the apartheid era

School level	School type	Name
Primary	Special Category Secular	Orient Islamic SAI
	Vernacular	Juma Masjid SAI for girls
		Anjuman Islam SAI
		Surat Hindu SAI
		Hindu Tamil SAI
		Manilal Valjee SAI
	Formal	Dartnell Crescent Girls' State-owned
		Saint Anthony's Catholic
		Durban Girl's State-owned
Secondary	Special Category Secular	Orient Islamic SAI
	Vernacular	Gandhi–Desai SAI
	Formal	Durban Girl's State-owned
		Sastri College State-owned for boys
		Saint Anthony's Catholic

Source: Adapted from Residential Development Memorandum of the Grey Street Area Indian Local Affairs Committee, 1979; Schedule of Community Facilities of the Central Durban Ratepayers Association, 1982.

Table 9.11 Tertiary educational institutions

Name	Type
M. L. Sultan Technical College	Technical and commercial training
Saint Aidan's Provincial Training College	Teacher training

Source: Adapted from Residential Development Memorandum of the Grey Street Area Indian Local Affairs Committee, 1979; Schedule of Community Facilities of the Central Durban Ratepayers Association, 1982; St Aidan's Mission Centenary Brochure, 1983.

No analysis of education in the Grey Street Complex would be complete without mentioning Hajee Malukmahomed Lappa Sultan. His trust, the M. L. Sultan Charitable and Educational Trust, made its mark in educating the Indian community via schools in various districts and the establishment of the first Indian technical college that trained many.[68] A singular note of distinction is that the M. L. Sultan institutions were open to all regardless of creed, race and ethnicity.

CONCLUSION

This chapter has assessed the development of culture, particularly in terms of education and civil society organizations, in the Grey Street Complex in the apartheid era. The study has illustrated that the Grey Street Complex was vital to the Indian community and their broader life functions from the arrival of indentured and passenger Indians in Natal until the late twentieth century. The success of this precinct was attributed to the sacrifices made by the Grey Street community, which demonstrated their innate ability and determination to live a successful life through the establishment of cultural organizations and community-built institutions under the harsh realities of the apartheid system. Through such endeavours, they maintained their cultural identities while still providing the essential components of a community life for their future generations.

Evidently, the community bears a mnemonic attachment to the Grey Street Complex through the role of culture in its various forms. In particular, religion and education were fundamental components to community life in this precinct, and great sacrifices were made to establish such institutions as an essential part of the value system for these residents. It is also evident that there was cultural connectivity in the community and harmony among all religious groups. Each of these organizations and institutions independently reinforced cultural identity and contributed to the personal and cultural profile of former and current residents. Thus, the memory and nostalgia of culture has played a significant role in historically connecting both former and current residents to this precinct.

NOTES

1. See Ahmad et al. (2014, 1).
2. Lewicka (2008, 212).
3. Hebbert (2005, 583).

4. Hebbert (2005); Lewicka (2008).

5. Maharaj (1999, 249).

6. Davis and Rajah (1965); Simon (1989, 193).

7. Hart and Padayachee (2000); Hiralal (2007); Stiebel (2010, 3).

8. The Groups Areas Act (1950) was enforced to divide South Africa's land according to race groups. This legislation emanated from a colonial history of European and British imperialism – which was inherited and schematized by Afrikaner nationalists for their apartheid doctrine to promote racial segregation.

9. Rajah (1981).

10. Stiebel (2010, 1).

11. Stiebel (2010).

12. Mamet (2007, 73).

13. Mamet (2007).

14. Simon (1989, 191).

15. Rajah (1981); Simon (1989, 191); Hiralal (2007, 103).

16. Simon (1989, 194); Maharaj (1997, 263).

17. Rajah (1981); Simon (1989); Rosenberg (2012, 11).

18. Rajah (1981); Jithoo (1985); Simon (1989).

19. Rajah (1981).

20. Hancock (2002).

21. Hancock (2002); Fox, Hunn and Mathers (2002, 3).

22. Yin (2011, 31).

23. Garson (2012, 9).

24. Garson (2012).

25. Garson (2012).

26. Rajah (1981); Padayachee (1988, 1); Vahed (1999, 19).

27. Rajah (1981).

28. Rajah (1981).

29. Rajah (1981); Padayachee (1988, 1); Vahed (1999, 19).

30. Rajah (1981).

31. Rajah (1981); Singh (1960).

32. For the variety of employment, see Singh (1960); Rajah (1981); Padayachee (1988, 1–3).

33. Rajah (1981); Padayachee (1988).

34. Brookes and Webb (1965).

35. Rajah (1981); Chetty and Omar (1983, 4–6).

36. Rajah (1981); Jithoo (1985, 365).
37. Rajah (1981); Chetty and Omar (1983, 6); Jithoo (1985).
38. Rajah (1981).
39. Chetty and Omar (1983, 6).
40. Rajah (1981).
41. Rajah (1981); Chetty and Omar (1983); Jithoo (1985, 366).
42. Rajah (1981).
43. Rajah (1981); Jithoo (1985, 365); Vahed (1999, 20).
44. Chetty and Omar (1983, 5).
45. Memorandum to Group Areas Board, Central Durban Property Protection Committee, 1961; Chetty and Omar (1983).
46. Interview, 30 November 2016.
47. Interview, 19 May 2016.
48. Interview with Mr Ahmed Mahomad, 19 May 2016.
49. Interview with Mr Ahmed Mahomad, 19 May 2016.
50. Henning (1993); Govender and Naidoo (2010).
51. Vahed and Waetjen (2015).
52. Sema (1985, 3–5).
53. Sema (1985, 3–5).
54. Vahed and Waetjen (2015).
55. Vahed and Waetjen (2015); Sema (1985, 8).
56. Desai and Vahed (2012). For a comprehensive understanding of the rise of organized Hinduism in Durban, see Gopalan (2010).
57. Gopalan (2012).
58. Interview, 4 May 2016.
59. Interview, 4 May 2016.
60. Interview, 19 May 2016.
61. Memorandum of the Central Durban Indian Area Protection Committee, 1969.
62. Govender and Naidoo (2010).
63. Memorandum of the Central Durban Indian Area Protection Committee, 1969.
64. Residential Development Memorandum of the Grey Street Area Indian Local Affairs Committee, 1979.
65. Interview with Karsandas Manjee, 5 March 2016.
66. St Aidan's Mission Centenary Brochure, 1983.
67. St Aidan's Mission Centenary Brochure, 1983.
68. Interview with Growfin Property Group, 22 April 2016.

BIBLIOGRAPHY

Ahmad, N., M. Dadras, B. Pradhan, S. Safapour and H. Z. M. Sharfri. 2014. 'Land Use/Cover Change Detection and Urban Sprawl Analysis in Badar Abbas City, Iran'. *Scientific World Journal* 1: 1–12.

'Brochure of the 50th Maha Samadhi of the Saiva Sithantha Sungum'. 2003. Bramha Sri Siva Subramonia, Founder and Ecclesiastical Head of the Saiva Sithantha Sungum.

Brookes, E. H., and C. B. Webb. 1965. *A History of Natal*. Pietermaritzburg: University of Natal Press.

Central Durban Indian Area Protection Committee. 1969. 'Memorandum Presented to the Group Areas Board at an Enquiry Commencing on 21 May, into a Proposal to Proclaim the Grey Street Complex for the Members of the White and/or Indian Group.'

Central Durban Indian Ratepayers Association. 1982. 'Schedule of Community Facilities of the Group Areas Investigation: Proclamation 106 of 1973 in terms of Section 19(i) – Grey Street Area'.

Central Durban Property Protection Committee. 1961. 'Memorandum Presented to the Group Areas Board Which Sat at Durban on the 13th and 14th November, to Enquire into the Proposal to Proclaim the Durban Central City for the Members of the White/Indian Group'.

Chetty, T. D., and S. M. Omar.1983. 'Grey Street Area: A Survey of a Community'. Institute for Social and Economic Research, University of Durban-Westville, Durban.

'Commemorative Brochure of the Shree Gujarati Hindu Sanskruti Kendra. 2001. 'The Official Opening of the Ekta Mandir and Sanskruti Kendra'.

Davies, R. J., and D. S. Rajah. 1965. 'The Durban CBD: Boundary Delimitation and Racial Dualism'. *South African Geographical Journal* 47 (1): 45–58.

Desai, A., and G. Vahed. 2012. 'Indenture and the Origins of Hinduism in Natal'. *The Hindu: Centenary Edition of the South African Hindu Maha Sabha.*

Emmanuel Cathedral Historical Guide. 2016. 'A Publication of the Emmanuel Cathedral Parish, Durban'.

Fox, N., A. Hunn and N. Mathers. 2002. *Research and Development in Primary Health Care: Using Interviews in a Research Project.* Leicester: Trent Focus Group.

Garson, G. D. 2012. *Sampling.* Asheboro: Statistical Associates Publishing.

Gopalan, K. 2010. 'Caste, Class and Community: The Role of the South African Hindu Maha Sabha in (Re)Making Hinduism in South Africa 1912–1960'. MA thesis, University of KwaZulu-Natal, Durban.

———. 2012. 'A Brief History of the South African Hindu Maha Sabha'. *The Hindu: Centenary Edition of the South African Hindu Maha Sabha*, 6–31.

Govender, B. G., and T. P. Naidoo. 2010. *The Settler: Tribulations, Trials, Triumph*. Durban: Barlow Govender Foundation.

Grey Street Area Indian Local Affairs Committee. 1979. 'Residential Development Memorandum to the Honourable Minister of Community Development on the Question of Removal of the Restriction on Residential Development in the Grey Street Complex'. 1–8.

Hancock, B. 2002. *Trent Focus for Research and Development in Primary Health Care: An Introduction to Qualitative Research*. Nottingham: Trent Focus Group.

Hart, K., and V. Padayachee. 2000. 'Indian Business in South Africa after Apartheid: New and Old Trajectories'. *Comparative Studies in Society and History* 42 (4): 683–712.

Hebbert, M. 2005. 'The Street as Locus of Collective Memory'. *Environment and Planning D: Society and Space* 23: 581–596.

Henning, C. G. 1993. *The Indentured Indian in Natal, 1860–1917*. New Delhi: Promila and Co. Publishers.

Hiralal, K. 2007. 'Indian Family Businesses in South Africa: 1870–2004'. *Anthropologist Special Issue* 2: 99–108.

Jithoo, S. 1985. 'Indian Family Businesses in Durban, South Africa'. *Journal of Comparative Family Studies* 16(3): 365–376.

Kathiawad Hindu Seva Samaj Souvenir Brochure. 1956. 'Commemoration of the Laying of the Foundation Stone of the Educational Institutions at Curries Fountain by His Honour, the Administrator of Natal, Mr. D. G Shepstone'.

Lewicka, M. 2008. 'Place Attachment, Place Identity, and Place Memory: Restoring the Forgotten City Past'. *Journal of Environmental Psychology* 28: 209–231.

Maharaj, B. 1997. 'Apartheid, Urban Segregation and the Local State: Durban and the Group Areas Act in South Africa'. *Urban Geography* 18: 135–154.

———. 1999. 'The Integrated Community Apartheid Could Not Destroy: The Warwick Avenue Triangle in Durban'. *Journal of Southern African Studies* 25 (2): 249–266.

Mamet, C. 2007. 'Fictional Constructions of Grey Street by Selected South African Indian Writers'. MA thesis, University of KwaZulu-Natal, Durban.

Padayachee, S. G. 1988. 'The Victoria Street Indian Market: 1910–1973'. Dissertation (Hons. B.A), University of Durban-Westville, Durban.

Rajah, D. S. 1981. 'The Durban Indian Central Business District: A Case Study in the Geography of Apartheid'. Unpublished PhD Thesis, University of Natal, Durban.

Rosenberg, L. G. 2012. 'A City within a City: Vestiges of the Socio-Spatial Imprint of Colonial and Apartheid Durban, from the 1870s to 1980s'. M. Soc. Sci dissertation, University of KwaZulu-Natal, Durban.

Croft, L. T., R. J. Davies, G. G. Maasdorp, P. N. Pillay, L. Schlemmer, G. L. Trotter and H. L. Watts. 1971. 'Group Areas and the Grey Street Complex, Durban'. Centre for Applied Social Science, University of Natal.

Sema, O.A.R. 1985. 'A Detailed History of the Juma Mosque from 1881 Onwards, and Its Progression to the Largest Mosque in the Southern Hemisphere'. A local history project of the Juma Mosque presented to the Department of History, University of Durban-Westville.

Simon, D. 1989. 'Crisis and Change in South Africa: Implications for the Apartheid City'. *Transactions of the Institute of British Geographers* 14 (2): 189–206.

Singh, S. S. 1960. 'The Pioneers on the Truro and the Belvedere'. In *The Hindu Heritage in South Africa*, edited by S. Chotai, B. D. Lalla and R. Nowbath, 1–10. Durban: South African Hindu Maha Sabha.

South African Hindu Maha Sabha Centenary Brochure. 2012. *The Hindu: Centenary Edition of the South African Hindu Maha Sabha, Durban*, 1–30.

St Aidan's Mission Centenary Brochure. 1983. 'A Publication of St Aidan's Mission, Durban'.

Stiebel, L. 2010. 'Last Stop "Little Gujarat": Tracking South African Indian Writers on the Grey Street Writers' Trail in Durban'. *Current Writing: Text and Reception in Southern Africa* 22 (1): 1–20.

Surat Hindu Association Diamond Jubilee Brochure. 1975. 'Celebrating the Surat Hindu Association: 1907–1975'.

The Durban Road Map and Durban Street View. 2016. https://www.maps-streetview.com/South-Africa/Durban/roadmap.php. Accessed 14 May 2016.

Vahed, G. 1999. 'Control and Repression: The Plight of Indian Hawkers and Flower Sellers in Durban, 1910–1948'. *International Journal of African Historical Studies* 32 (1): 19–48.

Vahed, G. 2010. 'An "Imagined Community" in Diaspora: Gujaratis in South Africa'. *South Asian History and Culture* 1 (4): 615–629.

————. 2013. 'Religion'. In *The Making of Place, the Warwick Junction Precinct: 1870s – 1980s*, edited by A. Hassim, S. Moodley, L. Rosenberg, K. Singh and G. Vahed. Durban: Durban University of Technology.

Vahed, G., and T. Waetjen. 2015. *Schooling Muslims in Natal: Identity, State and the Orient Islamic Educational Institute*. Scottsville: University of KwaZulu-Natal Press.

Yin, R. K. 2011. *Qualitative Research from Start to Finish*. London: Guilford Press.

10

ROOTING HISTORY

INDIAN INDENTURE IN SOUTH AFRICA AND THE SULTAN OF MANY JOURNEYS

Goolam Vahed and Ashwin Desai

The death of Hajee M. L. Sultan removes from the Indian scene one of its most colourful personalities. His story is in the best American tradition of the poor American boy 'who made good'. Farm hand, waiter, farmer, porter, small businessman, big businessman, he passed through all the phases of poverty and wealth, at one time losing all he had in a tobacco business, at another time risking more than he had in a commercial venture. Written up, the story would appeal to thousands as on a par with stories of the merchant princes of the Western world; rich in interest and a spur to everyone.... The story is touched too with the same human magnanimity that has brought a final lustre to the great names of the capitalist world.... Who knows but that in time to come another small boy provided with the advantages existing only as a result of Hajee M. L. Sultan's beneficence will not rise from poverty to wealth; and what is more important, from ignorance to knowledge; and become in the field of political leadership or literature or science or industry a great statesman leading the whole Indian community to new levels of attainment. For who can tell where the influence [of] a benefaction begins or of magnanimity ends. There is something more. A curious inspiration invests the memory of such a man as the late Hajee M. L. Sultan. It is the inspiration to emulate his example of munificence.

—*The Graphic*, 19 September 1953

The contribution of the Indian indentured of South Africa to the colonial economy was massive. Despite undertaking back-breaking work, from labouring on sugar plantations to building railways, most of the just over 150,000 migrants chose to stay in South Africa rather than return to India. Their impact was incredible, yet their histories were largely invisible in the public domain and continue to be marginalized. The promise of a memorial for the indentured made by the government in 2010, as Indians commemorated the 150th year of the arrival of the first indentured Indians in South Africa, failed to materialize even a decade later as the 160th anniversary was being marked. There is one indentured migrant, however, Sultan Pillai Kannu, whose name was emblazoned on a technical training college, and in post-apartheid South Africa, a street bears his name. However, his epitaph in *The Graphic* newspaper, a weekly paper owned by an Indian and aimed at the Indian community, interestingly chose not to use the word 'indenture'. His roots both in South Africa and India are erased and his life likened to that of a poor American boy who made good. But the signature of Sultan's life remains the fact that he arrived here in what the historian Hugh Tinker[1] called a 'new form of slavery'.

In researching Sultan's biography, we seek to confront both the *flattening out* of the indenture experience and its *writing out*. While the indentured were faced with similar working conditions, it is important not to paint them as victims of history. As the story of Sultan shows, they were also agents, making history as they contended with and manoeuvred around the strictures of a racist colonial economy. The French philosopher Jean-Paul Sartre once explained that the French intellectual Paul Valéry was petit-bourgeois, but not every petit-bourgeois was Valéry, encouraging us to try and understand how individuals who might share similar experiences can strike out in different ways. As Sartre elaborates in defence of biographical analysis:

> ... a man is never an individual; it would be more fitting to call him a singular universal; having been totalized and therefore universalized, by his epoch, he retotalizes his epoch by reproducing himself into it as a singularity. He is thus at once universal by way of the singular universality of human history, and singular through the universalizing singularity of his projects – he requires to be studied from both perspectives simultaneously.[2]

While Tinker's *A New System of Slavery* resonated with many left-leaning academics and activists in the context of the Vietnam War, the civil rights struggle in the United States and anti-apartheid activism in South Africa, the field of indentured studies has evolved too. More recent historians like the Fijian Brij V. Lal have argued that 'generalizations tended to be descriptive rather than explanatory' and he turned to biographies to provide a sense of how the indentured negotiated a system barely one step removed from slavery. From numbers, he was now turning the indentured into people with ambitions, cultures and agency even while accepting that the structural nature of indentured industrial agriculture was essentially unfree. Yet it was also a system that some migrants used to escape restrictions in Indian society or to assume positions of power (such as *sirdar*s or sub-overseers) within prevailing power mechanisms.[3]

Kumar has augmented this perspective and pushed the arguments further by making the case that many individuals made the choice to emigrate and that they often had ambitions, hopes and desires that they aspired to achieve through emigration.[4] Bahadur has written an excellent work on women's agency.[5] In a similar vein, we hope through the life of M. L. Sultan to help provide a more nuanced account of indenture.

Sultan was born on 15 February 1873, in Quilon (Kollam), Malabar District, Kerala, South India. He arrived in Durban in 1890 on the *Congella* at the age of 17, as part of the great movement of Indian labour to the sugar producing colonies in the nineteenth century. He died more than six decades later as Hajee Mulukmahomed Lappa Sultan on the evening of Sunday, 6 September 1953 at his residence at 80 St Augustine Road, Escombe, at the age of 80.[6] Thousands attended his burial at the Brook Street Muslim Cemetery in Durban the following morning.

For many years, both of us walked past the technical college that bore his name, on our way to school. It never struck us to ask: Who was Sultan? Where did he come from? How did a huge building come to bear his name? Given the nature of apartheid's history books, Sultan made no appearance in the section covering Indians, which most often bore the heading 'The South African Indian Problem'. In researching the story of Sultan, we were startled when we found that his family had struggled to retain his name on the institution and had engaged in a dogged attempt to find their roots in India and connect with family.

ROOTS

The Sultan family's drive to find their roots in South India is part of a wider and deeper interest among Indian South Africans in their Indian lineages. Narratives of descendants of Indian South Africans tracing their families are published regularly in newspapers,[7] usually in November when the arrival of the indentured is annually commemorated. This interest in roots took off from around 2010, when the 150th year of the arrival of the indentured was commemorated, and newspapers encouraged members of the public to submit family histories for publication. Since then, interest in family history has undergone an unprecedented boom, fuelled by knowledge of the material available in the archives and the greater contact between distant family members facilitated by social media and the telecommunications revolution.[8]

This urge to reconstruct family history has been explained in various ways. According to Ann-Marie Kramer, genealogy

> allows people to personalize the past. Genealogists have told me: 'I hated history at school. It was just a series of dates with no connection to my life.' But then they've discovered that their great uncle won a medal during the First World War, and the place where he fought immediately becomes more than just another battlefield.[9]

Robert Taylor has suggested that in a context of 'rapid socio-cultural change' where the 'social change appears to be getting out of hand', family is usually 'the most natural fount of sustenance.... The comforts of home become a palliative to social control.' While members of families reach 'inwards' they also 'reach out to living kindred, and reach back in time to recover ancestral heritages'.[10] Katherine Ellis writes that in a context of worsening conditions in late nineteenth-century America, 'the pursuit of stability, domesticity, and the sure knowledge of one's parentage became an integral part of middle class culture'.[11]

In the case of diasporic Indians, there is a practical reason for genealogical searches, in that they may wish to apply for the overseas citizen of India (OCI) card. Indians overseas can be classified into two broad categories: non-resident Indians (NRIs), who are Indian citizens living in other countries, and persons of Indian origin (PIOs)/overseas citizens of India (OCIs), who are Indians in the diaspora who are formally connected to India. The Hindu nationalist

Bharatiya Janata Party (BJP) created the PIO card in 1999, aiming to garner diasporic financial and political support. The OCI card was introduced in 2015, with some changes from the PIO card, which it eventually replaced. The OCI cards are the only valid documents. Descendants of indentured migrants take up this option for reasons ranging from ease of travel to a desire to invest in India, but rarely return to live permanently there.[12]

While many stories have been published in newspapers, others have put out their histories in the form of brochures and booklets. Tholsi Mudly's *A Tribute to Our Forefathers* (2011) marked a five-year search in which she outlined the journey of her paternal grandparents, Iyemperumal and Solai Pachai of Salem, Tamil Nadu, and maternal grandparents Chinnien and Nallamma Padachi, and maternal great-grandfather Madurai Padachi, also of Salem, who arrived on the *Congella XXVI* on 28 March 1898. Mudly traced their stories and grave sites, and the family annually pays homage to their ancestors. Another excellent and detailed family history is Mansingh Narrandes's *They Came from the East: The Narrandes Family* (2010). Some of these genealogical reconstructions are a means to hold family reunions. As Taylor points out, family reunions are usually 'marked by the glorifying of family histories, the filial pietistic inventories of family virtues, the exhortations to maintain interfamily affections and loyalties, the socializing and recreating, centered on inspiring kin unity'.[13]

In other instances, family members have traced their ancestors and made the journey to India, despite in some cases being uncertain as to where their ancestors originated, and the journey has ended in vain. Chartered accountant Kanthan Pillay of Reservoir Hills visited his ancestral village of Salem in Tamil Nadu when they discovered that his grandfather Mutha had left his wife and only child in India to travel to Natal in 1904. Here he married a second wife Mariamma and started a new family. Pillay did not find his family in India.[14] School principal Jay Naidoo related how he traced his roots back to the village of Godyattam in Tamil Naidu. When he visited in 2007 and asked for the 'Chetty family', he learned that all 500 families in the village had the name Chetty, which was a caste designation.[15]

Raj Govender, a high-ranking official in the department of arts and culture, traced his maternal grandparents, Tiruvengada and Valliammal Pillay, to Siruvallur, a village in Polur in the North Arcot district of Tamil Nadu. They arrived in South Africa in 1908 on board the *Umfuli X* and were assigned to the Cecil Prospect Sugar Estate in Isipingo, south of Durban. Govender and his wife Nirmala went to Chennai and drove the 140 kilometres to their village by taxi through many towns and villages 'with mostly single-lane roads where we had to stop a number of times to let cows and goats slowly pass'. A local councillor accompanied them to Siruvallur where Govender spoke to village seniors. He showed them photographs of his grandparents and was directed to likely 'family' members whom he met in an arranged meeting at the village temple.[16]

SULTAN PILLAI KANNU

Variously described as a porter, waiter, farmer, businessman and philanthropist, Sultan Pillai Kannu Madukannu Mahomed, indentured number 43374, was born in Travencore, south India, in 1873, and was compelled by the early death of his father to leave school at the age of 14. Finding his earnings insufficient, he decided to emigrate to Ceylon (present-day Sri Lanka). According to family legend, the ship's engine broke down during the voyage leaving him stranded in Triticurin, Tamil Nadu, with no funds. The ship repairs dragged on and when he was approached by recruiting agents, he agreed to indenture in the then British colony of Natal. On his arrival in Durban in 1890, he was assigned to the Natal Government Railways (NGR) and worked as a porter at the Berea Road Railway Station.

While indentured migrants are usually associated with the sugar industry, only 60 per cent were employed in sugar; others were employed by the Durban and Pietermaritzburg municipalities, the NGR and tea industry, and those with special skills worked in hospitals, hotels, private clubs and dockyards. Sultan was allocated to the NGR whose total allocation of just over 8,000 Indians made it the largest single employer of indentured labour. Indians were instrumental in the successful extension of Natal's railway network as gatekeepers, signalmen, and platelayers, or they collected tickets, copied letters and addressed envelopes in the office.[17]

It was during Sultan's time as an indentured migrant that the Colony of Natal underwent important political changes. By 1892, the number of Indians in the colony equalled that of whites, and white hostility towards Indians saw decisive action being taken when the colony was granted self-government in 1893. Britain wanted to end its financial commitment in the region, and approved a constitution that did not have protections for Africans and Indians. The new white government in Natal saw things like town planning, trade and politics in terms of racial distinctions. Whites felt besieged by an

'Asiatic Menace'[18] and the government passed legislation that would force Indians to reindenture or return to India upon completing their indenture and to legally subordinate non-indentured Indians in Natal. Laws were passed to restrict franchise, trade, residence, land ownership and entry into Natal which rendered Indians second-class citizens.[19] This was not confined to Natal but was evident across the empire in places like Australia, Canada and New Zealand during this period, when whiteness came to prevail in a context of empire.[20]

After completing his term of indenture in 1895, Sultan joined the gold rush to the Transvaal, where he worked as a waiter in several well-known city hotels. In the 1880s, what is now South Africa was made up of four separate territories. The two coastal provinces, the Cape Colony and Natal, were British colonies but inland, the agricultural Orange Free State and Transvaal Republic were under Afrikaner control. The discovery of gold transformed the Transvaal economy and brought thousands of European migrants as well as Indians from Natal and abroad. To a much greater degree than Natal, the Transvaal imposed severe anti-Indian legislation, denying them the franchise, attempting to segregate them in locations and forcing them to trade in areas reserved for Asians. The economic prospects of the Transvaal eventually led to war between Britain and the Transvaal that lasted from 1899 to 1902 and brought the Transvaal under British control.[21]

Sultan returned to Durban in 1899 as part of the stream of Indians who were forced out of the Transvaal at the outbreak of the Anglo-Boer War. The Anglo-Boer War has been renamed the South African War because of the acknowledgement of the involvement of blacks (Africans, Indians and Coloureds) in the war in terms of both fighting and suffering. Whites were initially reluctant to use blacks. An editorial in the Durban-based *Natal Mercury* noted that there was 'a natural disinclination to use Coloured soldiers to fight the Boers'.[22] This was so because 'we live in a country thickly populated by races still to a large extent steeped in barbarism'. Without a strong white race, there would be 'pandemonium' and 'chaos'. The war had to remain a 'White Man's war' so that the victorious British could impose their own brand of civilized order. Sultan was one of the many Indians forced to flee the fighting in the Transvaal.

Once the British had established order, Indian refugees wanted to return to their homes and businesses, but the British refused to allow them back. An Indian refugee committee was formed and after much agitation, in March 1901 they were given two permits, meaning that just two of the thousands of refugees could return to their homes. The committee wrote to Sir M. Bhownaggree, the Indian member of parliament (MP) in England, for assistance.[23] However, it was only from September 1902 that the permit office began issuing permits and by the end of 1902, 4,371 permits had been granted to Indians.[24] Many others were denied permits if they did not have the proper paperwork.

It is not certain why Sultan did not return to the Transvaal. In any case, as typified his way, he was already settling into his new life. According to family legend, Sultan's 'natural courtesy and willingness to render dignified service made him a popular figure' and many gratuities had come his way during his years as a waiter. He was prudent with his money and shortly after returning to Natal, he took up farming near Bellair. Farming and market gardening were common to large numbers of Indians who, after completing their indentures, began to grow fruit and vegetables for the local market on land rented from absentee landlords and land companies. According to the Wragg Commission of 1886–1888, 'Indians do remarkably well as cultivators of small parcels of land rented on short leases. Those settled in the vicinity of Durban have succeeded in winning for themselves, almost entirely, the supplying of the local markets with vegetables'.[25] The success of Indian farmers heightened white hostility towards Indians.

Sultan later took up banana farming at Escombe, south of Durban, where he spent the major portion of his life. There were around 14,000 Indians living in this area by the 1950s, specializing in banana farming. This area was lost to the Group Areas under the apartheid government, when it was developed as the township of Chatsworth for Indians. The Group Areas Act destroyed this vibrant rural community.[26] In addition to farming bananas, Sultan also tried tobacco cultivation. He had initial success only to suffer disappointment and losses. He also partnered a specialist in Vedic medicine in Grey Street, Durban, bringing spiritual and physical comfort to the many sick who patronized this business. Realizing the advantages of commercial endeavour, he opened a wholesale and retail business at 106 Victoria Street, Durban, known as M.L. Sultan & Sons (Pty) Ltd, whilst at the same time growing betel leaf at Stamford Hill. He made shrewd investments in property which formed the basis of his wealth.

Sultan married Mariam Bee, the granddaughter of an indentured migrant, Sayed Cassim Mothoo Saib, in 1905 and the couple had 10 children, four sons and six daughters, (in order of birth) Ameena Bee, Fathima, Abdul Hamid, Mariam, Ayesha, Abdool Razack, Kathija, Mohamed Ebrahim, Allimah and Aboobaker.

RELIGION AND CULTURE

Approximately 10 per cent of migrants indentured to Natal were Muslims. Two-thirds of those who migrated to Natal were from South India and arrived via Madras. In the case of Muslims this figure was 45 per cent, with 55 per cent coming from the north via Calcutta. The main recruitment areas in the south were Arcot, Malabar (now in Kerala, from whence Sultan came), Madras and Mysore.[27] Indentured Muslims were culturally, linguistically and ethnically diverse. While around half listed 'Muslim', 'Musalman', 'Mahomed' and 'Mahomedan' as their caste; other prominent castes were Fakhir, Hajam, Julaha, Labbai, Mappila, Rawther, Pathan, Sayyid and Shaikh. Migrants from the south consisted mainly of the Mappilas and Labbais, with Muslims from Kerala being mostly Mappilas, who, Kunju points out, emerged out of an Indo-Arabian community formed through marriage relations between the local women and Arab sailors and merchants.[28]

The 1901 Madras census described the Labbai, who were distributed throughout Arcot, as 'part-Arab, part-Tamil Muslims' who are mainly traders and betel-vine growers in south Arcot. Mappila was a Tamil mispronunciation of the Arabic *mu'abbar*, which means 'from over the water', and it was generally accepted that they were descendants of Arab traders and Dravidian women. They were traditionally involved in trade, agriculture and service.[29]

South Indian Muslims spoke Tamil, Telegu, Kannada or Malayalam, which is the language of the state of Kerala and which Sultan spoke. Both Tamil and Malayalam are languages of the Dravidian family, with Malayalam emerging as a distinct language centuries after Tamil. They are similar in many ways, with the main difference being in their syntax and semantics, and the fact that Malayalam borrows more heavily from Sanskrit. However, the languages have a great resemblance in their scripts and sentence formation. Sultan was an outstanding orator in the Malayalam and Tamil languages. Kesaveloo Goonam, the first female Indian doctor in Durban, following her qualification at Edinburgh University in the early 1930s, described her childhood experience of Sultan:

[T]he person I took great fancy to was Uncle Sultan who paid me a great deal of attention at a time of my life when I felt awkward, overlooked and ignored. My eldest sister won all the prizes at school and my younger sister was the pretty one. Nothing distinguished me. Uncle

Sultan doted on me. I thought he had the kindest of faces. He spoke in the pure Tamil of South India. Every time he called at our home he ignored my brothers and sisters and looked for me. He would put me on his knee. I had the feeling that Uncle Sultan alone understood what was going on in my mind. Sirkari Naidoo persuaded Uncle Sultan to establish technical education for blacks. The inscription at ML Sultan College is: 'Enter to grow in wisdom. Depart to serve better thy kind and thy country.'[30]

In his study on Tamil culture in South Africa, C. Kuppusami has a section on those who played a key role in 'nurturing and promoting the Tamil language in South Africa'. M. L. Sultan is amongst the persons acknowledged. Kuppusami writes:

M. L. Sultan was a lover of the Tamil language, having had a deep knowledge of Tamil literature and of the customs and practices of the Tamils. He was also well spoken and had a strong personality. As an indentured labourer, working as a porter, he found time to teach Tamil to all of his Tamil-speaking co-workers. He was a devoted Muslim who did his daily customary prayers. His associates, however, were mostly Tamils who professed the Hindu faith. He frequently addressed Tamil groups in the vernacular. He also chaired meetings of the Tamil organisations. He encouraged his Tamil adult friends and others to learn the mother tongue to advance their knowledge of Tamil and even advised them on the kind of Tamil books to read. He is said to have carried the well known text book in Tamil, the *Kurral* with him to quote lines from it on appropriate occasions. He had a fair knowledge of astrology and was able to read and interpret the Tamil almanac and advise his friends on auspicious dates and times for the performance of religious ceremonies. He attended numerous Tamil weddings at some of which he would give a congratulatory address in Tamil. He would often be seen in the company of small groups of intellectuals. Educated Tamils enjoyed his company because of the merit of his discussions and the impeccable Tamil in which they were expressed.[31]

Sultan was widely recognized for broadening his spiritual life while not neglecting the practical aspects of business. He was a deeply religious person with great insight into the writings of Muslim and Hindu philosophers, and was also able to read the latter in Sanskrit. It is said that he was familiar with *Saiva Sithantha* philosophy.[32] He would say 'El Wa'd Din' – 'A promise made is an obligation' – and never went back on his word. Despite his wealth, he was known to travel from Escombe to Durban, a distance of 12 miles, by train and once even walked the distance to keep an appointment.[33] I. C. Meer wrote that Sultan

> wore a red fez and the traditional Muslim tailored long coat. He had a car, locked up in his garage, but he used the train on his daily forays into town. M. I. (Meer) met him on one of those train journeys ... Sultan would invariably be reading something in the Tamil script ...[34]

Sultan felt the nostalgic call of the country of his boyhood and did visit India in search of his family and friends but, to his disappointment, most of those he had been close to had died, and he returned to Durban after spending 6 months in his own village. Sultan also went on the pilgrimage to Mecca.

DEATH

Early in 1953, Sultan suffered a stroke. He recovered after being bedridden for some weeks only to have a second stroke a few months later. Prayers were held in mosques, schools and other public institutions for his full recovery, but he passed away on 6 September 1953. Around 4,000 people attended his funeral service the next morning and he was buried at the Brook Street Cemetery, Durban. When a memorial service was held to publicly honour M. L. Sultan and his philanthropic contributions, the Avalon Theatre was filled to capacity. Many tributes were paid to his outstanding qualities and speakers at the service included H. Nattrass, first principal of the M. L. Sultan Technical College; B. M. Narbeth, chairman of council, M. L. Sultan Technical Collage; Alan Taylor, representing the minister of education; A. S. Kajee of the Natal Indian Organisation (NIO); P. R. Pather and A. M. Moolla of the South African Indian Organisation (SAIO); and S. Rustomjee and Ashwin Chodhree of the Natal Indian Congress (NIC).

Jalbhoy Rustomjee, a close friend of M. L. Sultan, emphasized that Sultan's charity knew no bounds of caste, creed or religion. He captured

the sentiments of many when he said that their one regret was that
M. L. Sultan had passed on 'before he saw the fruits of his labour'. He put
it thus:

> It would seem as if he was led to the heights but passed on before the
> beauty of the City broke open to his view, for when he left behind
> those handsome sums of money for Technical Education and other
> charities, I feel sure that all sections of the Indian community would
> have rejoiced with him – had he only been spared to see his many gifts
> of money built in Colleges and Institutions, though it will go down to
> his revered memory that thousands of scholars have already benefited
> and thousands more will benefit in future by his generous gifts. He was
> a man of singular character. He always preferred the Lovely Road, and
> being blessed with a character sincere and honest, he persevered in life
> amid many changing scenes and conditions, and to one who labours
> in that way success is bound to follow. One feature of his charity I
> commend to my countrymen, that is, that his charity knew no bounds
> of caste or creed or religion. The late M. L. Sultan was a man of singular
> character, sincere and honest, who persevered in life among amid many
> changes in scenes.[35]

Ashwin Choudree, vice-president of the NIC, paid the following
compliment:

> Such men are rare in human history. Such gems are Heaven's own gift
> to mankind. His destiny fulfilled, His life's labour done, Sultan Sahib
> has gone to the land of immortals, and we in this world will always find
> him enshrined in our hearts.[36]

Nattrass, in his tribute to Sultan, remarked that M. L. Sultan 'loved Natal
and will be missed by many, particularly the poor. His vision remains with us
to grow through the years. He gave thought for all the Indians throughout
South Africa and hoped that all would share in the benefits he helped to
establish'.[37] An editorial in *The Daily News* opined that Sultan's 'example was
that of a noble spirit prepared to put his shoulder to the wheel. Mr. Sultan set
an example in public spiritedness not only to the Indian community, but to
the whole of South Africa'.[38]

PHILANTHROPY

After the early death of his wife Mariam Bee in 1933, Sultan channelled his energy into philanthropy. The main financial contribution of M. L. Sultan was to the building of the M. L. Sultan Technical College on Centenary Road, Durban. Sultan had a great passion for education as a means of upliftment and was instrumental in the establishment of the *technikon*. The struggle for technical education assumed urgency after the Cape Town Agreement of 1926–1927 and its upliftment clause which specified that Indians should not 'lag behind other sections of the population'; and the South African government promised to 'uplift' Indians who remained in South Africa rather than accept the cash to return to India. Moderate Indian leaders like A. I. Kajee and P. R. Pather realized that Indian workers had to be educated to compete in an industrializing economy. The Natal Workers' Congress and the Indian Teachers Society initiated workers' continuation classes in August 1929. In June 1930, the Indian Technical Education Committee was formed with B. M. Narbeth as chairman. It provided part-time evening classes in commercial and technical subjects at Sastri College, which continued until 1956. There was no government help and the committee functioned with generous public contributions and free tuition from teachers.[39]

In 1934, B. M. Narbeth complained to the town clerk that 'the premises in which these classes are held … are a ramshackle building in a more or less dilapidated condition'.[40] Although the Medical Office of Health (MOH) concurred with this assessment after his investigation, reporting that 'the structural condition is substantially as described by Narbeth. The Hall is not suitable for educational purposes', no provision was made. The situation was critical, and the committee discussed the position with the Indian Agent General, Sir Syed Raza Ali. They met with the mayor of Durban in May 1938 and the finance committee in July 1938, but despite correspondence with the city council from 1939 to 1941, all pleas fell on deaf ears. The first development towards a permanent structure occurred in 1942 when M. L. Sultan donated 17,500 pounds (subsequently increased to 33,000 pounds) towards such an institution, which was half the cost of the proposed building. While the eventual cost was much higher, the initial contribution gave the proposal a fillip and embarrassed the government into committing to the scheme.[41] Sultan's contribution placed the question of Indian higher education in the public sphere and the city council eventually granted a piece of land in the Botanical Gardens area where the college and several schools for Indian children were established, such as Orient High and Gandhi Desai.[42]

M. L. Sultan formed the M. L. Sultan Charitable and Educational Trust on 28 June 1949, with a capital sum of 1,00,000 pounds for Indian spiritual, cultural, educational and economic upliftment. The first trustees were M. L. Sultan, Abdul Razack Sultan (son), Mahomedessuff Abdool Kader (son-in-law), B. M. Patel (friend), Vincent Lawrence (friend), G. B. Chetty (friend) and M. A. Desai (friend). It is important to note that this was established as a public trust, and was not controlled by the family. In fact, at the present time, only one family member, A. K. Sultan, is a member of the trust. The composition of the trust is significant in that although a devout Muslim, Sultan included his close Hindu and Christian friends in the trust, underscoring that he knew no barriers of caste, creed or religion. This point was highlighted by I. C. Meer in his biography, *A Fortunate Man*, where he writes of a visit to M. L. Sultan with his cousin M. I. Meer, editor of the *Indian Views* newspaper:

> During our tea we were disturbed by a delegation that came to see Mr. Sultan about a donation for a in which they were involved. They emphasised that the project was for Muslims, thinking that would attract Sultan's money. But Sultan said he did not support sectional causes. 'Allah is Rab-ul-a-lamen – Lord of the Universe. He is not Rab-ul Muslimeen – Lord of the Muslims. Show me anywhere in the Qur'an where Allah is described as sectional, favouring one group over another. Where does the Quran say Rab-ul-Muslimeen? He sent off the delegation disappointed.[43]

Sultan's openness may have had something to do with the place of Muslims in nineteenth-century Malabar society. Ghosh makes the important point that Muslims in Kerala did not

> have any claim of imperial or aristocratic traditions. And as they had no political ambitions, the rulers had no malice towards them also … Instead, the Kings in Kerala who realized the significance of Muslim contribution to trade and economic prosperity encouraged their settlement. Since the beginning, the Muslims have a cordial relationship with other communities …[44]

An editorial in *The Daily News* on 10 September 1953, titled 'Benefactions to his People', captured the importance of Sultan's contribution. The article stated that in the course of his lifetime, Sultan had given away 200,000 pounds, whereas the value of benefactions under wills in the whole of the Union of South Africa was 500,000 pounds per annum.

Full-time classes were initially conducted in private premises until the building which stands today was officially opened on 7 August 1956 by the then Minister of Education, J. H. Viljoen, with 19 classrooms and an enrolment of 240 full-time students.[45] There were over 1,500 full-time and 4,000 part-time students by 1965. Over time, the *technikon* offered courses in catering, hairdressing, nursing, dressmaking, engineering, draughtsmanship, bookkeeping, welding and others, which were instrumental in the upward mobility of the Indian working classes. The initial years also saw the enrolment of many African students, but after the National Party (NP) government passed a law in 1959 segregating tertiary education, African students were prohibited from attending the institution.

The M. L. Sultan Charitable and Educational Trust built a number of buildings over the years at the *technikon*, which shows the extent of its involvement in philanthropy in a specifically South African context.

- Ayesha Bee Building: named after the daughter of M. L. Sultan and officially opened on 8 September 1959 by P. R. Pather, well-known community leader, member of the moderate NIO and member of the M. L. Sultan Technical College council.
- Abdul Hamid Sultan Building: named after the eldest son of M. L. Sultan and officially opened on 6 September 1960 by C. A. Milne, mayor of Durban.
- Mariam Bee School of Home Craft: named after the wife of M. L. Sultan and officially opened on 8 September 1965 by the then minister of Indian education, W. A. Maree. The foundation stone was laid on 8 September 1964 by M. E. Sultan, son of M. L. Sultan.
- Dr M. E. Sultan Building: named after the third son of M. L. Sultan and officially opened on 8 June 1978 by Haydn Bradfield, mayor of Durban. M. E. Sultan became the first Black president of the M. L. Sultan Technical College Council when he was appointed by the minister of Indian affairs, Marais Steyn, in May 1975. He had been part of the thirty-member council since 1958, was a member of the South African Indian Council (SAIC), president of the South

African National Council for Child and Family Welfare, trustee of orphanages in Lakehaven and La Mercy, vice-president of the Natal Indian Cripple Care Association and chairman of the M. L. Sultan Educational and Charitable Trust. Amichand Rajbansi of the SAIC welcomed the move but said that he hoped it was only the first appointment of many aimed at 'Indianising Indian education'.[46] The University of Durban-Westville awarded an honorary doctorate to M. E. Sultan in 1978 for his 'dedicated leadership and outstanding devotion to the upliftment of Indians'.[47]

- Fathima Bee Building: named after the second daughter of M. L. Sultan and officially opened on 19 April 1991 by Arnold Zulman, chairman of Beacon Sweets and Chocolates.

Contributions were also made for the building of *technikon*s on the south coast and in Stanger and Pietermaritzburg.

In 1946, the minister of education declared the M. L. Sultan Technical College an approved institution for Indian higher education under the Higher Education Act No. 30 of 1923. The college was officially opened on 7 August 1956. In 1979, it was renamed the M. L. Sultan Technikon when its status was changed from a college to a *technikon*. This remained its name until 2002, when the M. L. Sultan Technikon merged with Technikon Natal to form the Durban Institute of Technology, now known as the Durban University of Technology (DUT).

According to Yunus Sultan,[48] the family learnt via the media on 25 November 2001 that the department of education intended to change the name of the M. L. Sultan Technikon with effect from 1 February 2002. The Sultan family members were 'gravely disappointed at hearing about this', since M. L. Sultan's name was not to be included in the new name. The Sultan family, Yunus said, 'were surprised as we did not receive any notification'. The family began a public campaign to ensure that the new name included 'M. L. Sultan' in it.

A committee comprising of the two vice-chancellors of these *technikon*s and the two chairmen of their respective councils was established to propose a name to the then Minister of Education, Kader Asmal. They recommended the name Durban Institute of Technology. The Sultan family appealed to the committee to retain M. L. Sultan's name in the new name of the merged institution, providing the historic context and strong reasons to do so. The community at large was equally vociferous through the press in demanding retention of the name. Hassim Seedat, the then chairman of the M. L. Sultan Charitable and Educational Trust, also wrote a strongly worded letter to the press. Yunus Sultan noted that while the family did not approve of the violence, some students of the M. L. Sultan Technikon 'went on a rampage, smashing windows and disrupting classes and examinations, in protest to the name change'.

Despite these protests, the naming committee stuck to its guns and the minister approved the new name. At this point, Yunus Sultan made contact with Minister Asmal's personal secretary, Nasima Badsha, to arrange an urgent meeting between the minister and Sultan family members. Yunus Sultan, a senior member and spokesman of the Sultan family, wrote a letter to Minister Asmal on 15 February 2002, outlining the reasons why the name should be retained. A delegation of eight met with the minister a week later on 24 February. Much to their disappointment, he conceded that he was heeding the advice of the naming committee. According to Yunus Sultan, 'we left the meeting with a sour taste in our mouths, when we realized that this was never going to revert'. However, it was eventually decided that the campus of M. L. Sultan Tecknikon, one of the seven in Durban and Pietermaritzburg that formed the DUT, would be called the M. L. Sultan campus.

The original M. L. Sultan Technical College (Technikon) used to celebrate Founders Day annually in memory of M. L. Sultan on 6 September, his death anniversary. This celebration ceased when the name change took effect. It is one of the ironies of history that while Sultan's benevolence is now enjoyed by all South Africans (over 80 per cent of the students at the DUT are 'Black African', as defined by the South African government), the one day on which his name was remembered, has been erased. Faced with this insensitivity, the Sultan family then approached the mayor of Durban, James Nxumalo, and succeeded in getting the road where the institution stands renamed from Centenary Road to M. L. Sultan Road in 2003, an appropriate legacy for his generosity, providing a little consolation for the loss of the name.

On 19 April 2011, the DUT posthumously conferred a degree of 'Doctor in Management Sciences' (honoris causa) upon M. L. Sultan in recognition of his yeoman services to the institution, and education and philanthropy more generally.

There have been countless other beneficiaries, especially in education.[49] The M. L. Sultan Charitable and Educational Trust's total donations to educational institutions throughout KwaZulu-Natal, in today's monetary value, have been estimated, according to Yunus Sultan, at approximately 320,000,000 rand.

'OPERATION KERALA'

The extended Sultan family has been resurrected, albeit in new forms and using new technologies, and Sultan's descendants have turned the family tree full circle by making the return trip to India. According to Sultan's grandson, Yunus Sultan, the son of M. E. Sultan, in the period from 1968 to 1980, there was contact between Sultan, the third son of Sultan, and Mulukmahomed Shumshudeen, the grandson of M. L. Sultan's brother Mytheen Kannu Labba. M. E. Sultan was the chair of the M. L. Sultan trust and much of this correspondence included information about the family in Durban, the philanthropic work of the trust and newspaper cuttings in regard to the work of the trust and the family. In June 1980, Yunus Sultan wrote to Shamshudeen to inform him of his father's death on 27 May 1980. Yunus received a letter of condolence a few weeks later but with everyone caught up in work, the correspondence between India and South Africa stopped.

Around two decades ago, due to interest in roots among the younger members of the family in particular, the Sultan family began a search for their relations in Kollum, Kerala, South India. The search was initially frustrating but continued intermittently until November 2015, when the extended Sultan family held a reunion in Durban. At this function, due once again to pleas from younger family members, the organizers, according to Yunus, gave 'a commitment to find our roots in Kollum'.

During this visit to Durban in 2015, Yunus' paternal first cousin, A. H. Sultan, who works and lives in England and had also come to visit his ageing mother, found M. L. Sultan's diary in his deceased father's satchel. This diary contained the addresses of family in Kollum, but it was the address of the post office as the practice at the time was for the postman to hand the letters to residents as he usually knew everyone in the village.

A. H. Sultan was sure that 'he must have had family in India. But there was no link. Our previous generation lost all contact.' He found Sultan's diary and discovered that he had written letters to relatives, care of the Mohammedan school in the village of Kollam in Kerala. A. H. Sultan noted that the desire to make contact with relatives was strong and visited India several times without success. There was a breakthrough when a Bini Ajay joined the hospital in England where he worked. He discovered that she was from Kollum. They contacted a lawyer friend in Kollam, Mr Joycutty, who, in turn, hired a resourceful local man, Feroz Khan, to search for the family.

There was a feverish search, with notices put up in mosques, public spaces and various shops. There was no luck even though Khan got onto his motorbike and criss-crossed the town looking for the Sultan family. One can appreciate the enormity of the task when it is noted that Kollum's population stood at 60,000. After two months of searching, by chance, one afternoon, Khan casually asked an elderly man whether he had family in South Africa and was shocked when the reply came: 'I am Mulukmahomed Shamshudeen, my father is the nephew of M. L. Sultan'. Khan showed him a photograph of M. L. Sultan and he confirmed that it was his family. Khan called Joycutty and as recorded by Yunus Sultan, the conversation went as follows:

> Khan: I have made contact.
> Joycutty: Take down his address and I will see him tomorrow.
> Khan: No, you must come now.
> Joycutty: It is late now.
> Khan: The elderly man insists you must come now!

Joycutty contacted Bini Ajay who happened to be in Kollum on holiday, and the three of them, Ajay, Khan and Joycutty, went to Shamshudeen's home, where he 'took out documents, photographs and letters, covering a period of 119 years' (the first letter was dated 1897). Shamshudeen had in his possession letters exchanged between his father and Dr M. E. Sultan and an obituary that appeared in a local Durban newspaper when M. L. Sultan died. It was sent to India by Yunus' father, M. E. Sultan.[50] According to Shamshudeen, he kept the dream alive that 'one day, my uncle's children will come looking for their roots'. And he hung on to every single heirloom, letter, piece of paper, newspaper clipping and just about anything associated with M. L. Sultan, who had left Kollam in 1890. When contact was made with him, he declared, 'I knew that you would come and I have kept everything and I resisted my children's demand that I throw away the bundle of documents because it was taking [up] too much space in our small house'.[51]

Ajay photographed the items on her cell phone and forwarded them to A. H. Sultan in England who, in turn, forwarded them to Yunus in Durban. 'You can imagine the excitement that was buzzing when this news was received by us in Durban', he said. The Sultan family in South Africa, England and Australia put together a team of descendants comprising of five grandchildren and three great-grandchildren to visit Shamshudeen and his family. It included England-based A. H. Sultan and Australia-based Iqbal

Sultan. The family dubbed this 'Operation Kerala'. Communication was sent to Fathima and Ajmal, grandchildren of M. L. Shamshudeen (who was the grandson of M. L. Sultan's brother, and thus Yunus' second-generation cousin), advising them that the team would visit from 25 March for a period of 6 days. According to Yunus Sultan, 'the news was received with much excitement, especially from Shamshudeen'.

According to Yunus Sultan, his own journey involved 13 hours of flying and two and a half hours by road. The delegation reached the hotel in Kollum around 6 p.m., accompanied by Khan and Joycutty. They contacted Fathima and though they told her to meet them the following morning, the family was overjoyed and insisted on meeting immediately. They lived close to the hotel and arrived within a few minutes. According to Yunus, during this meeting, 'emotions poured out and before long the floodgates opened and days gone by emerged in graphic detail'. They met Shamshudeen the following morning. He was 83 years old at the time. Yunus Sultan related what happened:

> After the formalities were done, Shamshudeen then took out the treasure trove. Going through all this, wonderful memories came to light. In this collection were 26 letters written between 1953 and 1980 between the patriarch's third son M. E. Sultan and Shamshudeen. Shamshudeen mentioned that he had this treasure trove as he knew that the Sultan family would one day find this. The oldest letter we found was dated 18 December 1897, written by M. L. Sultan to his sister Nuhoor in the Malayalam language, on a letterhead of the Masonic Hotel in Johannesburg, where he worked as a waiter. Thereafter we enjoyed a delicious South Indian lunch.
>
> Shamshudeen's family were so excited about our visit to Kollam that they invited the local media to be present, who in turn put a photograph with an article on M. L. Sultan in Kollam's local newspaper. After lunch the sharing of family history both ways brought tears to our eyes. Rich emotions reinvigorated us. 83-year-old Shamshudeen simply grew in strength and he was totally revitalized. He had a sharp mind and a good memory. He would every now and then remind us that he always knew that someday the Sultan family from South Africa would come. In a complete surprise he revealed that the patriarch of the family was Mulukmahomed Labba. We were always under the impression that it was Lappa. It now seems that the family name was lost in translation when M. L. Sultan emigrated to South Africa in 1890. Shamshudeen

then informed us that M. L. Sultan had four brothers, Mytheen, Pacha Pillai, Mazoor and Peer Mahomed, and one sister Nuhoor.

Yunus made the pointed observation that 'if Shamshudeen had passed away prior to 2016, then definitely we would never have been able to find our family roots'. Attempts to translate the 1897 letter from Malayalam have not been successful as yet. Yunus observed that besides his grandfather none of the other family members had emigrated, and that with the exception of two information technology (IT) professionals working in Dubai, the rest of the family is in India. He was impressed by the high levels of education, as the majority of the family were professionals in fairly good economic standing, living in an urban setting.

At the end of the four-day trip they discovered 168 cousins in Kollam; examined old documents, including letters written by the Sultan family in South Africa to family in India and visited the house where M. L. Sultan grew up, Juma Masjid opposite the house where their forefathers prayed and the cemetery where family members are buried.[52] In August 2016, a reunion was arranged at the Al-Ansaar Hall on West Road, Overport, with the hope of the English, Australian and Indian members of the family joining them in South Africa. Unfortunately, due to visa delays, the Indian members were not able to be present. With the benefit of technology family members in South Africa connected with Indian relatives.[53] This was the start of what the family hoped would be multiple ways to keep them connected across four continents.

AN 'ML SULTAN TRIBUTE'

The 1860 Heritage Centre organized an 'ML Sultan Tribute' on 13 April 2019 at its Durban home. The Heritage Centre is an official museum that falls under the auspices of the KwaZulu-Natal Department of Arts and Culture. It has been in existence for some time but was officially opened on 30 May 2017 at its present site after a long struggle by community members. Board member Satish Dhupelia told *The Mercury* newspaper at the opening of the centre that the aim was to make it a repository of indentured and Indian history. Importantly, Dhupelia said that history in South Africa should not be viewed in silos:

> While we all value our own cultural and religious practices, we all are part of the country's collective history. Our histories are all

intertwined ... The project is an important effort in our broader vision of locating the history of the SA [South African] Indian community within the broader SA struggle for freedom and democracy. It comes at a time when every effort in social cohesion must be supported by right thinking South Africans ... Our core business is to generate a broader understanding of the South African Indian community through understanding its history; its enormous contribution to South Africa's freedom struggle and its commitment to the deepening of democracy and culture of respect for human rights.[54]

Selvan Naidoo, volunteer curator at the centre, sees the museum as an opportunity to 'finally recognize and honour the heroes and heroines of our troubled past through dynamic exhibitions. We hope to educate the broader South African public about a much forgotten part of our common history'.[55] The centre has paid tribute to many South Africans, including anti-apartheid luminaries as well as others who have made a contribution to the country.

One such person is M. L. Sultan.

The programme director at the Sultan tribute on 13 April 2019 was attorney Aslam Mayat. In his opening speech, Mayat stated:

India is changing from the founding principle of the Indian nation to a Hindu Rashtra. Ironically, they choose to ignore that the Aryan invaders brought the Vedas to India. In South Africa we face calls to change from a rainbow nation, to an Afro centric one. History is rewritten by the victorious. The 1860 Heritage Centre aims to preserve the records of the desis. The Sultan family has obliged. Others must record the oral testimonies before they are lost.[56]

Mayat reminded the audience that Sultan had donated 17 properties to charity and that the total donations by the M. L. Sultan trust to various educational and other institutions throughout KwaZulu-Natal are estimated in today's monetary value at 320 million rand.

Following a list of distinguished speakers,[57] the programme director, Aslam Mayat, concluded by stating that the Sultan family wanted the audience to leave with three lessons from the life of M. L. Sultan:

First, philanthropy or ubuntu. The last wish of Alexander the Great was for his arms to hang out of his coffin to demonstrate that no matter how powerful, you leave this dunya with nothing. Ana Fakir, I am poor, praise be to God.

Second his embrace across ethnicity, caste, race and religion. During Indenture all Indians celebrated Coolie Christmas Muharram. Later Diwali was embraced by many. Lately we have become more parochial.

Third not to be apologetic. Sultan came lappa with 'niks' [nothing]. By hard work, skill and thrift (and no BEE [Black Economic Empowerment] to help him, only obstacles) he amassed a fortune which he used not for dependency charity, but to empower others.

Such tributes to Sultan and others are an important starting point towards acknowledging the history of the marginalized.

JOURNEYS WITHOUT END

The story of M. L. Sultan throws new light on the story of indenture and its aftermath. The indentured were tied down by contracts and their mobility was heavily circumscribed. But once indenture ended, many migrants took their chances in a South Africa that was dramatically changing. Diamonds and gold were discovered, the African populations were violently subjugated, and Boer and Brit went to war. In this environment some, like the newly released Chinakanoo Moodley, made their way to Kimberley and the diamond fields. Moodley accumulated wealth and sponsored the Sam China Cup for which Indians from all over South Africa competed in a soccer tournament on a provincial basis every few years.

Sultan went the other way to the gold fields of Johannesburg, finding work as a waiter. In the process both were to change or fiddle with their names. Chinakanoo Moodley became Sam China, probably because it rolled off the tongue of the British colonialists easier. Sultan dropped the Pillai. Was it to emphasize his Islamic roots and distance himself from the majority Hindus that bore this surname? Whatever the reason, it was in many ways a distancing from his roots in India as he dug deeper roots in Africa. He would go back, but the family tree he left behind branched into paths far from his own roots in Africa.

The banning of all immigration from India for much of the twentieth century and India's boycott of apartheid South Africa stretched and, in many cases, cut the umbilical cord with the 'motherland'. What for many started as a belief that indenture was a temporary exile, turned into a lifetime and then an eternity. But the demise of apartheid and the renewal of ties with India has created an explosion of interest in tracing roots, re-linking with family and of course securing a PIO card. The stay in India will be temporary. But the ties, as the Sultan family has shown, can grow tighter through future generations, given access to social media.

The quest to link with the land of our mothers and fathers after a long hiatus has literally taken off. As we finish this chapter, a man who served 10 years on Robben Island in the 1960s and who for much of his life was classified as 'Coloured', wrote to us wanting to find the roots of his father's family in India or Sri Lanka. This was a man who refused to be racially categorized! Nobody appears to be immune to this quest for the roots of their histories.

Descendants of indentured migrants who arrived in Natal at the height of colonialism are searching for their roots. The frequency of requests that we get from members of the public for help in tracing ancestors is on the increase, as are stories in newspapers and publications.

From an analysis of accounts in newspapers and publications, it appears that some are inspired by stories related by elders in the family. Saranya Devan, a university student in her early twenties and fourth-generation South African, maintained that while South Africa was the country of her 'birth and my home; I also have emotional and cultural links with India. It is important to understand one's roots. Therefore, Indians in South Africa must never forget that their forefathers came from India to sell their sweat to develop Natal'.[58] Raj Govender felt that the visit to the village of his ancestors brought his life full circle:

> Knowing who you are, who your ancestors are and where you come from can give you a sense of identity in this vast complex world. Learning your family history is a vital part of understanding yourself. Creating and building a family tree lets you leave a legacy for your children or future kin. Names from the past become alive and real, with insights and lessons to teach the current generation. Discovering the sacrifices and positive contributions our forefathers made to improve life for their family develops greater unity.[59]

According to Taylor, one of the common themes in most family reconstructions is 'portraying an idyllic image of the pioneer forebears, who are admired for their sacrifices'.[60] One of Sultan's grandsons remembered his grandfather as

> showing great courage and being strong spirited for making the long journey into the unknown. He showed a spirit of independence, humility, hard work, and made great sacrifices. It is this that has allowed us to make a contribution at the present time, not just in South Africa, but in many parts of the globe, in Australia, the United Kingdom, and elsewhere.[61]

Yet, while acknowledging this contribution across oceans, members of the Sultan family in South Africa were adamant that home is South Africa.

NOTES

1. Tinker (1974).
2. Sartre, quoted in Crittenden (1998, 32).
3. Vahed (2017, 73).
4. Kumar (2017).
5. Bahadur (2013).
6. Nattrass (1954, 3).
7. See Desai and Vahed (2019, 183–209).
8. Desai and Vahed (2019, 183–209).
9. Kramer (2011, 379).
10. Taylor (1982, 21).
11. Ellis (1975, 57).
12. Waetjen and Vahed (2014, 71).
13. Taylor (1982, 28).
14. Naidoo (2017a).
15. *Sunday Times Extra*, 21 November 2010.
16. R. Govender (2018).
17. Vahed (1995, 36).
18. On the 'Asiatic menance' see Swanson (1983).
19. Swanson (1983, 405–408).
20. Lake and Reynolds (2008).
21. See Desai and Vahed (2016, 49–65).
22. *Natal Mercury*, 13 October 1899.

23. Pillay (1976, 98–99).

24. Pillay (1976, 99–100).

25. Cited in Vahed (1995, 38).

26. Desai and Vahed (2013, xvi).

27. Vahed (2001, 195).

28. Kunju (1989, 278).

29. Vahed (2001, 196).

30. Goonam (1990, 17).

31. Kuppusami (1993, 76–77).

32. Kuppusami (1993).

33. Nattrass (1954, 5).

34. Meer (2002, 114).

35. *The Graphic*, 19 September 1953.

36. *The Graphic*, 19 September 1953.

37. Nattrass (1954, 7).

38. *The Daily News*, 10 September 1953.

39. Vahed (1995, 139–141).

40. Vahed (1995, 143).

41. Vahed (1995, 142–145).

42. See Vahed and Waetjen (2015, 189–190).

43. Meer (2002, 115).

44. Ghosh (1987, 1).

45. *Daily News*, 2 August 1956.

46. *Natal Mercury*, 17 May 1975.

47. *Natal Mercury*, 11 March 1978.

48. Interviews with Yunus Sultan held on 15 February 2019 and 18 March 2020.

49. There are too many beneficiaries to list here, but some of them include the University of Natal in 1955 for its Non-European Section which produced many of the first black professionals in the community, Sastri College, Villa Road Madressah, University of Durban-Westville (sports stadium, swimming pool, prayer room), Nelson Mandela Durban Medical School, M. L. Sultan Administration Building–Lake Haven Sea Cow Lake (Orphanage), M. L. Sultan Administration Building, David Landau, Asherville. Historically, the government did not build schools for Indians; rather the most popular schools were state-aided, where the local community had to build the school. For this reason, many communities approached the

M. L. Sultan Charitable and Educational Trust to assist in building schools for their respective areas. Beneficiaries included M. L. Sultan Technical College – Pietermaritzburg; M. L. Sultan Technical College – Stanger; M. L. Sultan Avoca Primary School; M. L. Sultan Escourt Primary School; M. L. Sultan Colenso Primary School; M. L. Sultan Ladysmith Primary School; M. L. Sultan Newcastle Primary School; M. L. Sultan Merebank Primary School; M. L. Sultan Kranskloof Primary School and M. L. Sultan Raisethorpe Madressah. See *Fiat Lux* (April 1982, 5). The government policy was to match community contributions on a pound to pound basis, which meant that the contribution was actually double in practice.

50. *Post Natal*, 24–28 February 2016.
51. *Post*, 17–21 August 2016.
52. *Post*, 17–21 August 2016.
53. *Post*, 17–21 August 2016.
54. Pillay (2017).
55. Desai and Vahed (2019, 207).
56. Aslam Mayat, Programme Director, Tribute to M. L. Sultan, 1860 Heritage Centre, 13 April 2019.
57. The long list of distinguished speakers included Shameema Mayat, chairperson of the Women's Cultural Group, who spoke of the various institutions making a contribution to society at large from some of the properties of the M. L. Sultan trust; professor Thandwa Zizwe Mthembu, DUT vice-chancellor; professor Jairam Reddy, former vice-chancellor of the University of Durban-Westville; principals of several schools that have benefitted from funding from the Sultan trust; M. L. Sultan's great-grandchildren, Shenaz Khan and Rashad Sultan; and there was a recorded message from Fathima Shah Jehan of India, who is M. L. Sultan's brother's great-granddaughter. Amongst those who attended were Member of the Executive Council (MEC) for Provincial Housing Ravi Pillay; the then Durban deputy mayor, Fawzia Peer; Dr Baker of the Iqra Trust; cartoonist and social activist Nanda Subban; and Miss UniWorld finalist, Al Hadia Shaik.
58. Naidoo (2017b).
59. R. Govender (2017), cited in Desai and Vahed (2016, 193).
60. Taylor (1982, 28).
61. Aslam Mayat, Programme Director, Tribute to M. L. Sultan, 1860 Heritage Centre, 13 April 2019.

BIBLIOGRAPHY

Bahadur, Gaiutra. 2013. *Coolie Woman: The Odyssey of Indenture*. London: C. Hurst.

Crittenden, Paul. 1998. 'The Singular Universal in Jean-Paul Sartre'. *Literature and Aesthetics* 8: 29–42.

———— (eds.). 2013. *Chatsworth: The Making of a South African Township*. Pietermaritzburg: University of KwaZulu-Natal Press.

————. 2016. *The South African Gandhi: Stretcher-Bearer of Empire*. Redwood City, CA: Stanford University Press.

————. 2019. *A History of the Present: A Biography of Indian South Africans, 1994–2019*. New Delhi: Oxford University Press.

Ellis, Katherine. 1975. 'The Limits of Domesticity in the Nineteenth Century Novel'. *Feminist Studies* 2 (2–3): 55–63.

Erben, M. 1988. 'Biography and Research Method'. In *Biography and Education: A Reader*, edited by M. Erben, 5–19. London: Falmer Press.

Ghosh, S. K. 1987. *Muslim Politics in India*. New Delhi: Ashish Publishing House.

Goonam, K. 1991. *Coolie Doctor: An Autobiography*. Durban: Madiba Publishers.

Govender, Neelan. 2008. *Girrmit Tales*. Durban: Rebel Rabble.

Govender, Raj. 2017. 'The Joy of Tracing My Family Roots'. *Post*, 29 November.

————. 2018. 'Visiting My Family's Village'. *Post*, 19–23 September.

Kramer, Ann-Marie. 2011. 'Kinship, Affinity and Connectedness: Exploring the Role of Genealogy in Personal Lives'. *Sociology* 45 (3): 379–395.

Kumar, Ashutosh. 2017. *Coolies of the Empire: Indentured Indians in the Sugar Colonies, 1830–1920*. Cambridge: Cambridge University Press.

Kunju, A. P. Ibrahim. 1989. *Mappila Muslims of Kerala: Their History and Culture*. Trivandrum: Sandhya Publications.

Kuppusami, C. 1993. *Tamil Culture in South Africa: Endeavours to Nurture and Promote It among the Tamils*. Durban: Rapid Graphic.

Lake, Marilyn, and Henry Reynolds. 2008. *Drawing the Global Colour Line: White Men's Countries and the International Challenge of Racial Equality*. Critical Perspectives on Empire Series. Cambridge: Cambridge University Press.

Meer, I. C. 2002. *A Fortunate Man*. Cape Town: Zebra Press.

'M. L. Sultan – Philanthropist Extraordinary'. *Fiat Lux*, April 1982, 5.

Mohabir, Nalini. 2014. 'Port of Departure, Port of Return: Mapping Indentured Returns to Calcutta'. *Small Axe* 18 (2): 108–122.

Mudly, Tholsi. 2011. *A Tribute to Our Forefathers*. Wandsbeck: Reach Publishers.

Naidoo, Arushan. 2017a. 'How You Can Trace Your Roots'. *Post* (Natal newspaper), 15 November 2017.

———. 2017b. 'SA Indians Ignorant of Their Roots'. *Post*, 12 November. https://www.iol.co.za/thepost/sa-indians-ignorant-of-their-roots-11946151. Accessed 6 December 2017.

Narrandes, Mansingh. 2010. *They Came from the East: The Narrandes Family*. London: Mansingh Publishers.

Nattrass, H. 1954. 'A Tribute to Hajee M. L. Sultan: First Patron of the College'. Durban: M. L. Sultan Technical College.

Pillay, Bala. 1976. *British Indians in the Transvaal: Trade, Politics and Imperial Relations, 1885–1906*. New York: Longman.

Pillay, Kamcilla. 2017. 'Revealing Our Collective History'. *IOL*, 29 May. https://www.iol.co.za/mercury/news/revealing-our-collective-history-9411036. Accessed 4 December 2017.

Swanson, Maynard W. 1983. 'The Asiatic Menace: Creating Segregation in Durban, 1870–1900'. *International Journal of African Historical Studies* 16 (3): 401–421.

Taylor, Robert M. 1982. 'Summoning the Wandering Tribes: Genealogy and Family Reunions in American History'. *Journal of Social History* 16 (2): 21–37.

Tinker, Hugh. 1974. *A New System of Slavery: The Export of Indian Labour Overseas, 1830–1920*. London: Oxford University Press.

Vahed, Goolam. 1995. 'The Making of Indian Identities in South Africa 1914–1949'. Unpublished PhD thesis, Indiana University, Bloomington.

———. 1999. 'Natal's Indians, the Empire and the South African War, 1899–1902'. *New Contree* 45: 185–216.

———. 2001. 'Uprooting, Rerooting: Culture, Religion and Community among Indentured Muslim Migrants in Colonial Natal, 1860–1911'. *South African Historical Journal* 45 (1): 191–222.

———. 2017. 'Brij V. Lal: Rooting for History'. In *Bearing Witness: Essays in Honour of Brij V. Lal*, edited by Doug Munro and Jack Corbett, 65–86. Canberra: Australian National University.

Vahed, Goolam, and Thembisa Waetjen. 2015. *Schooling Muslims in Natal: State, Identity and the Orient Islamic Educational Institute*. Pietermaritzburg: University of KwaZulu-Natal Press.

Waetjen, Thembisa, and Goolam Vahed. 2014. 'Passages of Ink: Decoding the Natal Indentured Records into the Digital Age'. *Kronos* 40 (3): 45–73.

ABOUT THE CONTRIBUTORS

Gajendran Ayyathurai completed his PhD at Columbia University, New York, and is an anthropologist and historian based in Göttingen, Germany. He has published on the culture, memory and history of the casteless Tamils and Indians in Tamil, English and German. His current book project is titled 'Deep Resistance: Buddhism, Caste, and the Marginalized in Colonial India'. He has initiated a new sub-field, critical caste studies, with scholars from India, Europe and North America.

Satnarine Balkaransingh is an acclaimed performing artist and author of numerous journal articles and books on themes ranging from development economics and commerce to folk performative traditions and the arts. He co-founded the Nrityanjali Theatre of Trinidad and Tobago. He has written, scripted and directed over 65 stage and television productions, including dance-ballets, at multiple international and Caribbean venues. A former musician, he was later trained at the Kathak Kendra, New Delhi, under the late Reba Vidyarthi and Birju Maharaj in Kathak classical dance. He has authored *Ramleela in Trinidad: 100 Years of the Felicity Open-Air, Folk Theatre Tradition* (2021) and *The Shaping of a Culture: Rituals and Festivals in Trinidad Compared with Selected Counterparts in India, 1990–2014* (2016), co-edited *Reigniting the Ancestral Fires: Heritage, Traditions and Legacies of the First Peoples* (2017) and co-authored *Kunuwaton: The Culture and Cuisine of the Santa Rosa First Peoples of Arima* (2014).

Crispin Bates is Professor of modern and contemporary South Asian history at the University of Edinburgh and holds a Honorary Visiting Professorship in the Graduate School of African and Asian Studies, Kyoto University. He completed his PhD at Cambridge University, where he was also a junior research fellow. He has held visiting professorships in Paris, Kolkata, Beijing, Kyoto, Tokyo and the National Museum of Ethnology in Japan. He has authored, co-authored and edited a total of 15 books, including a history of South Asia from 1600 to the present, entitled *Subalterns and Raj* (2010), and a series of seven volumes concerning the history of the Indian uprising of 1857, entitled *Mutiny at the Margins* (2013–2017). From 2015 to 2018, he led 'Becoming Coolies', an AHRC-funded project on the origins of Indian overseas labour migration in the Indian Ocean, for which he conducted research in archives throughout the Indian Ocean region.

Ashwin Desai is Professor of sociology at the University of Johannesburg. He is the author of the seminal *We Are the Poors: Community Struggles in Post-Apartheid South Africa* (2002). Among his recent books are *Reading Revolution: Shakespeare on Robben Island* (2012), *Reverse Sweep: A Story of South African Cricket since Apartheid* (2017) and *Wentworth: The Beautiful Game and the Making of Place* (2019). He, along with Goolam Vahed, has co-authored a seminal work on indentured labour, *Inside Indian Indenture: A South African Story, 1860–1914* (2010), and *A History of the Present: A Biography of Indian South Africans,1994–2019* (2019).

Kalpana Hiralal is Professor of history in the School of Social Sciences at Howard College, University of KwaZulu-Natal. An AfOx Senior Fellow at the University of Oxford and a South African NRF rated researcher, her two key areas of interest are gender and the South Asian diaspora and gender and resistance in South Africa. She has been the recipient of several research grants and scholarship awards – in particular, the Nordic Africa Institute Guest Researcher's Scholarship (2007) and the Inspire Erasmus Staff Scholarship (2017). She is the co-editor of *Satyagraha, Passive Resistance and Its Legacy* (2015), the editor of *Global Hindu Diaspora: Historical and Contemporary Perspectives* (2017), and the co-author of *Pioneers of Satyagraha: Indian South Africans Defy Racist Laws 1907–1914* (2017), *Gender and Mobility: Borders, Bodies, and Boundaries* (2018) and *Sisters in the Struggle: Women of Indian Origin in South Africa's Liberation Struggle 1900–1994*, vol. 1: *1900–1940s* (2022).

Ashutosh Kumar is Associate Professor of history at Banaras Hindu University, Varanasi, and the President of the Centre for Alternative Studies in Social Sciences (CASSS), New Delhi. He was a fellow at the University of Leeds; the Centre for the Study of Developing Societies (CSDS), New Delhi; the Centre for the Study of Slavery, Resistance and Abolition, Yale University; and the Indian Institute of Advanced Study, Shimla. He has published many books and articles in international peer-reviewed journals. His most recent publications include *Coolies of the Empire: Indentured Indians in the Sugar Colonies, 1830–1920* (2017), the study guide *The Indian Labour Diaspora* (co-authored with Crispin Bates) (2017) and *Indian Soldiers in the First World War: Re-Visiting a Global Conflict* (co-edited with Claude Markovits) (2021).

Archana Kumari is an Assistant Professor of History at Indraprastha College, University of Delhi. Her doctoral work looks at the ageing of people of Indian origin in South Africa during the colonial and postcolonial period. She has published articles in peer-reviewed journals and presented her research at international conferences.

Sarojini Lewis has completed her PhD in School of Visual Studies, Jawaharlal Nehru University, New Delhi. She has a background in visual studies and fine arts with a specialization in archival photography, video art and book arts. She is currently working as a researcher, artist and curator. Besides her research for her PhD, in her visual work and curated projects there is a fascination with history – of the landscape, the city, the environment and its user: what would unite them, what kind of view is there, on what is it focused? Recurring elements in her visual research are photographs of objects, people, migration and moments that reveal forgotten situations, and function as visual traces and fragments, creating narratives leading to new perspectives.

Heena Mistry is a research associate at the Global History Initiative, Queen's University, Kingston. She was formerly a visiting fellow at the Weatherhead Initiative in Global History, Harvard University, and the Centre for Indian Studies in Africa, University of the Witwatersrand. She researches on global Indian diaspora politics during the interwar years.

Tashmica Sharma is a PhD candidate in disaster management in the School of Agriculture, Earth and Environmental Sciences at the University of KwaZulu-Natal, Durban. Her chapter in this volume is based on her master's thesis entitled 'Memory, Nostalgia and Reality: A Socio-Historical Perspective of the Grey Street Complex'. She has lectured in the discipline of geography at the University of KwaZulu-Natal. She takes a strong interest in Indian diaspora studies. She currently serves on the Management Committee and Women's Group of the South African Hindu Maha Sabha. In 2021, she was inducted into the Provincial Climate Change and Sustainable Development Council, chaired by the premier of KwaZulu-Natal.

Bobby Luthra Sinha is a social anthropologist and political scientist who works as chief researcher (projects and advocacy) at the Adiwasi Samta Manch (ASM), a non-governmental organization (NGO) operating from Chhattisgarh. She completed her PhD at the University of Basel and holds the position of deputy director at the Centre for Asian, African and Latin American Studies (CAALAS), Institute of Social Sciences (ISS), New Delhi. She is also the co-chair of the Scientific Commission of Migration of the International Union for Anthropological and Ethnographic Sciences (IUAES). She writes for peer-reviewed scientific journals and digital news portals as an independent academic. Her areas of specialization include rights-based movements of environment and ecology, migration and diaspora studies as well as political ethnography and comparative politics.

Goolam Vahed is Professor in the Department of History at the University of KwaZulu-Natal. He has published widely, in peer-reviewed journals, on identity formation, citizenship, ethnicity, migration and transnationalism among Indian South Africans as well as on the role of sports and culture in South African society. Some of his recent books include *Chota Motala: A Biography of Political Activism in the KwaZulu-Natal Midlands* (2018), *Schooling Muslims in Natal: State, Identity and the Orient Islamic Educational Institute* (co-authored with Thembisa Waetjen) (2015) and *Crossing Space and Time in the Indian Ocean: Early Indian Traders in Natal: A Biographical Study* (2015).

INDEX